IN THE DRIVER'S SEAT

Interstate Trucking – a Journey

MARC MAYFIELD

With four or maybe five exceptions, I have changed the names and genders of people I met while I lived a trucker's life. I'll never know the identities of the men and women I heard on my CB radio. I can only thank them here for their words and hope the reader will laugh often, as I did, but consider seriously what they had to say.

The name "Linehaul" is an obvious fiction. The motor carrier it represents is real. Truck numbers, CB handles, and dog and coyote names are unchanged. Place names—except two— remain untouched, because truck driving is, for the most part, a profession of true geography.

For Gayle

All professions have their own little peculiarities of detail.

HERMAN MELVILLE, MOBY-DICK

Prologue

San Francisco, California, 1957.

Where does a circle begin? Tormented by schoolyard bullies, determined to fight back, a boy registers for boxing lessons. As his father completes the paperwork, the son glances through an open gymnasium window. Across the street, truck drivers back semi-trailers to loading docks set in the curbside wall of a brick warehouse. The vehicles perform a mechanical dance, graceful and efficient, and the boy watches, captivated by the sinuous, dependent movements of tractors and trailers. He never forgets.

Sebastopol, California, 1968.

My friendship with Don Emery deepens when I openly admire his tractor and semi-trailer—steel twins in black, yellow, and chrome. We are neighbors at The Apple Tree Motel, a moldy 1940s motor court. Don's truck is named Yellowjacket. Enameled script on the driver's door celebrates a way of life: *Gypsy*.

The Apple, as it is known to the college students and itinerants who call it home month to month, offers low rates, carports, kitchenettes, and room enough out back in the weeds to park an 18-wheeler. Don and his women drink, make love, and fight through thin walls for a few days and nights, then he is gone again. I hold his mail, most of it from Bakersfield, at the southern end of California's Central Valley. I think of Dust Bowl ballads and 1930s photographs of migrant farm workers. Don's people.

Thumbing through my record collection, he finds Hank Williams, Loretta Lynn, and two Merles—Travis and Haggard. Don reaches for a flat pick, tunes my guitar, plays an intro to "Your Cheatin' Heart," then sings the song like he owns it. I ask about life on the road, what he carries, where he goes.

"I feel good out there. Anything that fits in the box. Anywhere."

Then the subject is me. "What are you doing in school? I've seen the way you look at my truck." I ought to drop out, he says, and grab a gearshift or two. See the country.

"What would my family say?"

"Oh, hell. Just call 'em from Albuquerque."

One morning, tired of paying rent on rooms he sees three or four days a month, Don piles his gear in the coffin sleeper. As diesel smoke drifts into a clear autumn sky, we stand next to Yellowjacket and he asks again, "What are you doing in school?"

There is no good answer. We shake hands, road dog and long-haired student of philosophy.

Don says, "I'll bet I see you out there."

Chapter One

Sam, our Golden Retriever, whined and barked. My wife Gayle often said that he knew when I called from the road—he never barked if the phone rang and it was someone else. Then, always, after her eager hello, her questions. Where are you? *How* are you? How's the weather? Is it bad enough out there tonight to hurt you and the truck? You'll pull over if it gets worse or if you need to sleep, won't you? Do you miss me? When are you coming home? You've been away for five weeks. Sam just walks around the house looking for you. Do you miss me?

At times I missed her more than I could say at a public phone. At times I didn't want to go home and I hated my selfishness, staying out there, having a pretty good time of it while she was left to worry: does he love his truck more than he loves me? I hoped she would never ask. I didn't want to lie, but I didn't want to tell the truth.

Sam barked again and Gayle said, "You're gone. You're always gone."

—∞—

People asked me, "What's it like out there? What's long-haul trucking *really* like?" They always asked twice, as if I had a secret, and my short answer was always the same: "You have to like being alone."

What's it like out there? What's the long haul really like?

It is distances between loading docks and distances between people. Phone calls from truck stops on anniversaries and kids' birthdays. Long-distance marriage and long-distance divorce. Over-the-road means away-from-home. Families take the hit. Truckers' marriages survive on phone calls if they survive at all, and the strongest endure because they work for two or three nights once every four or five weeks.

Sometimes there's sunshine, dry pavement, and highway glory. Sometimes it's all-night drives through blowing snow and days when wind, rain, and the windshield wipers never stop.

It is seventy-hour workweeks without overtime. Piecework, but you're not paid for every piece. Driving without sleep, sometimes. Unpaid time at loading docks. Going without a shower for a few days. Truck-stop crimes committed in the names of food and coffee. Heavy traffic and threats by the minute to your life, your truck, and your customers' freight. An occupation of noise, vibration, health risks, and hearing loss. It is the best of jobs, it is the worst of jobs—Grand Tour, sweatshop, sweet dream, recurring nightmare.

Pay isn't always what recruiters promise. Your home-time is at a dispatcher's convenience, Tuesday and Wednesday one month, Sunday and Monday the next, Saturday afternoon to Sunday evening the next—your company will tell you that's a weekend. Drivers quit, sign on at other carriers, and quit again and again. Annual employee turnover at most trucking companies exceeds 100 percent, and with good reason—trucking isn't for everyone.

You arrive on time for a 5:30 a.m. loading appointment, open the trailer doors, and back in. The shipping clerk says, "I'll come out to your truck when the paperwork's ready," and he does, at 4 p.m. You've been up since 5 a.m. Your delivery is set for 4 o'clock the next morning, 768 non-stop miles away and you don't dare show up late, but that's not the clerk's problem. Have a nice night.

You're desperate for sleep but you can't find a place to park your rig. Your eyes start to close. You grip the wheel and keep driving. It's early in the evening and every rest area is already full; four-wheelers are parked in all the trucks-only spaces. Truck stops, on-ramps, off-ramps—you try them all. They're choked with idling trucks. The lucky drivers sleep.

Sleep.

Just the thought of it is enough to make you nod off. Your eyes start to close again and you roll down the window—maybe a draft of air will help you stay awake. Two blue men and a pink, laughing deer dart across the road. Your foot comes off the accelerator and taps the brake pedal. Drivers talk on the CB to keep each other's eyes open, and you keep moving because, like them, you can't sleep if you can't park first. You see the blue men again, and the deer, then a yellow clown with green hair stands on your hood and flips you off. Your foot taps the brake pedal.

You've got to sleep. You've got to sleep but you keep going. If a four-wheeler slips up, if a real deer streaks out, if any little thing goes wrong, that's it, you're done, your foot won't move fast enough.

Your eyes start to close a third time. You almost drove off the road back there and you don't want to be driving the next time your eyelids drop, but you keep rolling.

That light! I first saw it in 1992 near Celina, OH and I didn't know what it could mean, a sky that glowed dark and light and green and gray and black all at the same time, in mid-afternoon. Then wind slapped the truck, reminding me that my load weighed only 13,000 pounds.

South of Paducah, KY one year later, I saw the murderous palette again. Four-wheelers on I-24 were pulling over and scrambling to crowd in beneath overpasses. Truck drivers were yelling on the CB about a funnel cloud. Find cover! Pull into a truck stop! No, keep going, maybe you could outrun the thing! Pray! Kiss your ass and your truck goodbye!

Westbound on I-20 near Big Spring, TX.

I had the pedal on the floor and I was only going 45 miles an hour.

A driver keyed up and said, "Headwind. Crosswind. Bad wind. We're all gonna get blowed over and die."

The wind began to blow harder, truckers began to talk about it more, and I parked on an exit-ramp, not sure what I should do. With each howling gust the truck rocked back and forth on the suspension. A black Kenworth pulled in behind me and stopped a couple of feet from the back of my trailer. I grabbed my CB mic. "Black truck on the ramp. You copy?"

"Yeah. This freakin' wind! I'm s-s-s-scared, man. I ain't got a thing in my b-b-b-box! Jesus! *Listen* to that wind!"

I said, "I'd pull farther up the ramp for you if I could. But my leg is shaking so bad I can't push in the clutch."

"Mine is t-t-t-too. Damn wind! I don't like this p-p-p-part of New Jersey!"

At the Pilot truck stop in Laramie, WY, January 20, 1999, 7:30 p.m.

I stood close to my truck with another driver—the both of us bundled up while our fuel tanks filled—in a miserable sub-zero gale. He was headed east. I'd planned to push on to Rawlins, 100 miles to the west. His tractor and trailer were coated with thick hoarfrost. Mine were just covered with light winter muck.

I yelled over the noise of the engine and the wind. "What's it like between here and Rawlins?"

"It's hell froze over," he shouted back. "You'll get into ice and blowing snow at the 298 yardstick and you won't get out of it. Elk Mountain is as greasy as I've ever seen—they've got a wreck or two every mile. Temperature's falling, wind's blowing like a son of a bitch. If I were you, I'd stay here tonight, see how it looks in the morning. What'd you leave behind you?"

"There's blowing snow up on Sherman, then it's clear. Your troubles are over."

"Well, that's the only good news I've heard today. Winter out here really sucks."

—⁂—

People often wanted to know if I drove the same route all the time.

"No," I'd say. "I drive irregular linehaul. I'm all over the map."

"You're a Teamster, aren't you?"

"No. These days, most truck drivers aren't union members."

Non-union, irregular-route trucking isn't eight daily hours on the job then a commute home to the family, five days and 40 hours looking forward to another weekend, week following predictable week, and paid holidays. It is camping out two, three, four, or five weeks in your truck. Maybe a load gets you home for an evening, maybe not. Think of day shift, swing shift, or graveyard and of working any one, two, or three of them—or split parts of them—in the same 24-hour period, then other parts in the next 24, no two days ever alike, day after day. You take your time off 500, 1,600 or 2,500 miles from home.

Every load picks up and delivers at different times. Truck drivers don't speak of formal work shifts. There aren't any. You'll never see a time card. The job lasts until it is done, until freight is stacked on a dock, until a trailer is empty or dropped at a customer, whether it's 3 a.m. or 3 p.m., midnight or midday. Then you're off to the next load and the one after that.

They could have called it "unpredictable" or "sporadic"—it is both of those—but "irregular" is the preferred shorthand because no single, regular route is followed and no two routes are exactly alike. Truckload after truckload, year after year, you hardly ever see the same dock twice. You haul whatever to wherever, whenever.

You pick up from—or deliver to—malls, prisons, airports, breweries, copper mines, grocery stores, college campuses, military bases, deep-water ports, explosives plants, recycling centers, construction sites, warehouses in the middle of nowhere, and underground storage vaults carved out of limestone.

You take computers from Sacramento, CA to Elmwood Park, NJ. Big-screen TVs from Orlando to Atlanta. Whiskey from Baltimore to Columbia, SC. Furniture from Calgary to Santa Fe, NM. Hospital supplies from Green Bay to Nogales. Frozen hash browns from Othello, WA to Compton, CA. Automobile brake parts from Stockton, CA to Mississauga, ON. Toothpaste from Chicago to Reno. Gun safes from Spanish Fork, UT to Hagerstown, MD. Sphagnum moss from Rice Lake, WI to Phoenix. Turkey stuffing from Gary, IN to North Kingstown, RI. Ribbons and bows from Berwick, PA to Pueblo, CO. Evil-smelling plastic pellets from Yerington, NV to Fort Worth.

Your pathways on the continent cross and cross again, like scribbles on a blackboard. You see the country coming and going.

You earn extra pay for multiple stops, so you run Genuine American Oak tables (made in China) from Fife, WA to Lee's Summit, Sedalia, and Jefferson City, MO, Louisville, KY, and Norfolk, VA. Refrigerators from Denver to Helena, Great Falls, and Havre, MT. Paper towels from Portland, OR to Los Angeles, Commerce, Pacoima, Pomona, and Lancaster, CA.

Many of your loads are expedited: they emphatically cannot deliver late. They're "hot." A receiver's dock is 2,400 miles away and you have to arrive between 1:45 a.m. and 2 a.m. three-and-a-half days after your pick-up. You're an hour early. Or your load is due at a consignee 10 hours after you leave the shipper. You drive every minute of the 10 hours to get it there on time—freight couldn't be hotter than that.

You don't see most of your cargo but you see lots of trailers. They're preloaded or you back in and someone loads the one you've got, and maybe you stand on a dock to count boxes or pallets. You drop trailers at consignees or you watch someone unload or they unload while you wait in your truck. You stack cartons or roll pallets out onto a warehouse floor once in awhile and some unloads are sweaty headaches, but you shrug them off—it's the miles that count.

Miles.

You're paid for them, not for when you run them. A mile driven on Christmas or while your family is sitting down to Thanksgiving dinner pays the same as any other. There is no time-and-a-half mile, no double-time mile, no holiday-pay mile.

Miles.

Trucking's units of measure. We speak of revenue per mile. Cost per mile. Net earnings per mile. Loaded and empty miles. Miles per hour and miles per gallon. Fuel-tax miles. Household Goods Carriers' miles. Paid and unpaid miles. Practical miles. Out-of-route miles. Ton-miles. Average length of haul—in miles, of course. Miles driven in a day, week, month, year, or working lifetime. Miles a driver has gone without or since an accident. Miles until we replace a set of steer tires (figure on about 105,000) or drive tires (roughly 275,000). Miles we expect to run before a major engine overhaul (more than a million). Warranty miles for truck components (200,000, 400,000, or 750,000). Miles from home. Miles to go before we sleep. When we get a load assignment, our first question is, "How many miles does it pay?" Drivers ask each other, "Getting enough miles?" "What does your company pay per mile?" "How many miles did they give you last month?"

Miles.

Nothing is more important.

Miles.

Drive more, earn more, at 22 cents a mile, or 27 cents a mile, or 31 cents, or 37 cents, or 41 cents, or 88 cents, or 96 cents, depending on your carrier, how long you've been driving, and whether you're a company driver or an owner-operator. Truckers need serious miles to turn those pennies into take-home dollars. We've been led to expect 100,000 or 120,000 paid miles a year for solo drivers, 200,000 for teams. We say "Show us the money" *and* "Show us the miles."

Miles.

They're bread and butter, meat, potatoes, and gravy. Want to lose a driver? Promise him miles then break your promise.

Miles.

The word is a balm, a trucker's prayer, a request, a demand.

"I've got a lot of freight today," a dispatcher said to me. "Where do you want to go?"

"France."

He laughed, but he knew what I meant.

Miles.

Freight.

You run all over when it's good. You're happy just to run anywhere when it's not. You're always thinking about it and asking the same questions: Do they have freight today? Will they give me miles? When do I pick up and deliver? Can I do it without violating the federal Hours of Service regulations? All you know is that the answers will never be the same two times in a row, so you live with the different-from-one-load-to-the-next schedules of your freight, taking one irregular route at a time, and, most days, the view from your office window changes by the hour.

You might sit in your truck all weekend waiting for a dispatch, dreaming about freight and the money you'd make if you were rolling. Then you get a 1,300-mile load with a Monday morning pick-up and a Wednesday afternoon delivery, followed by a 1,700 mile jump from Thursday evening until Monday morning. You smile—you've got a 3,000-mile paycheck coming.

Maybe you're stuck on the West Coast because that's where the freight is and for five weeks straight you see only three states. You lose count of trips from paper mills in Oregon and Washington to grocery warehouses in California. I-5 becomes a blur. You could drive it in your sleep.

Some months there's a lot of freight and you stay out 30 days and run every one of them. Some months, it seems, you sit and wait as much as you drive. When the economy slows down trucking does too, but you're not out here to sit around, you're out here to get around. You don't make any money when the wheels aren't turning.

You drive 14,000 miles one month, 8,999 the next, 12,000 the next and 10,638 the next. You never know. There's usually less freight in the first quarter, but, two years in a row, January and February are your best months.

With irregular freight and irregular schedules come irregular rest periods. Truckers sleep one night and drive the next, sleep—if you can call it that—in the middle of the day, then drive all night and into midmorning, days and nights and driving and rest mixed back-to-back in a routine of non-routine.

Forget about Circadian rhythms.

Weight.

What your load weighs. What you, your gear, and your rig weigh. What you, your gear, your rig, and the load weigh. How much you've got on each axle or each axle group. Truckers don't always say 'pounds.' We know what a pound is.

"That dumbass forklift operator's got me at 37,600 on my drives."

"If I can slide 1,900 off my trailer I'll be legal."

"Forty-five thousand. That's a lot of dog food."

"I told my dispatcher, 'You know and I know an eighteen can only legally gross 80,000 and I can only do 12,000 on the steers, 34,000 on the drives, and 34,000 on the trailer.' He said, 'I don't care if it's over. Take it.' Lucky for me, the scales were closed."

On average, I carried about 26,000. Some drivers never carry less than 45,000. When you take the freight, you take the weight. Beer, rolls of paper, steel coils, copper anodes, grain, they're all heavy. Aluminum cans, potato chips, bubble wrap, and paper towels are light. Partial loads weigh next to nothing.

I preferred lighter freight—less than 36,000—but if the forecast was for wind I wanted weight every time. A driver I knew agreed. "I like weight," he said. "Weight holds me down." A tornado blew his truck over.

The heaviest freight I hauled—copier paper from Salem, OR to stationery stores in Reno and Las Vegas—brought the gross vehicle weight to 79,980. Call it 40 tons. My lightest load—eight mysterious cardboard boxes strapped to a pair of small pallets—weighed 102 pounds. I pulled them 1,600 miles in an otherwise empty 53-foot trailer from Salt Lake City to Bowling Green, KY.

"Well, I never," said the receiving clerk. "They sent a big truck across the country with two dinky skids. I could fit them in the trunk with my first husband. You married, hon?"

Truck scales. Chicken coops.

Do you want to know—do you *need* to know—if they're open or closed? You've got a CB in your truck, so key up. It won't cost anything to ask a question.

"Northbound, is the Bolingbrook scale open or closed?"

"Closed. The lights are off and nobody's home."

"Southbound, what's the Valdosta coop doing?"

"Just checking your weight and rolling you across."

"What's up with Truckee tonight—big word or little word?"

"Say what now?"

"*Open* or *closed*?"

"Little word. I heard they were checking log books."

"Do we got the big word or the little word at the North Platte scale?"

"Big word. Hammer down."

"Is Banning open or closed?"

"Four-letter word."

—⁓—

Most of the truck drivers I met out there were intelligent,

hard-working men and women, some with formal educations far beyond high school, many with the common sense no college degree ever conferred. Everyday people. The usual assortment of human and political persuasions. Rednecks. Liberals. Rush Limbaugh devotees. Some were openly gay and some were probably lesbians.

Straight or not, a woman in a driver's seat scared some guys and they gave it up on the CB.

"Ain't you got a husband to do the work?"

"Why don't you get back in the bedroom, where you belong?"

"You're taking a man's job away by being out here, little girl."

Crap, all of it. Trucking takes all kinds and if you stay out here long enough you'll meet them. Drivers who talk to themselves in parking lots. Hyper-social types who can't shut up in restaurants and truckers' lounges. Quiet, self-assured old hands. Cowboys who can't see past long hoods and chewing tobacco. Arrogant newcomers from white-collar fields who think they're smarter and better, who are nervous about getting down with the rest of us, who don't learn to truck faster than anyone else.

Truckers call interstates The Big Road. We speak of running The Top and running The Bottom—I-94 and I-10, respectively—and of driving Left Coast to Right Coast and back again, water-to-water, side-to-side. We drive up and down—from border towns in Texas, Arizona, New Mexico, and California into

Canada, and from Maine to Florida.

Roads are personal if you drive a truck. You feel every bad paving job. Deferred highway maintenance hurts. Your tractor hits the bumps then your trailer hits the bumps. Back slap. Kidney punch. You curse California's broken concrete and bone-jarring, leg-cramping turbulence. The scandal-built interstates of Arkansas. The bounce-and-slam along Big-Road miles in Illinois, Kentucky, Louisiana, Pennsylvania, and North Carolina. Missouri's pitch and yaw. The constant drubbing in Michigan, South Dakota, and Connecticut. I-8 from Casa Grande, AZ to the California state line is as smooth as polished stone. You think, Why can't they all be like that?

At the Beckley Travel Plaza on I-77, a trucker limped into the professional drivers' TV room and groaned as he sat down.

"Hey, Bobby," a woman said. "You look like you been in a fight."

"I have. Fought the damn turnpike all the way from the first cashbox."

"Should have seen the other guy, right?"

"I *am* the other guy. That road half beat me to death."

—⁂—

Work clothing.

Out there, you wear what you want. There's no need to dress up, just being dressed is good enough, but that's up to you. I'm sure some people truck in their underwear and some in less than that. Many drivers favor cowboy clothes—boots, duster, big hat.

You see steel-toed shoes and long-sleeve work shirts tucked tight into cheap jeans. I liked moccasins, because they're comfortable, and Levis, because they fit. I wore t-shirts and polo shirts—I didn't tuck them in—and displayed my trucker's tan—a darkened left arm below the sleeve—with pride.

—⚊—

Loads. Trips.

They're the same thing and they're not the same thing. If you're under a load, you're on a trip, and sometimes that's what it is. Each load is a separate job, a separate tour of duty, a separate mix of pleasure and pain, a separate piece of your puzzle. Each trip means miles and revenue for the truck, miles and income for you.

Trips—those journeys within your journey—don't last long, a week at the most. Many go from start to finish in a day or two. A few turn out to be memorable—what you hauled and what it weighed; how many miles the run paid and how many more you had to drive; where you picked up and delivered and everything you did to make the ends meet. What about traffic, weather, the route, fuel prices, showers (or no showers), sleep (surfeit or deficit), Hours of Service issues, voices on the CB, scenery, and lessons learned about life and about yourself? Was the passage drudge work or fun? Did you have adventures? Each load is different and each trip writes its own short stories.

At Sapp Brothers truck stop, Sidney, NE.

"What you want me to do is illegal," I said into the phone.

"We can't let this client down again," a customer service rep said. "He's hopping mad. The load should have been in Minneapolis yesterday. I've rescheduled for 11 o'clock tonight. We can't be late."

"We?"

"Please. You've got a fast truck."

"It's another 760 miles. I already drove three hours this morning and you're asking for 12 more. That violates the Hours of Service regulations big time—you know that."

"I do, but . . . Please? We screwed up. This is priority freight, but the trailer sat in the Salt Lake yard for two days before you hooked it—I don't know why. Please?"

"Okay. Why not?"

"We didn't have this conversation."

I bumped the dock 15 minutes early, earning a written commendation for exemplary customer service.

The trip:

Visalia, CA to Dallas, TX in three days; 1,546 paid miles; 1,603 hub miles on the shipper's designated route; extra pay for required stops at private truck scales plus reimbursement for the scale fees. Easy money.

The load:

One thousand, three-hundred eighty cardboard boxes of bagged potato chips in a 53-foot trailer. Weight, including the boxes: 5,175 pounds. Nothing at all.

You had to scale at the Flying J truck stop on top of the

Grapevine and the 4-K Truck Stop in San Simon, AZ. The scale tickets were proof that you ran south on U.S. 99 and I-5, then east on I-10 and I-20 (you didn't try to cut across on I-40 and climb up to Flagstaff and the Coconino Plateau—the logical, practical route), and that you understood: bags of potato chips filled and sealed near sea level would explode inside the trailer between 6,000 and 7,000 feet.

You're in Hillsboro, OR. You have six days until your load of kitchen cabinets is due in Framingham, MA. The weather looks good all the way. This will be the first time your wife is with you on a cross-country run and it turns out to be a second honeymoon.

In Waynesville, NC a dock foreman signed my bill of lading and said, "That's that. Thirty loads delivered out of 31 shipped. One truck didn't get past Indiana. Something to do with black ice and a ditch."

I deadheaded 19 miles in California—from Stockton to Lodi—for palletized breakfast cereal, drove 800 miles to Seattle, and backed to a dock behind a supermarket. A forklift operator took half the freight off my trailer and loaded it right onto another truck. I asked the driver where he was going.

"Stockton," he said. "It's a hot load."

I called in from Bishop, CA, about 200 miles south of my carrier's Reno terminal.

"They tell me you're a hard runner," said the dispatcher. "I've got a hot one in the yard. Three thousand miles. Delivers in Bangor. Would you like to come get it and go to Maine for Monday morning?"

Funny question to ask a solo driver on a Thursday—too many miles, too little time, I'd have to falsify my log book—but I couldn't say "Yes!" fast enough. I had never been to New England in the fall.

"The trees," I kept saying when I got there. "The trees."

—m—

You turn on your CB—part tool, part toy—and click through the channels: 15 on the Grapevine, 17 up and down I-5 in California and Oregon, 21 between Southern California and Phoenix, 19 just about everywhere else. Truckers key up to ask about road conditions and the weather, give each other Smokey Bear reports, tell lies and true-life tales. Everyone talks shop. Tell me about your company, I'll tell you about mine. When a carrier has trouble keeping drivers, when a fleet manager has trouble keeping promises, when a dispatcher is a habitual liar, truckers name names. Then they talk about four-wheelers, hunting, fishing, freight, trucks, truck stops, fuel prices, sports, politics, religion, food. Men talk about women and women talk abut men. Sometimes you hear whole conversations. Sometimes you catch a few words before the voices fade and the drivers are out of range.

"What do they call you?"
"Spider Man."

"They call me Basket Case."

"Do you know the difference between a billboard and a patrol car?"

"Most definitely."

"Good deal. You're front door."

"Peterbilt is the *only* truck I'd take to a desert island."

Near Van Horn, TX, two truckers—a man and a woman—were eastbound and angry on I-10.

The man said, "Catch me if you can, bitch."

"Listen to me, you pig. I just peed and bought fuel. You've got to stop somewhere. And when you do, I'm going to kick the snot out of you and I'm going to drop the lid on that potty mouth of yours."

"Westbound, you look good back to the state line. What's it like over your shoulder?"

"I ain't seen nothin' since I left New York."

"Friend, we're in Utah."

"Like I said, I ain't seen nothin' since I left New York. Night before last."

Near Evanston, WY.

A westbound driver said, "I've got a load of Rice Krispies from Canada. Been listening to them all the way across: 'Snap, Crackle, and Pop—eh?'"

Ten miles east of the truck stops at Youngstown, OH.

"That chicken sandwich you bought back there. How's it taste?"

"Kind of like chicken."

"Like chicken?"

"Kind of."

Near Moriarty, NM.

A woman said, "Sweetheart, my exit's coming up. It's sure been nice running with you."

Sweetheart's comeback was the sound of a big, slobbery kiss, a real wet smacker. The woman laughed and said, "What's that for, darlin'?"

"Honey," Sweetheart said, "you just put that where it'll do you the most good."

—⚏—

What I saw out there would have happened whether I'd seen it or not. A moment earlier or a moment later, a quarter of a mile in either direction, and I'd have missed one thing and caught sight of another. There's a lot going on, a truck driver's eyes are ten feet above the roadway, and he only has to turn his head and look down. Four-wheelers—men and women—drive and apply make-up; drive and scrutinize spread-out maps; drive and reach back to slap a child; drive and prop books, magazines, and newspapers on the steering wheel; drive and fumble in a footwell for cigarettes or a dropped CD; drive and stare at laptop computers sitting open in the passenger seat.

A young couple argues bitterly in a car. She is driving. He bangs a fist on his only leg.

Bored teenagers sulk in the back seat. Mom and dad sit in front, as far away now from each other as they can get.

The passenger in a BMW stands up through the sunroof and turns to look directly at me, her long ponytail a dark pennant in the summer air. She is beautiful, a contender for the runways of Paris, and she is fully unclothed in a fast-moving car on a California highway. Mouth shaped into an orgasmed 'O,' she lifts, squeezes, and fondles her breasts, rolls her head from side to side, fake-comes again, blows me a kiss, and sits down. The sunroof closes.

—∞—

A dog is good company on the road, some drivers say. He won't ask for much, he'll always listen in apparent sympathy, and he'll like you when you don't like yourself. Miss your exit, arrive late for a delivery, get into a snow storm or a fender bender. He won't even notice.

A trucker's dog is at home with him all day, every day. That's good for the dog and it must be good for the trucker—out there, I saw dogs in many trucks. I saw every kind of truck dog imaginable, pocket-size to pony-size.

On I-95 a few miles north of Miami, a yellow Labrador Retriever wearing sunglasses and a brown, sleeveless t-shirt rode shotgun in a lime-green Peterbilt day cab. Nothing unusual about that. Why would a Lab need sleeves in Miami?

A Bouvier des Flandres sat upright in a parked truck watching his driver, who held two sacks from Burger King.

"Louie's just another dog, really. Not many people know what he is. *He* doesn't know what he is. He gets a cheeseburger and fries whenever I do and I always carry his snack in my right hand, so he knows it's coming . . . here you go, Lou. Bone appétit."

In Raphine, VA, I walked by an old Freightliner and glanced at the driver's door: *Red–Olathe, KS*. A few minutes later the truck passed me on I-81 and I was able to read the passenger door: *Frank–Olathe, KS*. Red waved. Frank, happy to be along for the ride, aimed his Springer Spaniel nose at the open vent window and smiled.

—⁓—

I saw this on the back of a trailer: *A professional driver is one who stays out of trouble and helps his fellow drivers to do the same.*

A trucker in a coffee shop laid his hands flat on the counter. "So there's two left-turn lanes. I'm stopped in the right-hand one. A guy in a Hummer pulls up *on my right* and turns *left* in front of me just as the light changes. I almost ran over him. What an idiot."

On U.S. 20 in Oregon, four-wheelers passed me over double lines and on curves. A truck driver coming the other way keyed up. "They can't see around the next curve and they can't see around the truck," he said. "I guess they think it's a good day to die. I think they're all idiots."

Idiots. There's no shortage out there. I met a few every day.

A four-wheeler tried to get around me on the passenger side while I was making a right turn in downtown Nogales. If I hadn't been paying attention, I'd have dragged my trailer tandems over the hood of his car. I'd have had some explaining to do. Other four-wheelers tried the same thing in La Junta, CO, in Laval, PQ, in Gresham, OR, in Brownsville, TX, and in more places than I can remember.

On U.S. 395 near Bridgeport, CA, a motorcycle rider disappeared behind my trailer and stayed back there for 10 minutes. I slowed down and he slowed down. I sped up and so did he. I slowed gradually to 40 miles an hour. He pulled around, gave me a single-digit salute, sped off, then got in close behind another eighteen. I keyed up. "Northbound, you've got a two-wheeler glued to your butt."

"Yeah, I saw him. He's a dead man if I have to stop. Until then, he's just another idiot."

At a truck yard in Memphis I saw a car hood wrapped around the rear axle of a wrecked trailer. Someone had tailgated a truck that had to stop. Another idiot. Dead, probably.

New Mexico, I-40 westbound at mile-mark 175.

A young woman driving a minivan started up the short on-ramp. She held a yellow pad of paper to the steering wheel and she was writing and there were two children in the back seat. We'd get to the end of the ramp at the same time if she didn't speed up.

I wasn't about to swerve and risk a rollover. I couldn't change lanes—too many other vehicles around me. I grabbed a gear, braked, and blew the air horn. And kept blowing it. She looked up, suddenly afraid, aware of the truck for the first time. She kept pace with me, waving me off, waving—and yelling, though I couldn't hear her—that I should *get out of her way!* I downshifted again and braked again and . . . *she* slowed. I don't know what she was thinking. I passed the end of the ramp before she did. Moments later, she came around on my left side. Her passenger window dropped. She leaned toward it and expressed herself with a finger. She sped up and turned around in the seat—the mini-van drifted in her lane—screaming, it looked like, and, again, showed me her finger.

I expected her to phone my company, give them my truck number, and claim that I had tried to run her off the highway. I jotted down her license plate number and I knew what had happened and what hadn't happened, but how do you defend yourself against a call-in like that?

For me, it was simple. I'd braked hard and grabbed two gears to avoid a collision.

Collision. Not accident.

For her, it was even simpler. A truck was in the way when she looked up from her legal pad and the truck driver was supposed to do something about it.

At the I-24/I-40 split in Nashville, I came within inches of killing a woman. Driving and talking on her cell phone, she slowed suddenly from 65 miles an hour, *stopped*, and motioned with her right hand—the left one held a cell phone—to drivers on an entry ramp: come on out. I brought my tractor, a trailer, and 44,000 pounds of freight to a dead-stop less than a foot from her rear bumper and I did it without swearing or jackknifing the trailer. The CB lit up.

"Death wish. No doubt about it."

"Where do you suppose she learned that?"

"Mayfield, you just saved a four-wheeler's life and she ain't ever gonna thank you."

Come on out.

My mother worried when I was on the road. Most evenings, I pulled over to call her from a different city, town, state, or province, a fact of life out there that never lost its novelty. She began our conversations with laughter and a question. "Where are you, Ulysses?"

"Don't worry, mom," I'd say before I climbed back into the cab. "Trucking's perfectly safe."

Chapter Two

I've always wanted to drive a big truck.

Everyman

Bosselman's Travel Plaza, Elm Creek, NE, just off I-80.

Truck air-conditioning pumps and trailer refrigeration units wrestled the heat of a summer afternoon. Heavy smells—diesel exhaust, burnt motor oil, urine on hot asphalt—hung in the air. I unlatched the hood, pulled it open, and stood on the steer tires, first one then the other, to clean the windshield. Three words drifted up to me. "You know . . . wife." An old gentleman—white-hair and white leisure suit—leaned over a tire, peering at the engine. I jumped down, pushed the hood back, and he said, "I always wanted to drive a big truck. You know, get out on the road. Wife wouldn't let me. The name's Walter Dougherty."

We shook hands and talked for two hours.

Walter Dougherty heard big engines in the night. They sang to him of adventure and of waking up in a different place each morning. For many years, he had been eager to know America's highways with a trucker's familiarity and to be at home in a cab, but his better half wouldn't let him go. She must have known that he might not return once big rigs and the road seduced him.

I pulled out of Bosselman's and headed back to the Interstate, where three 18-wheelers moved left into the hammer lane as my truck rolled down the on-ramp.

"Mash on it, big truck," said a driver on the CB. "Come on out."

"Thanks," I said, and topped 9th gear, cancelled the turn signals, grabbed 10th, then accelerated to 65 miles an hour.

"No problem, sir. We're here to help."

"I do appreciate it. You're clear, back door."

"We thank you. Safe trip."

"You too. Thanks again, gentlemen."

This may sound like a lot of footwork for people who have never met, but we already know each other—we drive. We drive, most of us, more than 100,000 miles a year. We do it, many of us, without so much as hitting a curb or scuffing a tire.

I turned the CB off, settled in for a nine-hour ride, and thought about the dream Walter Dougherty never woke up to: drive a tall semi cross-country, ride high on 18 wheels and into Hollywood sunsets, top mountain passes in clear moonlight, catch sunrise and a truck-stop breakfast far down the line. See America through a windshield—her cities, her towns, and everything in between. The Columbia River gorge. Texas bluebonnets every spring. Fall colors in West Virginia, eastern Tennessee, the Adirondacks, and the Ouachitas. Fields of canola and winter wheat in the Palouse. The Mississippi Delta. Alligator Alley. White pelicans over Klamath Lake. Bald eagles at Echo, UT. The Atchafalaya Swamp at dusk. The soft light of dawn on Mobile Bay.

—⁓—

Released from the confinement of their vehicles at rest areas and travel plazas, casual travelers—civilians—often look around for a truck driver. They hope to peek under a hood or into a cab and sleeper, touch the trucking life, rub elbows with highway royalty.

"Nice truck," they say. "I've always wanted to drive one of these."

"Can I look inside?"

"Where did you say you were headed?"

"What does your truck weigh?"

"Why's it called an 18-wheeler?"

"Why do truck drivers flash their lights for each other?"

"Where's a good place to eat? John Steinbeck said truckers know such things."

"Is it true you guys take drugs and drive all night?"

Civilians took in the custom lettering on my cab doors: name, hometown, and, once I'd gone the distance, my proud words: *One million miles—no accident, no incident.*

"Oh, come on. Can a man *drive* a million miles?"

—Yes. And more.

"Why does it say Mayfield Transportation on the door, but the trailer says Linehaul?"

—I pull their trailers.

"Do you drive in all 48 states?"

—I drive in the *lower* 48. And Canada.

"Do you drive alone?"

—Yes. Two's a crowd.

"Don't you get lonesome?"

—It hasn't happened yet.

"Mr. Truck Driver, what kind of engine is that?"

—Detroit Diesel, Series 60. It's rock-solid. Reliable.

"That's not some kind of odd-ball V-8, is it?"

—No. Turbocharged in-line six. Seven hundred and seventy-eight cubic inches.

"How much horsepower?"

—Three-hundred and sixty, 430 on cruise control.

"*Two* power ratings for one engine?"

—That's right.

"Got that noisy Jake brake?"

—I never leave home without it.

"What kind of mileage do you get?"

—I average 6.8 miles per gallon.

"How many gallons of gas do you use in a year?"

—You mean diesel. About 17,000.

"I see you've got two fuel tanks."

—Correct. Each holds 140 gallons.

"How many spark plugs did you say?"

—Very funny.

"What's that little white dome up behind the sleeper?"

—A Qualcomm antenna. It's for satellite-mobile communications. We send and receive load information, directions to customers, that sort of thing. There's a keyboard and display in the cab. Type a message, send it to the satellite, and a few seconds later it's on a computer screen somewhere.

"Nice truck. It's not like a car in there, is it?"

—No, it's not like a car at all.

Where did you say you were headed?

I hadn't said. I never said. Hijackers like to know. Time and again, the question turned into a request for a ride. Unauthorized passengers are illegal in trucks, but most people don't understand that. I didn't reveal what I was carrying, either, not even to other truckers. You never know.

Can I look inside?

I could always tell when that one was coming. The cab and sleeper were my office, living room, bedroom, breakfast nook, and sanctuary. The privacy they afforded was at times the best reason to be in the trucking business and to stay in it. I ran a white-glove inspection every day and I was never comfortable with strangers trooping through, making themselves at home in the captain's chair, placing unclean hands on the steering wheel, gearshift and upholstery, grinding mud into newly-scrubbed floor mats and the carpet. But it depended on who asked.

"Can I look inside?"

—Sorry. Insurance, you know. If you slip or fall we're both in trouble.

"Can we look inside?"

—Sure, but only from the steps, please.

"Can I look inside?"

—Oh, heck yes. Come on in.

Friends asked. My dentist said, "You've seen my office. I'd like to see yours." My mother asked, leaned back in the passenger seat, and smiled like she hadn't smiled in a long time. My wife asked. And of course Sam had to sit in the driver's seat and bark.

Nice truck. It's not like a car inside, is it?

—No, it's not at all like a car. Excuse me, I've got to get back to work.

Then I climbed three steps to the cab, closed the door behind me, and dropped onto the driver's seat. Plush covered. Comfortable. Home. The seat frame fell under my weight and rose on its air-bag suspension to a preset height. My body adjusted to its customary position, sitting. More than anything, a truck driver sits.

I glanced at the rear-view mirrors for quick views down both sides of my trailer and checked the Qualcomm for messages.

Nine gauges, a tachometer, and a speedometer faced me from the wraparound instrument panel: oil pressure, oil temperature, coolant temperature, transmission temperature, differential temperature, charging system voltage, service-line air pressure, service-brake application pressure, and fuel level. The tach rested at 900 RPM, the fast-idle speed. I wouldn't need to buy fuel for another 1,200 miles.

Controls and paddle switches were grouped in the dash-board B-panel: a red, octagonal knob—the trailer air supply (*Pull to evacuate, push to supply*). A yellow, diamond-shaped knob—the parking brake (*Pull to apply, push to release*). Cruise control and engine speed. Headlights, marker lamps, and road lamps. Marker-lamp interrupt. Two-stage Jake brake. Suspension air-adjustment. Manual engine fan (for continuous cooling on long climbs like Vail, Cabbage, or Fancy Gap). Fifth-wheel slide release (*Must be locked when vehicle is in motion*). Inter-axle differential lock (*Do not engage during spin-out*). Cab and sleeper heater controls. Air-conditioning.

Just above the tach and speedometer was the driver message center, a two-line LED display in the dash. At the touch of a button it showed the outside temperature, miles on the truck since the build date, hours on the engine and gallons of fuel burned since they first fired it up, average miles per gallon, trip miles and hours, leg miles (the distance traveled between pick-up and delivery points), total idle hours, the two first lines of an incoming Qualcomm message, or fault codes: low coolant; low oil level in the sump; abnormal exhaust gas temperatures; low injector pressure; a problem with the ABS braking system or one of the truck's computers.

Overhead, in a console above the windshield, my CB radio—a Cobra 29 LTD WX with NOAA weather channels and an emergency weather alert. Toggle switches on the driver's door armrest controlled electric windows, door locks, and side mirrors. A steering wheel 20 inches across capped the steering column. From the dash, my CD player pumped 40 clean watts to each of four speakers.

Three pedals in the driver's footwell—clutch to the left, brake in the middle, accelerator on the right.

Accelerator. Not gas pedal.

Between the seats a gearshift lever jutted up three feet out of the flat floor. It worked an un-synchronized 10-speed manual transmission.

Across the cab, a passenger seat with arm-rests. At times, it was my evening easy-chair. At times, I spent my days there, reading and waiting for a load.

Behind the seats, the sleeper. Room to stand up. Refrigerator. Pull-out desk. Floor-to-ceiling cabinets. Bunk with inner-spring mattress—not quite big enough for two, but big enough. Above that, a pull-down twin-sized bed, and, below, storage compartments for tools, extra clothing, spare parts, coolant and distilled water for the radiator, gallon jugs of motor oil.

A heavy vinyl curtain divided the cab and sleeper. Closed, it shut out the lights of truck stops at night or darkened the sleeper for day-time rest periods. Drawn around the doors and windshield, insulated shades sealed off cab, sleeper, and driver from the world.

I've always wanted to drive a big truck.

Try it.

Step up to the cab and slide onto the driver's seat. Check the mirrors. Shut off the fast idle—the engine RPM will drop from 900 to 600. Fasten the seat belt and snug it against your chest. Depress the clutch pedal nearly to the floor to engage the clutch brake. (This stops the transmission main shaft from spinning—you'll be able to shift into 1st without grinding any gears.) Cover the brake pedal with your right foot. Push in the parking brake control knob and the trailer air supply knob to release the brakes. Press on the brake pedal.

Look at the shift-pattern decal on the dash. Gears 1-4 are in the low range and 5-10 are in the high range. Follow the pattern. Shift into 1st gear from neutral. Make sure the range selector switch on the gear shift lever is down—you need to be in the low gear range.

Ease up on the brake pedal and pull down on the trailer-brake arm (it's on the steering column, where you'd expect to find a gearshift lever) to lock the *trailer's* brakes, and gently let out the clutch part-way for just a moment, to tug the fifth wheel against the trailer king pin—we don't want the tractor and trailer to part company. Depress the clutch and release the trailer brake. Place your foot on the brake pedal.

Check your mirrors. You'll be turning left and the trailer has to clear the truck parked on that side. The trailer will off-track (in a turn, its wheels will describe a smaller arc than the tractor's) and pass close to your neighbor's truck. There's no need to rip his hood off, nor, in turning left, for the trailer's rear overhang to smack the truck on your right.

Look around again. Yes, again. Check the mirrors and the gauges. Did the air compressor cut out? It's good to know there aren't any air leaks and that you'll have air for the brakes if you need to stop. Are your turn signals on? Truck turn signals don't cancel automatically, the driver has to do it—you'll need to remember that. Gently ease up on the clutch and brake pedals. Don't press down on the accelerator yet—there's enough torque at idle to get 80,000 pounds rolling in 1st gear.

Now slowly let the clutch out all the way.

Okay, you're moving, but don't be in too much of a hurry. Check your mirrors. Look left, look right, and pull straight forward before you start your turn. Check the driver's side mirror. Be damn sure you'll clear the truck on your left.

To shift up, depress the clutch pedal an inch to take up the free play, then an inch more. (After 1st gear, you don't use the clutch brake. Rookies often try to shove the pedal through the floor every time they shift.) Move the stick to neutral, engage the clutch, let the engine speed fall 300-400 RPM (the fall is known as a droop), depress the clutch two inches, and shift into 2nd. Re-engage the clutch. This is called double clutching—you pump the clutch twice for each shift.

Check your mirrors.

Straighten the rig and, double clutching, shift up to 3rd.

Check your mirrors.

You're driving now. Pay attention. Keep your eyes moving. Are there people anywhere near your truck? Are trucks pulling out or backing up? Leave the radio off and the CB on, and be ready to step hard on the brake pedal if someone yells. Keep it slow and take it easy. Stop at the curb. Don't forget to push in the clutch pedal or you'll kill the engine.

Check the mirrors and look both ways for oncoming traffic, depress the clutch fully and shift back into 1st, pull out, then double clutch up to 2nd as you turn the big wheel hand-over-hand and swing the rig wide, wide enough to clear that parked car—never forget that every trailer off-tracks. Always use the mirrors. Remember, you're in control of two vehicles—you *always* have to know where they are. Keep your eyes moving. Straighten out and shift up to 3rd and 4th, double-clutching each time, glancing at the tach, and following the droop. Flick the range selector up, find 5th, and shift. Keep looking around. Check your mirrors.

Up ahead a signal light has changed to orange and you'll be coming to a stop, so try a down-shift or two. Drop the range selector, double-clutch back to 4th and then 3rd, *raising* the engine speed 300-400 RPM with each downshift. Do it right and you won't grind any gears, over-rev the engine or stress the driveline, and you'll be at the proper engine speed for the next lower gear. Push in the clutch just before you stop—you don't want to kill the engine.

After you've been driving for awhile you won't have to think about any of this. You'll feel it. You'll know the RPM and the gear you're in, so you'll know your road speed. The road speed and the RPM will tell you the gear—you won't have to guess. When you know the gear and the road speed, you won't have to read the tach. Drive long enough and you'll know what truckers know.

See? You forgot to cancel the turn signals. Give it time. Soon enough, you'll know how to shift without the clutch and when to skip a gear. Soon, maybe sooner than you think, you'll find that steering and gearing have become part of you, like breathing.

Chapter Three

Everybody is ignorant, only on different subjects.

Will Rogers

Santa Rosa, California, 1971.

Circumstances collided. Events dovetailed. A relationship collapsed and I dropped out of school—not for the first time and not for the last. Through a community college, I earned a Class-A Chauffeur's License, which qualified me to drive anything on the nation's highways except motorcycles. I looked for a trucker's work at union hiring halls, grocery warehouses, a refinery, van-and-storage companies, and a lumber mill in the Shasta-Trinity National Forest, but there was a recession on—every day, experienced drivers took home layoff notices. Who needed an untried man? "No experience? You're not a truck driver yet." "We don't hire virgins." "You've got your Chauffeur's, sure, but no seat time. Sorry." I let my Chauffeur's expire. I gave up on trucks and trucking.

—⚬—

Donner Pass, one morning in 1991.

I glanced at an 18-wheeler in my rearview mirror and it was as if I'd never seen a big truck.

After that, whenever I saw a tractor and trailer I'd wonder where the driver was going, where he'd been, what he'd seen, and I'd remember Don Emery and Yellowjacket. I still wanted to drive. I'd tried other things—college, a factory job, more college, geology, real estate. Nothing satisfied me. Why not try trucking again? *Grab a gearshift or two. See the country.*

I expected it to be more than sightseeing. I expected it to be hard work, without knowing exactly what that might mean. If I had to get dirty, I knew I'd be able to clean up and if I was tired I would sleep. I didn't know what I'd find down the road. Travelers rarely do. That is why we go.

I didn't—couldn't—know about unpaid miles and unpaid dock time, unforgiving delivery schedules and all-nighters, or how long truckers' workweeks can be. It never occurred to me that someone had to unload all those trailers and that sometimes it was the drivers. There was no Internet for research, no blogosphere, no logging onto a truckers' forum to learn about the highway life.

But you could park at truck stops and talk to truck drivers. Some said union jobs were the best. Others wouldn't go near an outfit that pulled freight under the Teamsters logo. Drivers told me, "Trucking is easy and trucking is hard. I don't know how to explain that." "I like the road. Maybe you will, maybe you won't." "If I had it to do over, I wouldn't go to long-haul. Been divorced two times, going on three because of it. Women don't like to be left at home." "It'll be like a fever. It'll grab on to you and keep you. Are you sure you want to do this?" I said that I was as sure as I could be. "Then don't let no one stand in your way."

—〰—

I thought I could renew my lapsed Chauffeur's License simply by taking a written state exam, but I learned that within a year Chauffeurs' Licenses would no longer exist. As of April 1, 1992, every interstate truck driver would carry a Commercial Driver's License issued only by his home state and tracked by the federal government. Gone were the days when truckers stored up violations on one license, moved across state lines for another, and carried two or three in their wallets. Now, you'd surrender your old CDL before you got near your next one.

And to get a *new* CDL you'd have to pass a drug screen and physical at a doctor's office, keep a medical card that showed you were fit to drive, pass a basic written exam plus written exams for the endorsements you wanted—air brakes, say, or double trailers, or hazardous materials, or all three—then pass a skills test in the type of truck you hoped to drive.

I would have to start over.

I paid a visit to a driver-training academy where the CDL program lasted six weeks and cost $5,000. Pass the final exam, a salesman said, and I'd have a license to be proud of. Everyone passed—the school guaranteed it.

What about jobs? Who hired someone with a new CDL and no experience?

The salesman handed me a stack of recruiting brochures. "They're all horny for drivers," he said. "Take your pick." The trucking companies were in Oregon, Idaho, Washington, Nebraska, and Arkansas. One in particular—Linehaul—was based in Arizona. A regional truckload carrier, it also ran cross-country and into Canada, hired nationally, and operated two terminals within 100 miles of our house—getting home wouldn't be a problem. Most Linehaul tractors were less than three years old and each was assigned to just one driver—no one else drove the truck. That meant you wouldn't be sweeping someone else's trash out of your cab. The company ran a school in Phoenix and hired its graduates. Three weeks of instruction cost $1,200.

"Your background check came back squeaky-clean," a Linehaul recruiter said. "You're hired. You'll have to get yourself to Phoenix for orientation and the school. You'll need air brakes, doubles, and haz-mat endorsements."

I took a drug screen, a physical, and a fitness test, then studied for and passed the California written CDL exams—the state would issue my license if I made it through an on-road skills exam at Linehaul's school. After that, I'd spend six weeks on the road with a trainer, pulling loads and living in a truck, and, after that, I'd take a Linehaul road test. Then I'd climb into a tractor and go to work, driving solo.

—⚏—

Gayle and I stood at our front door, trucks and the road already a wedge between us.

She said, "I'll miss you. And our friend here will miss you."

She reached down to pet Sam, who was sitting still and glaring at me, ears down, his way of telling me he wasn't happy.

One hug for the dog. No tail wags for me.

One hug for Gayle. She turned away.

I tossed my duffle bags into the back seat, started the engine, and turned out of the driveway. I don't think I looked back.

—ɯ—

On the way to Phoenix, I paid attention to big trucks in a way I never had before. Soon, I would be driving one. I'd never noticed big rigs at rest areas. I'd never thought about truck scales—I didn't know that drivers were grabbing their mics.

"What's the word on the Wheeler Ridge scale?"

"Closed. Californy don't need your money today."

"Eastbound, what's Banning up to?"

"The inspection bays are open for business. Got your checkbook? Oh—they just closed the ramp."

"Goody."

"Oh—they just opened it again."

"Damn."

I would learn about scales and inspection bays just as I would learn about all the rest of it. I promised myself that I'd be a good student, for a change.

East of the old Burns Brothers truck stop near Coachella, CA, I-10 runs 24 miles up to Chiriaco Summit and the General George F. Patton Memorial Museum. Truckers gear down for the long pull, but the road flattens out eight miles from the crest. Getting over is easy, even with a heavy load. Then you coast downhill toward Phoenix, past rugged mountains and empty desert valleys.

Seen from the highway at sunup, the broad basins and distant ranges looked peaceful and untouched, the kinds of quiet places I like to think about and wake up in, but I was held captive, instead, by highway dreams and white line fever.

Blythe appeared, then the Colorado River and the Arizona state line. Unshackled from California's 55 mile-an-hour truck speed limit, most truckers cruised at 70. Linehaul's rigs slogged along at 57.

From Quartzite it was just two hours to the brown stain in the desert that is Phoenix. Long, nondescript streets. Strip malls. One dreary intersection after another, an urban patchwork extending for miles under a blanket of smog and dust, Arizona's answer to Los Angeles. I found a cheap motel minutes from Linehaul's terminal and called home.

"Hi," Gayle said. "Where are you?"

Sam barked.

—ɯɯ—

The next morning, orientation for 30 new-hires began with a video: blood dripped from covered stretchers. A sheeted body was wheeled to an ambulance. Someone was crying, "No . . . Please . . . No." In dense fog near Fresno, CA, a Linehaul driver and a four-wheeler missed their stop signs. They couldn't see beyond the windshields and didn't realize that they were both crossing an intersection at the same time. Their vehicles were moving fast, fast enough to wedge the car under the trailer, fast enough for the truck to roll 50 yards after impact, fast enough to decapitate one or two of the car's occupants. A woman screamed at the truck driver, "*You* did this! Look at what you did! *Look* at what you did!" Cut to the trucker, who covered his face with one hand and tried to hold the other in front of the lens. Fade to black.

"It can be rough out there," said a rep from Linehaul's safety department. He passed around photographs of wrecked trucks and bloodied windshields.

"This one was a suicide by truck—the guy stepped onto I-40 just west of Flagstaff. And this one here. Notice the antlers and the leg? The deer came over the hood and into the cab. The co-driver was hurt bad. Blood everywhere, as you can see. They had to replace the seats and all the upholstery."

This one hit a moose. This one hit an elk. This one hit a cow. Blood everywhere.

"This one. Rollover. Asleep at the wheel. Terminated, of course."

Knocked over a fire hydrant, water everywhere. Terminated. Drove under a low-clearance bridge in Chicago, ripped open the roof of a trailer, and didn't report it. Terminated. Forgot to set the brakes—tractor and trailer rolled off an embankment. Terminated. Overheated the brakes on a long, steep descent in Colorado—tires burned up, trailer burned up, tractor burned up, cargo a total loss, what can you say? Jackknifed on ice. Jack-knifed on dry pavement. Another rollover. Terminated. Terminated. Terminated.

A driver from a flatbed outfit recently acquired by Linehaul said, "How do y'all pay on miles?"

"We pay on Household Movers' Guide miles."

"They gave us hub miles before," said another flatbedder. "HHG stinks."

"Yeah. Now we're losing money."

"Yeah."

"Yeah," said the flatbedder seated next to me.

I asked him what the problem was.

"This outfit don't pay for all the miles you drive."

What? The brochure and the recruiter said Linehaul drivers were paid by the mile. I whispered to him, "A mile is a mile isn't it?"

"Not here."

Reps from different departments told us about the company. Founded in 1966 with two trucks, it was now up to almost 1,500. They hoped to be near 2,000 the following year and to add more each year after that. "The owner is a big guy and he wants to be the biggest. He bought a company in South Carolina a couple of years ago. And you flatbed operators, he just bought you."

"He didn't buy *me*," said a flatbed driver.

"We book a lot of retail freight, paper products, non-perishable foods, building materials—things people use. That keeps our trailers loaded and it keeps you moving. Remember this: don't *ever* say you'll deliver a load then drop the ball. *Never* deliver late. *Never* make a dispatcher look bad. Dispatchers have long memories."

"So do I," said the flatbedder next to me.

—ⁿⁿ—

The school.

Monday through Friday, 6 a.m. sharp to 5 p.m.

One week of classroom instruction, one week of learning to drive trucks at a training site known as The Range, one week of Range practice and supervised driving on streets and highways. The final exam would be a driving test and the diploma a CDL with air brakes, doubles, and hazardous-materials endorsements.

Monday.

At exactly 6 a.m. the instructor sneezed and said, "Call me Bob." There were introductions all around and a short bio from each student. Cab driver. Divorcee. Cookie salesman. Grocery clerk. Unemployed minister. Downsized computer programmer. Our ages varied—mid-twenties, forties, early fifties, sixties—and we all said the same thing: "I have always wanted to drive big trucks."

Bob shuffled his notes and began his first lecture: the responsibilities of driving a big truck. Then he talked about night driving, winter driving, and mountain driving. He told us to shower every day, to brush our teeth morning and night, to eat vegetables for proper digestion, to steer clear of truck-stop prostitutes. "You don't know what that lot lizard's got and you won't know until it's too late. You don't want to bring it home to your wife."

Tuesday.

Two students walked in fifteen minutes after Bob started his lecture. He frowned. "Late and trucking don't mix. You're both off to a bad start. You need to get with the program."

Wednesday.

Bob said, "Today we'll talk about the Hours of Service regulations and log books. Your trainers will tell you more when you get on the road, but I'll show you how to fill in a driver's daily log sheet. We'll spend the afternoon on word problems I've cooked up—I'll tell you what a driver did and you'll do the logs."

In one of Bob's log book exercises, a trucker drove from 9 a.m. to 3 p.m., slept from 3 p.m. to 9 p.m., drove from 9 p.m. to 1 a.m. then slept from 1 a.m. to 3 a.m. He unloaded until 8 a.m.

"It may be okay with you if I rest for two hours and get up at 3 a.m.," the divorcee said. "But you should ask me first. A gal needs her beauty sleep."

Everyone laughed. Sleep two hours. Throw freight for five hours, starting at 3 o'clock in the morning. Yeah, sure. How about some examples from the real world?

Thursday.

Surprise quiz. Safety videos. Lectures, with examples, on defensive driving.

"Always use turn signals and look before changing lanes," Bob said. "It doesn't cost anything to use your mirrors. Not using them can cost a bundle. Stay alert and respect other drivers on the road. Trucks and truck drivers are always on display, so show people that you're a pro. Don't get mad if someone passes you or gives you the finger and don't try to get even. Your truck is not a weapon."

Friday afternoon.

Bob said, "I want to leave you with this: the stopping distance for an empty rig is greater than the stopping distance for a loaded one. At 60 miles an hour on a dry road, you travel 90 feet before you touch the brake pedal, then you need more than 100 yards to stop. One hundred yards is the length of a football field. Things will happen within inches of your front bumper and they'll happen damn quick. Be prepared. Drive safe. Good luck. Report to The Range Monday at 6 a.m. Do not—any of you—show up late."

The Range.

Two graveled acres at the edge of Linehaul's yard. Orange traffic cones laid out to simulate corners, alleys, and loading docks. Four old tractors. Four old trailers. A few students were there Monday at 5 a.m., just to look around. We said, "Can't wait." "One step closer." "Gonna be good."

At 6 a.m. the chief instructor said, "Welcome to The Range. Here you will learn to inspect trucks and drive them forward and backward. We'll start with the pretrip inspection. You do not—ever, ever, ever—drive until you pretrip."

A second instructor stepped forward.

"The federal safety regulations say a truck driver has to satisfy himself that a vehicle is in good working order. You can't be satisfied unless you inspect your equipment. So you always conduct a pretrip inspection before driving and when you hook up to trailers and when you jump into a tractor for the first time. You pretrip with a flashlight in the middle of the night when it's raining and the trailer is parked in a mud hole, when the wind is blowing dust or snow in your face, when it's 110 in the shade, and whether a trailer is loaded or empty. Look for what is wrong. If something *is* wrong, get it fixed pronto. You wouldn't fly a plane if you knew one of the wings was going to fall off."

He handed out inspection checklists and led us over to a tractor and trailer. "We'll go through the pretrip inspection as a group, then you'll work in pairs, then by yourselves. You'll be doing this alone out there. Learn it."

We started at the steering tire on the driver's side of the tractor.

Another instructor said, "As professional drivers you will look at 18 tires and wheels—more if you're pulling double or triple trailers—at least once a day, more often than that if you're carrying hazardous materials. Look for cuts or bulges in both sidewalls, nails in the tread, low air pressure, uneven tread wear, and low tread. Check tread depths with a tire gauge if you're not sure—by law, we're allowed no less than 4/32" for steers and 2/32" for all others. If they're down that low get the shop to replace them. Some states will ticket you if you don't have metal caps on the valve stems. Are any missing? Carry spares. Make sure there aren't any loose or missing lug nuts and that there's no grease leaks around the hub. Is a wheel bent or damaged? Get over to a shop for a replacement. Let's move around to the front of the tractor . . . You don't want broken headlamps or a cracked windshield. Does the tractor lean to one side? Check for broken leaf springs."

We walked to the right-hand side of the tractor then to the right-side fuel tank area, just in front of the trailer.

"Check everything on this side like you did on the driver's side. You want to be sure the tank doesn't leak and isn't ready to fall off. Don't laugh. It's happened. While you're here, check the exhaust pipe. You don't want that to come off, either. Check the drive tires and rims. Check the mud flap and its bracket. Make sure there's no rocks stuck between any of the duals or on the landing gear. They could fly off and chip a windshield or hurt someone. When you hook a trailer or trailers, check the registration and annual inspection stickers—you and the company can be fined if they're missing or expired. Check for rust, holes, damage of any kind, air leaks and electrical problems. Look underneath. Check every tire and wheel. Adjust the brakes—we'll show you how tomorrow. Check the brake drums for cracks. Check hub oilers and grease caps. Make sure all the lights work. Look for missing rivets and broken welds. If the trailer is loaded and there's a seal, check the seal number against your paperwork. If the trailer is empty, climb in and look around—is it clean? Shippers won't load a dirty trailer."

We walked down the right side of the trailer to the tandems.

"You may find a bent rim back here. It'll usually be on this side—some drivers hit curbs and don't report the damage."

At the back of the trailer, the instructor said, "Check for a license plate, a rear bumper, and tail lights."

We looked at the tandems on the left side and walked along the trailer toward the tractor.

"Look at everything on this side that you looked at on the other side."

The instructor stopped at the fifth-wheel.

"Be sure the kingpin jaws are locked. The air and electrical lines can't hang down and rub the catwalk or the frame. That could get you a ticket, at least in California. Look at this fuel tank just like you did the other one. Look in the sidebox and check for three reflective triangles and a charged and properly-rated fire extinguisher."

We stopped at the driver's door.

"Before you start the engine, raise the hood and check the oil level. Look at the fan belts—should be three of them. Look for oil leaks. Is the water pump leaking? Are the alternator brackets cracked or broken? See that they're repaired—it's your responsibility. Grip the steering column to be sure it isn't loose. When you start the engine, watch the gauges. Be sure air and oil pressure come up right away and the compressor cuts out at 120 pounds. Test the horns. Check your voltage. Turn on all the lights, get out, and make sure they work. Run an air leak test and a low-air warning test. Check the tractor protection valve—if it doesn't pop out, find out why and get the thing fixed.

"Okay, I guess that's it. Get everything down cold. You'll have to perform a pretrip inspection and explain it to an examiner to get your license."

Tuesday. Wednesday. Thursday.

We learned to adjust brakes and practiced pretrip inspections. We backed under trailers, pulled them around traffic-cone corners, and backed them into traffic-cone docks. Instructors shouted, "Use your mirrors!" "Turn the wheel! No, the other way!" "Let the clutch out gently!" "I said gently, damnit!"

We learned about trailer off-track when the divorcee turned a corner and flattened three cones.

"People, people, people," said an instructor. "You won't pass the test if you run over anything. Learn to turn. Someday, there might be pedestrians at a crosswalk and you could crush them with your tandems if you turn wrong. 'Sorry' won't be good enough."

Friday afternoon.

An instructor said, "The pretrip inspection and back-ups are exactly what you'll do for the skills test. You're practicing. Next week, you'll practice more and we'll go outside and play in traffic."

Monday morning.

"I want you all to pretrip this tractor. Let me know if you find anything that's not right."

None of us did.

"Everybody look at the fan belts again. They're loose and one is cracked in three places on the inside. It's ready to break."

Monday afternoon.

"Pretrip this tractor and that trailer. Tell me what's wrong."

We didn't have a clue.

"There's no license plates! You don't want to cross a scale without license plates! The violation will go on your driving record and the fine will be your problem. Look for what is wrong. It's cheaper."

Tuesday.

We practiced pretrips and went out one-on-one with instructors to make deliveries. I backed to docks in Phoenix and Tempe then drove down to Nogales and back toward Phoenix. In Casa Grande, my instructor said, "You're starting to get the hang of it, but this dock is a famous rookie buster. Best let me do it. Did they tell you? Tomorrow, the class will convoy to Los Angeles. We'll deliver loads, stay at a motel, pick up trailers Thursday, and come back. I hope you're not fussy—the motel is a pit."

Wednesday.

We pretripped tractors, hooked loaded trailers, pretripped again, and set out for Los Angeles, the students driving and chattering on the CB.

In the consignee's lot my instructor said, "Back 'er and drop 'er." At dinner he leaned across the table and grinned. "I told you this place was a pit, didn't I? Holes in the walls, drunk truck drivers, hookers, hookers, and more hookers."

Thursday.

Halfway through the trip back to Phoenix the instructor said, "Well, how do you like driving?"

"Don't tell my wife, but I think I could get used to this."

Friday.

Each student pretripped a rig then drove off with an instructor, pulling a trailer around a few city blocks, out onto I-10 for several miles, and back to The Range—the exact route of the exam. I ground the gears on a downshift coming off the Interstate.

"You did good," the instructor said. "That shift bomb is the only thing I'd mark you down for."

Saturday.

"No one fails," said an instructor. "You will take the test until you pass, even if we have to stay all night. Our job is to get you into a trainer truck."

One by one, we went through our pre-trip exams. I pointed out a missing tail lamp and a bent ICC bumper but forgot to check the heater and the air conditioning. I backed in between the cones and ground the gears at the same off-ramp. The chief instructor shook my hand and said, "Congratulations. You have a CDL. Welcome aboard."

I drove home to California.

Chapter Four

Education is hanging around until you've caught on.

The Linehaul recruiter called from Stockton. "Come on down. Your trainer will be here this afternoon. His name is Eric. You'll like him."

"You've only been home for two days," Gayle said. "When will you be back?"

Sam sat down and glared at me.

Eric Le Clare repeated his truck number and handed me a key. "Don't lose it, like the last guy. Put your things in the closet behind your seat and take your shoes off before you step between the seats. No shoes in the sleeper. Ever. Keeps dirt out, keeps the inside clean. No smoking in the truck. Ever. No chewing snuff, either. Sneezing is okay, but not too often. The upper bunk is yours."

Eric's company-issued Kenworth T600—a model known to truckers as an Anteater because it looks like one—was clean inside and he didn't use tobacco, two pluses. My only request had been to train with a non-smoker, but I'd have put up with almost anyone and anything for six weeks now that I was this close.

"We're deadheading to Hayward," he said. "That will take

about an hour. We'll hook a set there and run up to the company's Wilsonville yard, in Oregon—it's near Portland. I'm hoping to come right back to Hayward and go right back up to Wilsonville. I'm trying to build a dedicated I-5 run. I try to stay on I-5 because it keeps me close to my daughter. And I-5 will be good training for you: it's got hills, curves, straight stretches. It's the real world."

On the way out to Hayward I had time to get a closer look at Eric. He was short and thick-set, with a heavy salt-and-pepper moustache and a receding gray hairline.

He said, "We're the same age and you've got a lot more hair. That has to stop."

Eric drove and we talked, mostly about our lives and ourselves. He'd barely made it through high school, but I would learn that he was capable, intelligent, and possessed of a photographic memory and an enduring passion for all things trucking.

"I'll be bad-tempered once in a while," he said. "Don't take it personally. I'm going through a divorce. I guess I wasn't home enough."

He had been driving trucks for 22 of his 45 years.

"It's all I've ever done, all I want to do, and all I'm ever going to do. I started when I got out . . ."

Eric checked the mirrors and changed lanes to pass a slow-moving truck. He shifted down one gear, checked the mirrors again, grabbed the mic, said, "Thanks, Schneider," switched the turn signal off and shifted up, all in one seamless movement. He barely pumped the clutch. He was smoother than an automatic transmission.

". . . of the army. Look. I'll teach you what I know. That's my job, so ask questions. I'm supposed to show you how to chain up, but I don't really expect snow in June. I'm not carrying chains anyway. You'll have to get it on your own."

I said I was there to learn and that I could figure things out for myself.

"Good. Not like the last guy. He knew it all before he got into the truck."

We broke our set apart in the shipper's lot, Eric said, "Let's see how you back up," and I sweated my way through pull-up after pull-up.

I said, "Tough dock."

"This is nothing. Practice. You'll get it. The loads come out between 6 p.m. and 8 p.m. It's all doubles freight and it's got to be in Wilsonville no more than 14 hours after we sign the shipping papers. It's 625 miles. We go zip-zip, nonstop. We'll split the driving."

At 8 o'clock he began glancing at the dock every few minutes. At 8:30 he looked at his watch and sighed. "Better get some sleep. I'll put the set together and start driving when our trailers are ready and wake you up a couple of hours after we get moving, whenever that is. Some loads come out late. That's your first lesson."

Get some sleep? At 8:30 on a summer evening? I didn't know what it was like to be in bed before midnight, but I climbed up to my bunk. Eric switched on his TV and put a tape in the VCR:

Good Morning, Vietnam.

At 2 a.m. on an off-ramp 75 miles from Hayward, he tapped my shoulder. "Tag. You're it. The load came out at midnight, those jerks. Well, we know you can sleep in a moving truck. You were out cold."

I adjusted the driver's seat—Eric was the shorter driver—and showed him my log book.

"Looks okay," he said. "Ready?" He sat sideways in the passenger seat for a few minutes, yawning. "Smooth shifting. You're using the mirrors. Good. I'm going to bed." He disappeared behind the sleeper curtain.

So this was it. The truck rumbled and shook. The engine droned on, diesel-loud. Air whistled through a gap in a door gasket. The seat frame creaked. The gear-shift lever wobbled and the dash gauges glowed. Outside, rural darkness was broken only by our rig's headlights and marker lamps. In just five weeks and six days, I'd be on my own. I'd sleep every night, too. None of this 2 a.m. foolishness for me.

I checked the mirrors and turned on the CB just to listen.

"Man," a driver said. "What a night! Is this a night or what? I love running at night."

"Me too," said another. "There's no traffic. It's just me and my rig."

Three hours later I saw the start of my first trucking sunrise, a pale blue glow off to the east, beyond the Sierra Nevada. The stars disappeared. Early light streaked high, distant clouds pink and orange. The colors faded. The sun rose behind Lassen Peak and pinned Mt. Shasta to the sky. I had driven up and down the Sacramento Valley many times and I thought I knew the place, but today everything was fresh and exciting. Today, everything began again.

Eric stepped from the sleeper, half-fell into the passenger seat, and said, "How's it going?"

"Good. Great."

His head dropped to his chest and he was asleep.

We stopped for coffee in Weed.

"Second lesson," Eric said. "'Check' calls. Find a phone and call in before 8 a.m. every morning except weekends. Give them the hours you logged the day before. If you need fuel, a cash advance, directions, whatever, tell your fleet manager. Call when you get empty or when you're loaded and ready to leave a shipper, even on weekends. Call anytime something hits the fan."

Eric drove the rest of the way to Wilsonville. I watched from the passenger seat as he pulled hills, descended grades, changed lanes, and worked through shift after flawless shift without even a glance at the tach or the speedometer. He was completely relaxed behind the wheel, careful and alert, his eyes always moving, constantly checking the gauges and mirrors. He kept his CB on, eager to chat or cheerfully trade insults with other truck drivers.

"'CB,'" he said, laughing. "Know what that means?"

"No."

"Children's Band."

I stayed up all day, high on a beginner's adrenalin.

We dropped the trailers and Eric called dispatch for our next load assignment.

He said, "We've got one from Portland to San Leandro, right next door to Hayward. If things go the way they should, we'll load in Hayward tomorrow night and be back up here the next day. For now, we'll put a set together, get showers and food at Burns Brothers, then go into town and see if they'll load us early. Maybe it's yes, maybe it's no. You won't know if you don't ask. Might want to remember that."

We waited at the shipper's dock for five hours. I dozed off around 7:30.

"Tag," Eric said, at 9:30. "You're it."

He hooked up and rode shotgun while I drove south out of Portland and across the Aurora truck scales on I-5. He crawled into the sleeper. I drove for three more hours. Before I realized what I was doing, I had slapped my face several times to stay awake. Then Eric was shouting at me.

"Pull over! Get into your bunk! Always tell me if you're tired! Always! Not good! Not good at all!"

The next morning he said, "You didn't want to admit you were tired. That's a good way to get killed out here."

I'd slept two hours in 23—as Eric knew—but he was still mad and he had every right to be.

"Okay," he said. "You got that out of your system. Most people wait a couple of weeks. Third lesson: don't do it again."

Eric later confided that he hardly ever rested when a new trainee drove. He lay on the bunk and listened, or watched through a slit in the curtain, ready to grab the wheel. When he slept, he believed, it was with one eye open. "If I'm asleep and you miss a shift, I know. If you head off toward the fog line or the median, I know. If you're thinking of having an accident and killing me, I know."

We ran like a true team once I figured out what Eric called the sleep thing. If I was tired, I said so. He did the same. One evening—just one—he pulled into a rest area and we both slept for seven uninterrupted hours, but most of the time we rolled up and down I-5. I began to enjoy night driving. Backing to docks, hooking trailers, load manifests and paperwork, Hours of Service regulations and log books—none of it was hard to understand.

Two weeks went by quickly.

The Hayward loads never came out at the same hour. I often fell asleep to *Good Morning, Vietnam* and a couple of times I woke up to it. If one of us was awake, the loaders waved from the dock. If we were resting, they beat on the door—harder, I thought, than they had to. I hated that sudden shock out of sleep.

Linehaul lost the Hayward account and we began to go where the freight went: Phoenix, Los Angeles, Lewiston, ID, Salt

Lake City, Phoenix again, the Bay Area, Portland, then back to Phoenix, back to the Bay Area, back to Los Angeles, and back to the Bay Area. I liked it best when we ran hard miles, the more the better.

"You want to keep moving," Eric said. "Not like the last guy."

I got home for two days after running for two weeks, then for half a day a week later.

Gayle said, "Is this how it's going to be? I see you when I see you?"

"Classroom in the cab," Eric said one night. "Things to know. 'Cabover'—no hood. 'Conventional'—hood. 'Dry van'—that's what we pull, as opposed to reefers. Stay away from iceboxes. A lot can go wrong. Who do you think pays for it? You go to a refrigerated warehouse, and you can wait a day or more to get loaded. 'Pups' you know. 'Set' you know. 'Doubles' you know. Any questions?"

I asked why the air-line connectors between tractors and trailers were called glad hands.

"Beats me."

What did LTL mean?

"Less-than-load. The trailer's not full or there's more than one shipment inside."

Bobtail?

"Your tail's bobbed off—there's no trailer behind you."

Pigtail?

"The electrical line between a tractor and a trailer. It's coiled, like that thing on an oinker's rear-end."

Deadhead?

"Going to get a load or running empty—a driver will tell you he's got a load of dispatcher brains, nothing but air in the trailer. Speaking of dispatchers' brains, get yourself a dispatch buster."

"A what?"

"Dispatch buster. Tape recorder with a little microphone that clips to the phone. Could save your butt someday. When you play a dispatcher's words back to him, he can't say he didn't say them. It's fun. Illegal, but fun. Recess. You drive. I've got a movie waiting. Wish I had some popcorn."

At the Phoenix terminal the company moved us into a brand new Freightliner.

"This is more like it," Eric said. "The Anteater's about dead anyway."

At the Stockton terminal the next day he said, "They've got two red-hot loads. You're going to see new country and make new friends."

We were off to Dallas with another trainer, a long-time friend of Eric's named Mike, and his trainee.

"You'll drive days and I'll drive nights, because Mike likes to drive at night and he and I like to gab on the CB."

Eastbound on I-40, five miles west of Amarillo.

I staggered out of the dark sleeper into the sunlit cab and dropped onto the passenger seat, rubbing my eyes. Eric and

Mike were deep into a CB discussion about divorce.

I said, "Coffee. Now."

"Mine just got up," Eric said. "What about yours?"

"Sawin' logs. I'm gonna let him sleep."

"Mine told me this'd be his first time in Texas."

"Well, what does he think?"

"Well, what do you think?"

"Uh," I said, looking out the window, "It's flat."

"Says it's flat. Wants coffee."

"Ten-four. Let's stop at the Petro. I've got to take the dog for a walk."

I said, "Mike's got a dog with him?"

"No," Eric said. "He means wee wee."

"Good idea."

Eric went into the sleeper to watch *Good Morning, Vietnam* and Mike led the way. We talked on the CB. A sedan passed from behind and I looked down at two matrons, their skirts hiked high.

"Mike," I said. "Don't look at those two chicks in the Lincoln."

He did, hoping to see young legs and maybe more. "Is that what Eric is teaching you?"

"No, I sort of invented that one."

"You'll do fine out here. You'll fit right in. Damn, but it's gonna be a hot day. If I was wearing a dress, I'd pull it up too."

Like Eric, Mike trained for the money—trainers were paid for all dispatched miles the truck ran—and, like Eric, he had never done anything but drive. "Seems like I've been out here my whole life. Owned a truck once. Went broke. Got divorced. Got married again. We're holding it together."

He wasn't home with his wife and kids more than a couple of days a month. It took a lot of miles to put food on the table, even with a trainer's pay.

We dropped our trailers in Dallas, found empties, and dead-headed to Fort Smith, AR for our next loads, one to Stockton and one to Los Angeles. The trainees hooked up, drove, and talked on the CB—the trainers slept. The trainers drove and the trainees slept. I drove and Eric watched *Good Morning, Vietnam*. The trainers split up in Barstow while the trainees were asleep. I pulled the curtain aside in Mojave and said, "I've got to . . ." and Eric joined in, "Take the dog for a walk. Have mercy! Mike told me about the grannies and the Lincoln."

In Stockton, he said, "I need a real Saturday-Sunday weekend. How about you? Yeah? See you Monday."

When we got back together again at the terminal, he was hooked up, grinning, and ready to go.

"We've got another hot one: display cabinets for a department store in a fancy Miami mall. Mall deliveries are a pain in the rear, but it's good miles. Florida, here we come! Kind of far from my kid, though. The thing is, we've got to deliver early Friday morning, Florida time. That gives us four days, but it's only about 60 driving hours so we should be okay. You're going to see more new country."

And I did, all along I-10 through New Mexico, Texas, Louisiana, Mississippi, and Alabama.

"We'd stop at the battleship museum if we had time," Eric said near Mobile. He laughed and shook his head. "I say that every time I drive by."

And Florida.

Eric said, "You're not going to tell me it's flat, are you?"

At 1 a.m. Friday in Miami we argued about freeway exit numbers and pulled into the mall after taking what should have been a wrong turn. Our directions brutalized east and west, left and right, a street name, any number of stop lights and stop signs, and had been given to us by someone who thought a truck coming from California would be headed north.

"Directions from hell," Eric said. "Get used to it."

Our next load, beer from a brewery in Jacksonville, wouldn't be ready until 1 a.m., Monday. The deadhead, 340 miles, would take, at most, six hours. Once loaded, we'd only pull the trailer to the Linehaul terminal in Greer, SC—400 miles.

"Seven hundred and forty miles," Eric said. "Three and a half days. Not good. Not good at all. Oh, well. You take the freight as it comes and you go where it goes. We ought to drop the trailer somewhere and check out the beaches, but we wouldn't have jobs if we came back and it was gone. People steal these things all the time down here. They think every trailer is full of TV sets."

We found a motel with truck parking, a swimming pool, and cable television.

I called home. Gayle said, "Where are you? When will I see

you?" And Sam barked.

At the Greer terminal, dispatchers put us on a hot load to southern California. "Team freight. Balls to the wall." Eric said. "You've got to love it."

In Jackson, MS he said, "When a hooker knocks on the door and you want her to go away, tell her to wait a minute, you've got to ask your wife. It works every time."

Near Weatherford, TX it was, "Tag. Wake me near El Paso." He closed the curtain and launched Robin Williams.

At the Phoenix terminal, a driver jackknifed while trying to back into a parking place and crushed a fairing behind his sleeper. Eric groaned. "Some drive, some just hold the wheel. You know, there's guys out here who've gone one or two million miles without an accident. Look around. It's easy to tell who can drive and who can't."

We grabbed a Seattle load in Los Angeles, drove north on I-5, and stopped at the Stockton yard for the night. Eric banged on the sleeper early in the morning.

"They have a truck for you and a load to Anaheim for this afternoon if you're okay with leaving me a week early. I told them you know what you're doing."

We shook hands. I said goodbye and thanks and see you down the road. Eric said, "Chicks in the Lincoln," and walked off, laughing. Then he turned around, as solemn as the night I'd been too tired to drive and too green to admit it. "Hey, Marc. Work on your first million miles. Keep the shiny side up and the dirty side down. Not like the last guy."

Chapter Five

It was a new world to him, with a new population.
SHELBY FOOTE, JORDAN COUNTY

I carried my duffle and sleeping bag to my first truck, passed the Linehaul road test, and met my fleet manager. He said, "I go by the name of Jimmy. You only take orders from me. Understand?"

I started back down I-5 and turned on Linehaul's cheap CB. "Hey, Linehaul truck 7405," a driver said. "Are you gonna wash that road commode sometime this year? That is *completely* disgusting. Somebody ought to call your company and give 'em your truck number."

I had to laugh, thinking how Eric would have answered that.

7405. A single-screw Volvo with rookie written all over it and 525,000 hard miles on the odometer. Not much bigger than a day cab inside. You couldn't stand up under the low roof. Instead, you squeezed up from the seat, took one hunched-over step to the right, and quickly sat on the narrow mattress, your legs stretched forward, your feet almost touching the firewall. Under the bunk, in the only storage compartment, spilled coolant and oily trash competed for space with your clothing.

7405. Nine gears. No overdrive. Governed at 57 miles an hour. A weed burner—the muffler and exhaust pipe were mounted directly below the sleeper. Without a vertical stack to carry it away, exhaust seeped up and into the cab and sleeper. Idling meant a carbon monoxide headache for the driver and anyone parked nearby.

7405. The dirtiest vehicle I had ever seen, inside or out. But I would degrease, disinfect, hose down, scrub, wax, and polish until it stood apart from every other truck on the road as soon as I found time.

I drove 200 miles nonstop, bought a cold root beer in Lost Hills, drank a toast to the arrival of a new life, and saluted the new man reflected in a truck-stop window. Out there had, at last, become out *here*. My training, what the company called driver finishing, was over, but my CDL was still little more than a license to keep on learning. Out here, I would finish myself.

South again, to the Grapevine and a sign at Wheeler Ridge: *All Trucks Stop At Scales*. My load wasn't heavy—18,000 pounds was nowhere near enough to put me over. The registration and permits were up-to-date. I'd done a thorough pretrip and adjusted the brakes under the watchful eyes of the yard boss. Nothing to worry about.

A loudspeaker detonated outside the driver's window. "Driver of Linehaul truck 7405, drive around to door number three."

What had I done? California wouldn't pull me in for a filthy truck, would they?

An officer inside the inspection station said, "Show me your log book, driver's license, medical card, tractor registration, trailer registration, and shipping papers."

He gave the tractor and trailer a once-over.

"Everything's okay," he said. "And your log book looks good. Neat. Legible. Current. I can hardly read some of them. How long have you been driving?"

"Five hours. It's in the book."

"I mean, how long have you been driving professionally?"

"Five hours. I have been driving professionally for five hours."

My load was set to deliver in Anaheim six hours after Jimmy handed the papers to me. The distance from Stockton, 360 miles, took about seven hours on California freeways in a governed truck, if you kept moving.

"Get down there anyway," Jimmy had said. "They'll take it."

"Come back at 6 p.m. tomorrow," said the receiving clerk. "Not 6:01. If you're late again I won't accept the load. Your company needs to get its on-time numbers up. What? Hell no you can't park in my lot until tomorrow night."

I called Dispatch.

"That's what happens when you're late, driver. You'll have to sit with it."

Three hundred and sixty paid miles in one day became 360 paid miles in two. I parked on a side street, a dangerous thing to do in southern California, the truck-and-cargo-theft capital of the United States. In those days, Linehaul didn't say anything to new drivers about that.

In the morning I walked two blocks to a phone booth.

"Hi," Gayle said. "Where are you?"

Sam barked.

"Anaheim. I've got my own truck."

"I didn't think they'd take it," Jimmy said during the check-call.

"Well, well," said the receiving clerk. "He's on time tonight. Let's see if he can get into door 13—that's the one between door 12 and door 14. The last Linehaul driver had a lot of trouble with it—entertained us for half-an-hour. Guess he was just unlucky. Thirteen. Unlucky. Get it?"

Mindful of drivers in the lot—any one of them had more experience—I took a deep breath and started to back in, certain they were all watching, eager for a mistake and the chance to tell me I didn't know how to drive. I turned the wheel, the tractor swung around, and the trailer slipped down between the guide lines then bumped the dock dead-center. I set the brakes, exhaled, and looked around. No one had paid any attention to me.

Mexican lumpers handled the unload, a full-trailer sort, hand-stack, and fingerprint. Two coffee breaks for union warehousemen stretched the job to seven hours. I called in as soon as the last boxes came off.

"You have to call when you're empty," said the dispatcher. "Not the day after. Didn't you get empty last night? Deadhead over to Fontana and pick up for Woodland. Got a pencil and paper? Here's directions and your load info . . . Deliver as soon as possible. It's a drop. And from now on, call as soon as you're empty."

I swapped trailers in Fontana, drove through the night and into mid-morning, parked at the Stockton terminal, and slept for six uneasy hours. I dropped the load in Woodland, bobtailed 40 miles back to the terminal, took my things out of the truck, and went home.

—ᗰ—

I was back at the yard two days later with tools, clothes, bedding, groceries, and a milk crate full of waxes, polishes, scrub brushes, and cleaning rags. I couldn't find 7405.

"They got rid of that old clunker," Jimmy said. "Take 8239. Put a set together then come see me."

The tractor turned out to be a single-screw Volvo abandoned by a driver from the company's Oklahoma City terminal. 8239. Dent-free. Clean and like-new inside. Seventeen thousand miles on the odometer, barely broken in. It wasn't a weed burner.

I began to run irregular freight up and down the West Coast, from Seattle to San Diego, to and from cities in and around Los Angeles, and out to Phoenix. Trips to Utah, Colorado, the east coast, or the South were rare and welcome changes of scene, and every load taught me something—where to park and where not to park; where to eat and where not to eat; how to beat the Hours of Service and get enough sleep; how to make my log book look legal when it wasn't.

I started a list of places to go back to, small towns, cities, scenic highways. I'd call Gayle and say, "You've got to see this." I bought my first CB and my first truckers' road atlas.

The places that were new to me!

The small towns of the Midwest and the South, each town a page in our national book. Factory towns, river towns, Bonnie-and-Clyde towns. Towns boomed and busted, towns where the last picture show was screened years ago. Picture-postcard towns in New England, beautiful enough to make a man want to walk away from his truck and settle down. Towns in Oklahoma, the Texas panhandle, and southeastern Colorado still scarred by the Dirty Thirties.

Every time I drove to a new town I highlighted its name in my road atlas. Soon there were highlights on almost every page, real places that had only been names to me before, and scenic routes—routes to go back to someday. I'd seen a lot of the intermountain west and some of the northern plains and the northeast, but, before driving trucks, never the South—I was unprepared for its natural beauty and the strong, heartbreaking pull of its history. I'd never been to Appalachia, the Gulf Coast, the Dakotas, Michigan, or Wisconsin. Because there's nothing like the excitement that comes with new lore and new country, I eagerly took every load—short-haul, medium-haul, long-haul—just to go where I hadn't gone before, just to add names to my life list.

During a Sunday-morning pretrip inspection in Grand Junction, CO, I discovered a leaking hub seal on a trailer axle. Linehaul's service department gave me the number of a local repairman who answered his phone and said straight away that he didn't work on weekends. "I'll fix it first thing tomorrow. Go park at GJ's, downtown. They have good showers. There's a market across the street you might like and a laundromat two blocks away. I know what you need. I used to drive."

"If you have to get around," Eric had told me, "use the truck as your personal car."

I dropped the trailer and bobtailed out to the Colorado welcome center in Fruita, saw a brochure for Colorado National Monument, and called the park—I had a road tractor but no trailers. Would it be possible to drive through?

"Come on over," a ranger said. "We'll call your tractor an RV. It'll be two dollars extra."

I drove into the monument, up onto the Uncompahgre Plateau and along Rim Rock Drive, stopped at every scenic overlook, and enjoyed a picnic in the cab. If trucking gave me opportunities like this, I wasn't going home. I was out there to stay.

Grand Junction became a personal watering hole. I always found the same safe parking place across the street from GJ's, where the shower was clean and cost only $5. The market across the street had friendly cashiers, a good deli, and a better bakery. I would look up at the mesas and say, "I've been there. Gayle's got to see this."

—∽—

"Oklahoma City wants 8239," said a Stockton dispatcher. "See if 7425 will start."

7425. A Volvo weed burner twice as old as 7405 and twice as grubby. It stank of oil, diesel fuel, the men who had driven it, and a dog or two. A loosely-capped pee bottle rolled around under the bunk. Something that could have been either blood or ketchup stained the floor in the passenger's footwell. Dirt and matted dog hair coated the upholstery. I pressure-washed the interior, air-dried it for a day, bought painter's drop cloths to cover the seats and floor, wrapped a thick tarp around the stained mattress, and didn't even think about wax or polish. I sat through unpaid downtime in San Diego for an air leak, unpaid downtime in Stockton for oil leaks, and unpaid downtime in Phoenix for electrical repairs. I asked Jimmy about Linehaul's advertised new equipment. He said, "New guys drive old trucks."

Late on a Friday afternoon.

Jimmy called me to the Stockton dispatch window. He had a hot load to Bessemer, AL that would be overweight on a two-axle tractor and he needed to put a lightweight Volvo under it. 7425 was the only one in northern California.

"It's 2,400 miles, it delivers Tuesday morning, you can't be late, and you have to leave now. Do you want it or do I force-dispatch you?"

I said, "I'll need an extra log book."

"Take two. Log it legal, okay?"

I drove until midnight. Saturday, Sunday, and Monday were

perfect 14-hour days behind the wheel. I slept in the consignee's yard Monday night and called in empty the next morning.

"You're on a tire load to Reno," said a dispatcher. "Deadhead to Opelika, swap out, and call me when you hook up."

It was true! Back-to-back long hauls really did exist! This was what I'd been looking for. This was miles with a capital M.

"Deliver Friday morning," said the dispatcher when she took my load call.

"It's Tuesday afternoon. I can't drive 2,400 miles in two and a half days."

"I am telling you to be in Reno Friday morning! Drive! Don't be late!"

"I can do it for Saturday."

"They're closed on weekends. We can't reschedule."

I called the safety department, they called her, and she rescheduled for Monday.

On Saturday afternoon I dropped my trailers at the Reno yard and took the truck home. I had driven 4,800 miles in eight days, never at more than 57 miles an hour. Linehaul's safety department didn't question my logs.

—⁕—

I didn't see a paycheck for three weeks.

"I'll look into it," Jimmy said, each week.

"Look here," he said at the end of the third week. "I told you I'd look into it. Say, you're not going to quit on me? You're not mad at Jimmy, are you?"

"I'm not going to quit and I'm not mad at anyone, but I'm working and I'd like to get paid."

"Ha! We screw you and you don't freak out. Amazing."

"Tell your fleet manager," said a payroll supervisor.

"I did."

"Well then, what do you expect me to do?"

I drove 165 out-of-route miles to the house, collected my trip sheets, took a load to Phoenix, and carried my papers into the payroll office.

"It's just growing pains," said a friendly clerk. "The company's growing *so* fast. You fell through a crack. It happens all the time. Oh, *I* see. The computer shows that you're out of the trainer truck, but you weren't switched over to OTR, so its kind of like you don't exist. Your fleet manager is responsible for that. No one knows you took those trips."

I knew. Dispatchers knew. Customers knew. Jimmy knew, and we talked every day.

He said, "As soon as your pay gets here from Phoenix I'll mail it to you." "No, nothing yet. Like I said, I'll mail it the moment it shows up." "Didn't I mail that to you?"

"We're selling 7425," Jimmy said one morning. "Take a load to Phoenix. They'll put you in another truck if they have one."

"I'm gonna give you 6119," a Phoenix dispatcher said. "It's a Reno truck. The driver just quit."

6119. A twin-screw Freightliner FLD120. Cleaner than 8239. Cloth upholstery instead of vinyl. Storage cabinets in the sleeper *and* under the bunk. A stain-free, twin-size inner-spring mattress. An upright stack. Only 36,000 miles on the odometer. A built-in phone wired to call a single number—Phoenix Dispatch—but only, a note on the handset cautioned, in case of emergency.

6119. Nice truck.

I sat in the driver's seat and smiled. I lay on the bunk, folded my arms back behind my head, and laughed. I took my time moving in and it was late afternoon before I had everything— each tool, each book, each item of clothing—in its place and went to the window for a load. The dispatcher said, "Stockton driver in a Reno truck? I don't know what to do about that. See Richard. He's in charge."

Richard said, "Deliver in Santa Clarita, CA at 8 a.m. Don't be late. The trailer's here in the yard."

I drove for three-and-a-half hours, slept at Chiriaco Summit, and got up at 3 a.m. I'd allowed five hours for the 183-mile morning drive to Santa Clarita, but in Pasadena rush-hour traffic on the 210 freeway came to a standstill. Accident, the radio said. We'd all be there for awhile. I called Phoenix on the truck phone and said I believed in customer service and the courtesy of telling a customer when a truck would be late. Would they call the consignee?

A dispatcher said, "Why don't *you* call?"

"The truck phone only dials Phoenix."

"Do you expect me to believe that? Richard . . . Richard! It's some guy in a truck . . . I don't *know* what he wants."

Richard said, "Why are you calling me?"

"I'm stuck in traffic. I'll be late. I'd like you to please call the consignee."

"Why would I do that?"

"Uh, good customer service?"

He said, "Horse crap." Then I was talking to a dial tone.

The receiver said, "Your company called. They said you told them you'd be late. They're *always* late and they *never* let us know. Thank you."

"Got one for you," said a California dispatcher. "Delivers Thursday, the day after tomorrow. Pick up in Los Angeles right away and scoot over to Greeley and Boulder. Do you know where Colorado is?"

I called in empty from Boulder late Thursday afternoon and told the Colorado dispatcher, "I won't have hours to do anything until tomorrow. Just letting you know." I thought he'd say, "Okay. Get some rest and call me in the morning," but I heard, "I've got you preplanned." To load in Denver that night and deliver in Salt Lake City the following morning.

"That's 500 miles not counting the deadhead," I said. "I don't have the hours for it."

"So? Cook a book. Get moving. Forced dispatch—you know how it works."

Six hours later at the northbound I-25 scale near Fort Collins, an inspector asked for my log book, flipped its pages back and forth for what seemed like an hour, then suggested that I park behind the scale house and take eight consecutive hours off duty. I said, "Thank you," slept like I meant it, and called the same dispatcher when I got up.

He said, "Why aren't you in Salt Lake?"

"You'll have to ask DOT."

"What are you talking about?"

"Well, I did tell you that I was out of hours."

"So?"

"They agreed with me. But don't worry—I didn't give them your name. This time."

He put me on hold for five minutes then came back on the line. "Deliver Monday morning. I'm not taking you off the load. You'd better watch your attitude."

Three days in the doghouse. Five hundred paid miles on a weekend. I bought a dispatch buster.

In time, Jimmy forwarded a package that contained two pay envelopes, one postmarked the day after my visit to Payroll, the other three days later. Both had been mailed to the Stockton terminal, where he'd kept them in a desk drawer. I called the manager at the Reno terminal, said I was already driving one of his trucks, and asked if he could use another driver.

He said, "Eric Le Clare is here. Says you're a good man. Love to have you."

Jimmy whined when I told him. Said I'd regret leaving his fleet. Said I'd get more miles in a single-screw tractor and that my pay would go up and up if I stayed with him. Said they were jerks at Reno. Said they didn't treat their drivers right and everybody knew it. He didn't want to talk about envelopes in desk drawers.

—⁂—

The Reno terminal. A potholed dirt lot inside a wire fence. Two tiny rooms squeezed into one corner of an ancient concrete building. Twenty-two trucks and 22 drivers. The company's beachhead in a growing urban area, part of a plan to build local accounts and balance inbound-outbound loads. A lot of freight came into Reno, the terminal manager told me, but not much went out in Linehaul trailers. He was working hard to change things.

"All our drivers help out," said my new fleet manager. "I'll ask you to make in-town deliveries once in a while, for hourly pay."

"Good," I said. "I like backing up."

He laughed. "Yeah, Eric said you did. There's docks in this town that'll test your manhood. Actually, you'll be surprised at the outbound loads we're starting to book. If you're looking for miles, variety, and excitement, this is the place. We'll keep you rolling and rolling and rolling."

They did.

I nodded off at the wheel for just a moment, once, in Oregon. After that, I didn't try to go from Reno to suburbs of San Francisco for two or three deliveries—all driver unloads—drive back to Reno, and, on forced dispatch, run all night to meet morning appointments—all driver unloads—in suburbs of Portland.

At the old Cherokee Truck Stop in Stockton.

I parked in a line of trucks then waited to scale my load. I checked my mirrors, let out the clutch, and started to turn. The truck shuddered and right away I knew I'd hit something on the driver's side—my first thought was a light pole or a dumpster—or something had hit me. I got out and saw a tractor wedged against my trailer. Where had it come from?

A trucker ran up to me and said, "I saw the whole thing! He was going way too fast. Man, he was flying! You were turning and he plowed right into you. It *looks* like you hit him, but *he* hit *you*."

The driver who'd hit me—or who I'd hit—stumbled from his cab and stared at his truck. The sun had been in his eyes, he said, and he couldn't see.

"I'd write that down," my witness whispered to me. "Look at him. He hasn't slept in a week."

He couldn't see? But he'd kept coming. Fast. In a parking lot full of trucks. And *I* hadn't seen *him*. That wasn't an excuse, just a fact. I *should* have seen him. *I should have been paying attention.*

One crunched hood. One undamaged trailer. Two inattentive drivers. Stupid, stupid, stupid.

I didn't hear from Safety or Claims after I reported the collision and a few weeks later I asked my fleet manager about it.

He said, "That little bumper cruncher? Wasn't your fault. Forget about it."

I couldn't do that. Twenty-three thousand miles into the life, I reset my million-mile clock.

Eight hundred miles and 15 driving hours separate Seattle and Billings, MT. Running legal, a solo driver could make the trip in about 23 hours, weather permitting: 10 hours behind the wheel, eight off duty and/or in the sleeper, a 15-minute pretrip inspection, then five more hours in the seat.

There were other legal work-rest combinations, depending where you were on hours when you started driving and how much dock time you logged. If your delivery window was wide open, you could run it any way you chose. If not, the load ran you.

I backed to a dock in Seattle for my 6 a.m. pick-up, hoping to get loaded and rolling toward Billings in an hour or two. I'd have just enough time to make my 8 a.m. delivery the following day, but the shipper didn't push the last pallet into the trailer until 2 p.m. I called the local dispatcher.

He said, "Can you help us out and still be in Billings by 8 a.m.?"

If I said 'no', he'd give my trailer to another driver and ask him the same question, and the company wouldn't pay me for detention. Or maybe, since this was a Thursday and the consignee was closed on weekends, they'd reset the delivery for Monday, leaving me with 800 miles over four days—$44 a day.

I said I'd try. I drove nonstop until 4 a.m., slept two hours, continued into Billings, and wearily stacked cartons on a dock for five hours.

"This wasn't supposed to come in until 3 p.m.," the receiving clerk said. "But we appreciate the hustle."

I placed the empty call and brought up my need for sleep.

"I don't want to hear about it," said the dispatcher. "Sleep after your next pick-up."

He went on: deadhead 30 miles and live-load 45,000 pounds of wheat in Broadview, MT then take it to a Lewiston, ID grain terminal for Monday. Or sit in Billings all weekend without a load and without pay. My choice.

Five hundred and eighty-seven paid miles in three days. Not good. Not good at all. I was too tired to refuse.

In Broadview, the loader blew the wheat into a pile that put me at almost 38,000 pounds on the trailer.

He said, "Oops."

I said, "What do we do now?"

"There's only one way to shift the wheat. Gun it down the street and slam on the brakes. Then come back to the scale and we'll see how you did."

It took several tries—going to the scale each time—to get all that weight off the trailer. One last bump leveled the load and I was legal all-around, grossing 79,400. I drove back to Billings, showered at the Flying J, collapsed on the bunk, and slept for nine hours. Two illegal dispatches in a row, I decided, was my limit. And no more all-nighters. My resolve would last two weeks.

Saturday, I drove west on I-90, seeing country that I'd missed two nights before. I stopped early at Muralt's truck stop—in Missoula—and the next morning turned onto U.S. Highway 12. I drove up Lolo Pass for the first time, parked at the summit, rolled the windows down, and listened to the wind in the trees for three hours.

U.S. 12. The Lewis and Clark Highway. Two lanes winding through the forested canyons of the Locsha and Clearwater Rivers, winding down from Lolo Pass to Lewiston, where grain elevators tower over the Snake River and a sprawling pulp and paper mill sits beside the Clearwater.

At the Lewis and Clark grain terminal on Monday I said, "I've never unloaded here before, so you'll have to show me how it goes."

"Least you asked," said the ramp operator. "Most Linehaul drivers don't use the smarts they were born with. They don't know but they don't ask. Damn fools. Okay, pull onto the ramp. Back against the stops, set your brakes, turn off the engine. Get out and chain the tractor to the ramp—see that chain in front there? Open the trailer doors part way. Loop this short rope over the handles so the doors won't swing full open. Stand clear when I raise the ramp. I'll weigh you loaded and empty and give you a scale ticket. Then you go to the trailer washout, right over there. Gets the loose grain out. Be careful with liquids in the cab—a

Linehaul driver dumped his pee bottle last week when the truck went up. Damn fool."

I stood clear. The ramp lifted the rig into the sky at a 45-degree angle, the wheat rushed out of my trailer and into a hopper grate, and the ramp came down. Elapsed time, less than two minutes. Fastest unload in the west.

My next load, paper towels from the pulp mill for Salt Lake City, wasn't due out until 2 a.m. After the washout I parked at a truck stop, opened the doors to let the trailer dry, and spent the day puttering in the cab and watching TV in the truckers' lounge. During a commercial one driver sniffed the air and said, "That mill sure stinks. Chlorine, chemicals, who knows what. They ought to clean it up or shut it down."

"Smells like jobs to me," said another. "Jobs for the folks in town and jobs for truck drivers like us. You need to respect that."

Two a.m. at the pulp mill.

A forklift operator said, "Just back in. We'll come get you when we're done."

I said, "We're supposed to count cases."

"Nah, we told your company last month: there's no more driver counts here. We load and we count. You can wait in the break room if you like. Most guys sit in their truck. It won't take but about 45 minutes."

It took just 25.

In Salt Lake City the load checker told me that one case of

paper towels was missing. I called Linehaul.

The claims rep said, "Did you count the load? Did you count? It's always driver-count there."

"Not any more. They . . ."

"Don't tell *me*. *You* just drive. If you didn't count it, I'm holding back $11 from your next settlement to pay for the shortage."

Linehaul kept the money for a year then returned it once it became clear, they said, that the mill wasn't going to file a claim.

Chapter Six

I hear, and I forget. I see, and I remember. I do, and I understand.

Confucius

At a paper mill near Frenchtown, MT a Linehaul trainer came over to talk while we waited for our loads.

He said, "Where you headed? The envelope factory in Pomona? I feel sorry for you. They've got one dock. There's stacks of pallets and junk and rolls of paper in the way and it'd be tight even without all that. I won't let a trainee back up in there. I do it. How's your backing?"

Backing.

It's one of the industrial arts. If you can't do it, you can't call yourself a truck driver. Your peers will know you're just holding the wheel and you'll hear about it.

Eric Le Clare told me to practice and I did until I didn't have to anymore, until I wasn't just holding the wheel.

Going forward or backward, you're always steering two vehicles. Your trailer leads when you back up, and when you're done there should be a perfect 90-degree angle between the trailer and the dock. Before you back up and while you're backing up, you watch for things that are easy to hit—parked cars, fire hydrants, telephone poles, other trucks. You don't want to bump anything but the dock. If you're not sure, you set your brakes. Then you GOAL: you Get Out And Look.

At some docks, white or yellow guide lines on the ground define a long parking place with a roll-up door at one end. "Put it in door 7" means "Back into the parking place in front of the seventh door and don't take all day." If there aren't any lines or if they're covered with mud, snow, or trash, you feel your way to that 90-degree angle 65 feet behind you.

I learned to back up sight-side (backing clockwise—you can see your path but not what's directly in back of the trailer) and blind-side (backing counter-clockwise—you can't see your path *and* you can't see what's directly behind the trailer). I learned that it's all in how you set things up. That you want to make as few pull-up corrections as possible. That you want to look good and get it in on the first try. That you've already won the battle if you line up your tractor and trailer before you shift into reverse and let out the clutch.

Backing tractors and trailers was one of the most satisfying things I've ever done. I looked forward to it, enjoyed watching drivers do it, and—there's no other word—loved bumping a dock on the first try. I always laughed when that happened and I laughed even more when I had an audience. If a back-up without corrections wasn't possible, I took pleasure in the challenge and the tussle and I realized one day that I favored the tough docks—docks without guide lines; docks poorly-lit and deep inside buildings; narrow, crowded docks where trailers and outside mirrors were an inch or two apart; docks where there didn't seem to be enough room to back in, let alone pull out ("If you can get in there," a driver said to me, "we're gonna have us a new definition of 'tight.'"); docks where you backed in blind-side off a narrow street or you didn't back in at all ("Last week, a Linehaul driver couldn't do it, so my boss called your company and told them to fetch someone else. He said, 'Send a real truck driver next time.'").

—◦◦◦—

An hour before sunrise on a winter morning in Reno, 53- and 57-foot trailers were jockeyed to doors at a tire distribution center. Snow covered the guide lines. A driver pushed and pulled a single pup through set-up after set-up, oversteered to correct, and had trouble backing straight once he turned into his space. Drivers sat in their cabs—engines idling, heaters running—and watched. They warmed up the CB.

"My momma can back up better than that."

"My dog can back up better than that."

"We all have longer trailers and *we* made it."

"How'd he get his license?"

"Oh, it was the prize in a Cracker Jack box."

"Here comes another pull-up."

"And another."

"And another."

"Is he going to get it in *this* time?"

"I'll bet that's what his wife says."

"Jeez. Finally. *Eleven* corrections."

A Chicago warehouse opened its gates at midnight and thirty truckers rushed to drop empties, hook their loads of paper products, and head out on the road. A driver keyed up. "This is my first time. Can somebody please help me back in?"

Other drivers said, "Go back to truck-driver school." "Why'd they hire you if you can't drive?" "You shouldn't be in the seat if you can't back up on your own." I said, "I'll help you."

I stood on the rookie's running board and explained the fundamentals, talking him slowly to the dock. He was unsure, nervous, and ashamed.

"Relax," I told him. "You weren't born knowing how to back up and neither was anybody else. You have to practice. There's no other way to learn it."

"This is a really hard dock."

"This is nothing. Practice until you don't have to practice anymore."

Chapter Seven

Whether you think you can or you think you can't, you're right.
HENRY FORD

I was talking with a friend in my living room, telling him road stories, telling him that trucking was the best job I'd ever found.

"It's great," I said. "I've never been so at-home with my work."

"Yeah, but are you making any money?"

Not really. No.

Pay started at 22 cents a mile. A six-hour grunt-work unload got you $40. At most, a Linehaul solo driver in 1991 might gross $24,000 during his first full year after training and that took more luck than brains, but I didn't complain. I was there to learn and my labor came with a bonus that didn't cost my employer anything: I was able to keep almost completely to myself.

I never ate at truck-stop lunch counters—too much friendly banter, too much whining, too many know-it-alls. I hardly ever keyed up, and, once, faked partial deafness to avoid a conversation in a truck-stop coin laundry. I tapped an ear and shouted, "Sorry! Left both aids in the cab! Can't hear a thing without them!"

When I had to, I'd share a few words with a dispatcher, another driver, or a cashier at a fuel desk, then climb back into the truck with only my thoughts for company, but I craved seclusion and I lived for the perfect anonymity of the days when I didn't talk to anyone. Gayle didn't realize at first that I had a problem. I kept it hidden, but after two nights at home I was climbing the walls, I needed to be alone again, I needed to get back to the highway.

"You're hooked," my terminal manager said. "You're a run junkie. Just what we're looking for."

He had no idea.

Trucking had grabbed onto me and whether it was more drug than fever I couldn't say. I was as devoted to my in-cab isolation as any addict is to his habit. Above all else, truck driving meant solitude to me. And time. Time to roll and reflect. Time to rub the veneer from lies I'd been telling myself for years. Time to get below the surface and relive every wrong turn and discarded relationship. Time to revisit my failures and awkward moments, public and private. Small stuff, really. Little ticks in a life. No big deal, no one got killed, just disappointed. In me.

—m—

It seems I've always been in search of solitude, my own unquestioned best way.

Grade-school summers were spent alone, riding to the ends of city bus lines just to see what was there; watching ships unload at old wooden piers; reading in musty public libraries, going everywhere in the world by book, awed by issues of *Life* magazine from the 1930s and 1940s.

Latchkey kid. Practically an only child. Bound to isolation, bound to himself, alone even among friends and family. Alone, but never lonely.

Later, there were solo backpacking trips in the Sierras; solo weekends on Oregon beaches; a summer-long solo trek through Utah and Arizona; a road trip east across the country and back through Canada—solo, most of the time; week-long solo escapes to the rain-shadowed Owens Valley and its towns nestled beneath the high wall of the Sierra Nevada. I often thought, Move to Bishop—you'll find something to do there. It's small. It's perfect. Instead, ever unsure about where to go and what to do for a living, I registered for one aimless college semester after another.

Professors' notes, written on term papers. Canaries in my coal mine.

"You've done a *great* job. Don't have the heart to knock you for being late."

"Good job, but it's late. Try to focus on your work—you'll get more done. I wish you had more confidence in yourself."

"Your work is very good. I hurt because you can't turn things in on time. You need help."

Who, me? Listening to advice and counsel was for other people. Learning from mistakes was for other people. Getting on in life was for other people.

I often left term papers, homework assignments, songs, and short stories unfinished. Sustained by the tension of works-in-progress, I was always busy being busy. I never went from "I'm doing something" to "I've done something. What's next?" The projects were trustworthy companions and I took good care of my friends, kept them, neat and tidy, in manila folders arranged and rearranged on my desk every day. If something was troubling or difficult, it went to the bottom of the stack. I didn't understand that you stay with a job until it's done, even if it makes you uncomfortable; that you set goals for yourself and don't make promises you won't keep; that you turn your work in on time; that you pay attention.

I put aside thoughts of the Owens Valley and began to think I'd look for a town on the Oregon Coast, get away from college and keep away from it. Learn carpentry. Build houses. Work on fishing boats. I was always going to do these things.

I grew a beard, hid behind it for 20 years, shaved the thing off a few months before I got into trucking, and saw a pale clown in the mirror, a con artist who talked about honesty while he held the truth at arm's length. I didn't know him at all. When had he started running in ever-tightening circles, making the same mistakes again and again, repeating his life's cycles? I didn't want to deal with that.

—∞—

Hauling a load across Wyoming one night, I started thinking about bullies I'd known. The teenage foursome that beat me up when I was nine. The kids who punched other kids at recess. The big kid who always wanted my grade-school lunch money. The bigger kid who borrowed my prized Rawlings baseball glove, refused to give it back, and threatened to brain me with a bat if I told anyone. The junior high school gym teacher who brought a camera into the boys' shower room, snapped the shutter nine or ten times, and warned everyone not to tell. The guy who liked to hit his employees in the stomach—hard but not too hard, he was just fooling around, right?

"What are you going to do about it?" The voice came out of the sleeper and I knew that if I turned around the speaker would be sitting on the bunk, one of those punks from fifth grade, grown up and looking for a rematch.

I said, "Get out."

Then I was yelling, "Get out!"

Then I was screaming, "Get out! Get out! Get out!"

"Deal with it," said another voice. "Now or never."

There are things you don't get over and memories you don't want to keep, but when it's time for a visit it doesn't matter what you want. They know where to find you. Wherever you go, there they are. They showed up for me as unauthorized passengers and I wasn't peacefully alone in the truck anymore. They came, first one then another and another, in rushes of loud and bitter feeling. They came at night, like hookers banging on the sleeper. Mile after mile, I stumbled down memory lane while they used me for a punching bag, no holds barred, no apologies, no defenses, no escape. I'd knock one down and another would pop up, targets at my inner shooting gallery: people, events, and mistakes I hadn't thought of or agonized over in years; everything I'd ever said or done wrong; every lie and missed cue; every paralyzing flash of self doubt; every choked emotion. Sweat and blush—as if the things were crawling again, as if a remembered slip of the tongue wasn't three full decades old, and the person I'd insulted had died a long time ago, and no one else had heard what I'd said, and so it didn't matter, did it? Why did it gnaw at me? What could I do about it? Nothing, no more now than when I'd said it.

Still embarrassed after all these years.

Deal with it.

Deal with all of it.

I began to dissect my segmented life—four years doing this, nine years doing that, three years here, five years there, moving around, going nowhere. I totaled up my missteps—the could-haves, would-haves, and should-haves. The repeated, unlearned lessons. I had stayed in school, hiding, I guess, from the world. I wouldn't have admitted it, but I wasn't there to learn. I was there because I had to be somewhere. I should have dropped out and I should have been told to leave, and whose fault was that? I looked at the man in the mirror every day and we never spoke. I never thought to ask him what he thought he was doing.

Driving, always driving, I relived the times I understood nothing. The times experience taught me nothing. The time I looked in a mirror and saw—literally, one stoned night—nothing.

Life.

I was in over my head.

I wasn't paying attention.

I had a lot of catching up to do.

Maybe I would start by bringing the truth in a little closer. Maybe I would start by talking to the trucker in the mirror, asking questions and listening to his answers. Our conversations took place day and night and I'd come home from the road and Gayle would say, "You look tired," and I would answer, "I feel like I'm working two jobs." I was in process and the past was in motion. I thought of it as psychological warfare, and I had time for the fight, all the time I'd ever need. I just had to drive a truck and be myself—as soon as I found out who that was.

It took two years, some 240,00 miles, and I don't know how many sleepless nights.

—ɷ—

Early one morning at a truck stop in Portland, OR.

A well-rested driver—he'd been sleeping a lot better lately— smiled back from a shower-room mirror. He was neither handsome nor ugly, inside or out. I liked him. I knew him fairly well. I could read between the lines on his face. He said, "The answer, as you now know, is that you have to find your own answers, learn every lesson, and keep rolling. We all make mistakes. We all have regrets. You can't change the past. You have to believe in yourself. Henry Ford was right."

Chapter Eight

It's an anywhere road for anybody.

Jack Kerouac

Freight in the Northwest could be slow to nonexistent and if you wanted to keep moving, you took what dispatchers offered. The best load one afternoon was sacks of silica sand to San Francisco, 626 paid miles. Deliver the next day at precisely 3:30 p.m., the customer service rep said, and she included the standard patronizing lecture: don't be late. But at 3 o'clock the consignee told me he *closed* at 3:30—"We've told 'em a thousand times. Maybe two thousand."—and that his yard crew would need at least two hours to muscle the load off. I asked about overnight parking. He pointed to a high chain-link fence.

"See the razor wire? They get in anyway. They won't steal the sand but it's better if you're not here at night."

We agreed that I would bobtail out and return around noon for the empty trailer.

"I grew up in this town," I said, "and I can't think of a safe place to park tonight."

"You grew up here? What high school did you go to?"

"Baytown."

"What year did you graduate? Don't you dare say 1964."

"1964."

"You didn't."

We looked at each other, two guys from the same graduating class, now in their forties. We introduced ourselves.

He said, "Mrs. Manteno won't believe it."

David Manteno didn't remember me until he thumbed through his yearbook that night, and I still couldn't place him when he opened it the next day and pointed to his picture. He turned a page and touched the photograph of a girl I recognized.

"We're still married," he said, and his voice jogged my memory.

"Wait a minute. I recognize you now, *Loverboy* Manteno."

Working back through 29 years, we talked of teachers good and bad, life since high school, head shots in alphabetical order. I paused at one a few names from my own.

"We lived together for a few months," I said. "It didn't work out."

I hadn't seen that picture since I was twenty and decided that memories of her were best left behind. I'd thrown my yearbook into a campfire.

I felt the familiar heft of the book even before David passed it to me. Padded vinyl cover. Pre-digital paste-ups. Typewritten text. Just yesterday. The years fly by, people say. In high school, you think that's for everyone else, and 45 seems a long way off, a lifetime, forever.

—ⱳ—

I didn't think I'd find a parking place in the overcrowded Stockton yard at midnight, but I was more than tired and it was worth a try. You never know.

I stopped at the entrance and waited for the contract security service to check my truck in. And waited, as men and women walked confidently into and out of the yard and past the guard shack. Inside, beneath sputtering fluorescent tubes, the lone watchman sat folded over a newspaper and an ashtray, asleep at his wheel. I found a space, a tapered slot at one end of the last dark row, and congratulated myself. The terminal beat street parking in a neighborhood where whores and drug dealers knocked on truck doors day and night. I rolled the windows down several inches and dropped onto the bunk, safe from the parasites outside Linehaul's fence.

Awakened by muttering, a rasping cough and wheezy breathing, I looked at the clock—2:45—then through a gap in the sleeper curtain. A dark figure stood on the sidestep, peering into the cab, stretching an arm through the lowered passenger-side window. I sat up, ripped the curtain open half-way, and yelled.

"What are you doing?!"

Surprised to hear a loud voice and startled to find a driver in the truck, the intruder jumped. He didn't leave.

"I'm . . . a truck driver," he said. "Yeah . . . a truck driver. My girlfriend's pregnant, man. Loan me five dollars for a motel room. Yeah . . . a motel room. So she can have her baby. Yeah. I need five dollars. Come on, man. Come *on!*"

A frantic hand tugged at the outside latch. Another swept like a pendulum for the inside handle—it opens a truck door, locked or not.

Interstate truck drivers who carry firearms violate any number of laws and ordinances. What constitutes a concealed weapon in a vehicle? The definition and the firearms you may transport depend on the communities you enter and the communities you leave. Cross a state line or a city limit and you break a law or two—drive back and you're legal, all without touching or even looking at your gun. "Out of reach and separate from the ammunition" works in most states. In some, it is no gun at all. In others, you keep your heat in the trunk. Oregon and Vermont prefer weapons in plain view, otherwise they're "concealed." Many cities, notably Chicago, Boston, and New York, write their own rules. The Canadians have theirs: gun, truck, trailer, and cargo are sure to be confiscated. The driver will be arrested.

The Federal Motor Carrier Safety Regulations have never addressed the subject of firearms in trucks, but Linehaul, like other carriers, forbade weapons on—or in—company property. Caught with a hand gun, a driver could expect to be out of work immediately. He would never drive a truck again. I knew this, but, for awhile, I carried a 9mm semi-automatic pistol in the sleeper, out-of-reach and separate—but not too separate—from a loaded clip and my ammunition.

"Come *on!* . . . I need five dollars *tonight!*"

"Get lost," I said. "Get away from my truck. Get the hell out of here."

The panicky snap-banging of the outside door handle drubbed on and on. Wide-eyed and more than awake three hours before dawn, this guy was buzzing along on something.

I reached for my gun case. If the man climbed into the cab and over the passenger seat, if he lunged at me, I would have every right to fire. A decent pistol shot at 40 feet, I couldn't miss at two or three.

"You'd better leave," I heard myself say. He punched the window.

I slapped in a clip, pulled the slide back and released it to chamber a round, the metallic clatter a sharp counterpoint to his drugged mumbling. He made another grab for the inside latch. I took a fast, deep breath then raised my weapon.

I said, "Get away!"

He drew back a fist and looked through the glass again. He moaned, his hands dropped from sight, and he vanished. I held the pistol long after his footsteps and wheezing faded into the night.

I think, sometimes, of the way things might have gone. If the door had been unlocked, my visitor would have opened it, trapping me in the sleeper. Perhaps he tried the doors on every truck in the yard and ran if someone yelled. He found mine locked but the windows were down a few inches, enough to stick an arm through and feel around for the latch. Maybe he wasn't up for more than petty theft. Maybe he was ready to kill someone. That made two of us. You never know.

On occasion, I revive the attempted break-in and play it forward. The street rat surprises me, knocks me cold, breaks my jaw and the bones in my face. He takes my wallet, searches the sleeper, finds the gun, and pistol whips me. My skull is split open. Blood and brains soak the mattress. He kicks in a few ribs as an afterthought and my wife receives a call from the county coroner. The Big Guy's attorneys press her for a quick settlement. Concerned only with its financial exposure, the company never admits that the security guards doze in their shack at night, and that thieves and hookers brazen their way into the gateless yard while the rented men sleep.

I've played it the other way, too. I shoot the punk. His blood and brains soak the upholstery. I never drive a truck again.

I later recognized my would-be thief among the wasted men and women who lived on the streets near the yard. Forever jobless, with nothing to lose and little to gain, they hustled what they had: stolen car radios, bald tires, themselves. One tried to sell me a Kmart shopping cart for $2. Another offered her body while I swept out a trailer at the terminal.

She said, "Hi there, sugar."

I didn't answer.

"My, my. You don't talk much, do you? I like quiet men. Anything you want?"

"I don't think you've got a thing I want. Bye bye."

"I've got *everything*. Don't these look good? There's more, baby."

I kept sweeping and she kept trying.

"Say, quiet man," she said finally. "You want me or not?"

"No."

"I got it *all*, baby."

And she did have it all at that moment, all the trash I had swept into a neat pile near the door. A flick of the broom and it was hers. No sale. Just a face full of dirt.

I tried to sympathize with the men and women who hung around truck stops sponging off drivers, but at times all I felt was anger. Some of them colonized street corners with homemade signs. *Spare change? Anything will help. Will work for food.*

So? Those of us in the trucks worked for food, often long and ridiculous hours. I didn't care to get badgered for spare change when I was tired and covered with sweat after an unload, had a short night's sleep coming up, and a shower wouldn't be possible until late the next day. Still, I gave when it seemed that giving would help—$15, food, and a gallon of water to an old man in Tucson; $20 to a pregnant Navajo teenager in a New Mexico convenience store; $25 to a fiftysomething woman begging in an Oklahoma rest area. She said, "I am not a prostitute." I said I knew that, the money was hers with no strings attached.

I understand that many street people have issues and mental problems. The world must be a terrible and baffling place for them, a place where they live short, desiccated lives, a place where they do hard time all the time. But the grinning young men who frequented intersections and freeway ramps and held signs—*Spare change? I just want a beer! God Bless!*—got nothing from me.

At a Phoenix off-ramp.

Desperate, said a hand-lettered cardboard square. *Will do anything for a meal.*

I asked the sign holder if he wanted to earn seventy-five dollars for four hours' work.

He said, "What is it?"

"Unloading a trailer. You just stack boxes."

"I don't do that job! Do you know who I am? Do you know who the hell I am? I'm getting out! Out! I don't have time for this!"

—⁓—

In downtown Los Angeles a lumper rolled off the last pallet and said, "Yo. Driver. Hey, bro, check this out." I looked into the empty trailer and saw, in one corner up front, blue sky. I dutifully took photographs and called Linehaul's claims department to report the damage.

The rep said, "6119, where and when did you do this?"

I laughed. "I didn't do it. I'm just reporting it."

"You're reporting it, so you did it. You drivers *always* say it was someone else."

I laughed again. "Well, I don't see how I could have knocked a hole in the roof of a trailer from the outside; I picked it up loaded and sealed—check the dispatch info. I couldn't see the hole until the trailer was empty. Neither could anyone else."

"Why are you laughing, 6119? This isn't a joke. If you're reporting damage, you did it. No one else has reported it. Why would you report it if you didn't do it?"

—∿—

I parked at the top of Loveland Pass and stood on the Continental Divide to watch the last minutes of a summer sunset. I heard the SUV before it raced up the last switchback to the summit, leaning hard on squealing tires, the engine wound tight, the interior lights on. Two men and a woman were inside, laughing. She was driving. Each of the passengers had a hand in her blouse. The vehicle shot by and disappeared over the crest.

Then, something. Some *thing* on the wind. A whisper? A rock fall? Far off? Nearby?

I climbed into the cab and started down the hill toward Denver.

Just north of the pass, U.S. 6 curves gently to the left then to the right. There's a gravel turn-out before the road curves back to the left and heads toward thin air. Straight and true, like railroad tracks, black skid marks led off the asphalt and into the turn-out. Someone had taken a wild ride, fishtailing through the gravel and skidding back onto the pavement. Around the next curve, the SUV teetered on its crushed roof five feet from the top of a steep slope, doors open, windshield blown out, windows shattered, the driver a silent heap in the road. I didn't see anyone else. I set the four-ways, ran to her—she was alive—ran to my truck, and called Phoenix Dispatch.

"This is 6119," I said. "There's been an injury accident. We're not involved. I'm at Loveland Pass, just north of the summit."

"Say, hoss, why are you sneaking around in the high country? I was there once, I . . ."

"Listen! There's a rollover up here, and two missing people. Call the Colorado state police. Tell them to send an ambulance and a patrol car right away. I'm about a quarter of a mile north of the pass."

I ran back to the wreck. The driver—she appeared to be in her late forties—lay on her side, motionless, bleeding from cuts in her scalp. Two young men stood beside her. One was crying and saying, "Oh, my God." The other whispered, "Button her top, Felipe. She's dead."

"No," I said. "She's breathing."

I kneeled next to her and asked how she felt and she said, "Cold. Can't move." I brushed dirt, glass, and bits of black plastic from her face. "You'll be okay," I said, but I didn't know if that was true.

Felipe said, "Can we put her in your truck? You have beds in there, don't you? It's warm. Don't tell me it isn't!"

I said, "We can't risk moving her."

"But she's *freezing*. You've got to do something! I'll have you arrested if you don't! My God! How do you expect me to get home? I'm cold! *Do* something!"

"Your friend may have a broken neck. If we move her, she could be paralyzed. I called for help. We have to wait for the medics."

The woman groaned and said again that she was cold. I pulled a goose down comforter out of the sleeper, tucked it around her, and said to the boy toys, "I'm not going to say a word when the police get here, but I smell beer and I see a lot of empty beer cans."

"Oh, my God!" Felipe started kicking cans over the edge and down the slope where I had expected to find two bodies.

We'd been alone on the hill when they crashed and that had been everyone's good luck—the tumbling vehicle could have plowed into cars and trucks, maybe knocking one or two off the road and down the hill, maybe killing a few people, maybe leaving a family in wheelchairs for life. But now traffic filled the road. Four-wheelers slowed to gawk and shake their heads. Truck drivers asked if they could do anything. Felipe paced back and forth, shivering and wringing his hands.

He said, "She wrecked her Mercedes three weeks ago."

"You're not hurt," I said. "Do you think you can help direct traffic?"

"Why do *I* always have to do everything? What's that sound?"

"Ambulance siren."

"We'll take it from here," said a state trooper. "Good of you to stop and help. Almost went down hard, fast, and dead, didn't they? Do you smell beer?"

—⋙—

I wanted to go to the East Coast, but the only loads out of Reno that Friday went to Kmart stores in Oregon, Idaho, and Wyoming.

"Wyoming," I said to the dispatcher. "Where in Wyoming?"

"Jackson. The first stop is in Idaho—Pocatello. Both deliver tomorrow. There's no freight in Wyoming. You might be stuck for the weekend."

Ah, Jackson and Jackson Hole and the upper Snake River. Ah, Grand Teton National Park, mountains for the imagination, and indelible memories of a childhood vacation: chuck-wagon cookouts, real log cabins, horses for a city kid to ride. This load was a gift, a chance to revisit an old haunt and tap into one of trucking's pleasures—time off in a beautiful corner of America. I would drop the empty trailer and bobtail to the park. Call the tractor an RV. Hike. Enjoy the scenery. Watch the river flow. Ah, Jackson Hole and its Teton backdrop. I couldn't think of a better place to be stuck for the weekend.

After the unload in Pocatello I called Linehaul to confirm my time off.

"We need a favor," said a customer service rep. "A rookie dropped the ball. After Jackson, we'd like you to swap trailers in Idaho Falls and make one delivery in New Jersey and four in New York. You're our only truck in the area, and, uh, we're already two days late on this."

Of course I said yes. Late or not, a load to the East Coast was also a gift.

The new-hire had picked up 45,000 pounds of potato flour then realized that he fell short of the hours needed to deliver legally. He drove 15 nervous miles, parked, and sat on his knowledge for a day before he called Dispatch.

"The driver told us he's at the Yellowstone Truck Stop," the rep said. "He may have abandoned the truck there. Call me if you can't find him."

I drove around the lot at the Yellowstone, parked next to a grimy, mud-spattered Linehaul tractor, and knocked on the sleeper. The driver's door opened to reveal a carpet woven of half-eaten fruit, French fries, cigarette butts, greasy food containers, unraveled cassette tapes, corroded flashlight batteries, and crumpled pages torn from a trucker's atlas. A disheveled troll slid out.

Where the hell had I been? Why the hell did they take him off the load? Didn't they understand that if he holed-up until tomorrow he could build enough hours to make the deliveries back east and make them on time? Would I explain how to cheat on the log book?

"Sorry," I said. "You'll have to learn on your own."

He watched while I hooked up and walked around the loaded trailer.

He said, "What the hell *are* you doing?"

"Pretrip inspection."

"Why? Seems okay to me."

I looked for holes, dents, and damage of any kind, but found only surface rust. The tires, mud flaps, hub oilers, and underride guard looked good and the annual inspection sticker was valid. The registration certificate had gone missing, but the company could fax me a duplicate. I replaced the glad-hand seals, two marker lamps, and a tail light.

He said, "Repairs are the company's problem. I don't carry tools. I don't carry spare parts. I don't do nothing but drive my little ol' truck. I'm damn good at it, too."

I put on my overalls and scrunched under the trailer tandem to check the brakes, fit a box wrench to an adjuster nut, pushed against the locking ring, and pulled down.

"Jesus, man," I said. "Three turns of the wrench? This one's way out of adjustment . . . so is this one . . . and this one . . . and this one. Do you ever look at your brakes?"

"Why the hell would I?"

He had been hooked to the trailer for two weeks, he said, and hadn't personally seen anything wrong. Didn't I think he would have noticed? The lights, brakes, and lost registration—all of it seemed very strange. And Linehaul, those idiots, they should have checked his available hours before the dispatch. It wasn't *his* fault if they couldn't do their jobs. After two months' driving he knew plenty about trucking and he could tell of things to make my hair stand on end, but then he'd have to kill me. Anyway, he figured he'd dump Linehaul real soon and track down a company that would appreciate a man who was a professional and nobody's fool.

I asked for the scale ticket.

"Now, why the hell would I weigh this load, driver? It's only 22 pallets." He climbed into his truck and slammed the door twice before the latch caught.

I drove onto the Yellowstone's scale. If the load wasn't right and I couldn't legal it, I'd have to go back to the shipper for a pallet shift. Would anyone be there on a Saturday afternoon? With the trailer all the way forward on the tandem—the rookie said he liked the way that looked—I had 12,400 pounds on the steer axle, 36,000 on the drives, and 31,000 on the trailer. I drove off the scale and set the trailer brakes, released the slider pins, shifted into reverse and pushed the trailer back on the tandem. I locked the pins and went around for a reweigh. The scale settled at 11,990, 33,500 and 33,900.

The consignees—one in East Orange, NJ, two in Brooklyn, one in Nyack, and one in New Rochelle, NY—didn't know yet that their potato flour would be at least two days late. It had been left to me to explain, apologize, negotiate a new delivery schedule, and nail down directions. On Monday, I called my customers from a Nebraska truck stop where the coffee was hot, the phones were close to a big-screen TV in the truckers' lounge, and off-duty drivers laughed at Robert De Niro's patter in *Midnight Run*.

East Orange took the news without comment or complaint and I made a new delivery appointment.

The first Brooklyn consignee wanted me to know that he

was upset. His flour had been promised for today and he needed it today.

He said, "So it's going to be late again? *Again?*" He sounded like De Niro.

"Sir," I said, "we owe you an apology. If you will . . ."

"I want to let you know that you're a dead motherfucker! Do you understand me?!"

"Hey," I said. "Calm down. Oh . . . the movie."

I explained that I was 1,600 miles from New York.

"Then I guess you won't be here tomorrow, either. Well, you seem to be a nice guy."

I asked for directions.

"To where?"

"Your warehouse."

"Warehouse? You call this shoe box a warehouse? Here's what you do, Mr. Nice Guy. You know the Green-Wood Cemetery?"

"Greenwood *Cemetery*?"

"Green. Wood. May I presume to say you are not from New York?"

The second Brooklyn consignee said unkind things about Linehaul.

Nyack was displeased. Without the flour they'd have to temporarily shut down their specialty foods plant. Their customers and employees wouldn't be happy. But things were what they were, when would I arrive, and what size trailer did I have?

"Fifty-three foot dry van."

"I told them short trailers! I told them! My lot is small! Small! You can't fit in here! Small! I told them!"

New Rochelle just wanted to know when I might get there. Did I need directions? I should look for a big gray building—the owner's name was painted on the side, they were right at the corner, I couldn't miss it if I tried, I was to ask for Frankie. Would I please call the day before I planned to deliver? And thank you, driver, for calling.

In East Orange I learned that appointments meant nothing. I waited three hours for a door, watched my delivery plan crumble, and called the other consignees.

"Very nice of you to call again. My daughter should be so thoughtful."

"What kind of truck driver calls when he's late?"

"You called again! It's like we're old friends."

"You'll be here the day after tomorrow? That's fine. Don't forget to ask for Frankie."

I crossed the Verrazano Narrows Bridge into Brooklyn, found my exit, and followed the directions to what looked like the correct intersection. I saw row houses. Children playing. Neighbors visiting on front steps. Cars parked bumper-to-bumper on both sides of a narrow street. I reread the directions. They were clear and I could see the cemetery, but I couldn't get my rig around the corner. Down the block, a man waved from the seat of a forklift. Two teenagers jumped from a stoop to move their cars and I made the turn.

"You called. You said you would be here and you are here. You are a prince. Four skids, yes? As you can see, there is no dock. But a chain I have. You wrap one end around each pallet, one end I wrap around the mast, I back up, the chain pulls tight, the pallet comes to the rear of your trailer, I roll forward, you unhook the chain, I lower the pallets to the street without dropping a single one, God willing."

I showed him the directions to my second Brooklyn stop.

He said, "No, my friend. Your truck is too big," and drew a map. "Go like this to the river."

A warehouse district near the East River.

I parked on the street, ignored honking horns and the shouted curses of a cab driver, and knocked on a steel door. A view panel swung open. "So. You are here at last. Go down the block. Turn left. Another block. Left. Another block. Left. You will see our dock. Don't hit *The Mercedes*."

Parked directly across the street from the dock, *The Mercedes* took up space a truck driver needed to maneuver. I made many corrections. The owner appeared and stood by his car. The receiver spat on the pavement and rolled up his sleeves. The men celebrated their feud with raised voices and arm waving. The receiver apologized for his neighbor's behavior.

"No problem," I said. "I like a challenging dock."

"You are not from New York, *bubbie*. I can see that."

Inside the warehouse an unloader raced back and forth

on a forklift, singing and fingering worry beads. He sped into the trailer, skidded, and hit the brakes. He screamed. "Son of a whore! Who turned these pallets around in here? That Idaho *schmuck* knows not to load this way! *Gott in himmel!*" He turned a pallet with the forks, hooked it, brought it to the back of the trailer, looked at me, grinned, and drove off, singing. Each time he barreled into the trailer the bilingual swearing started. Each time he backed out, it stopped.

"Not from New York," he said, wagging a finger. "We can see that."

The lot in Nyack was, as the man said, small—too small to swing a long trailer. I handed off sacks of flour in the employee parking area. The voice from the phone drifted down from a second story window.

"Please tell them once more only very short trailers. Thank you for calling." He pointed at the truck. "You are very clever with that thing. No one ever got so close to my dock. Small!"

I parked behind a shopping center for the night. After a sponge bath in the sleeper, I put on clean clothes and called home.

"Hi," Gayle said. "Where are you? Are you having fun?"

Sam barked.

Then I sat in the cab with the doors and windows open, thinking about the day, enjoying the evening air. A tall, thin man ambled by several times then stopped to talk. He wore a bright red bandana, a white, skin-tight t-shirt, sharply-creased lavender pants, pointed black boots, eye shadow, and lipstick. His Chihuahua, he said, understood only Spanish.

"Tell him something in English, he won't do it. He just looks at you."

He invited me to his apartment. Would I like a shower? He knew a few truck drivers and *they* liked showers. I declined, in English. The dog just looked at me.

At 4 a.m. I drove to New Rochelle and found the big gray building. Inside, damp, chilled air. Smells of bleach, old vegetables, and wet cardboard. Laughter, as warehousemen on their mid-shift break huddled around pink boxes of doughnuts. A raised eyebrow invited my inquiry.

"Good morning," I said. "I'm looking for Frankie."

The other eyebrow went up. Its owner made eye contact with every man in the room. One worker stopped eating and shook his head. Another asked if I wanted a closed casket.

"You are looking for Frankie? Have a doughnut."

"Thanks. Yes, I've got four late pallets from Idaho."

"Late? Frankie does not do 'late.' Frankie will fuck you up."

"Tell him," a worker said. "He is going to die today."

"Testify, brother. This man is going to die today. And soon."

They pointed down a long, dark hallway and hummed a death march.

"Just listen. You'll find him. Take another doughnut. It will be your last."

A dead man walking, I searched for Frankie in a chaotic grid of stacked pallets and shadowy aisles. Off in a distant corner, someone delivered a tongue lashing with rage and enthusiasm. I followed the sound out to the loading dock. A short man with the square build of a weightlifter turned to me and growled. Muscles bulged under his gray suit. He wasn't wearing a shirt.

I said, "Frankie?"

"Yeah. What do *you* want?"

"I called about the late potato flour."

"Oh. Oh, hey, Babe, thanks for calling. Your own people can't use a phone? You are on time? Believe me, that makes you one in a million. Babe, we're running a bit late this morning." He glanced at two men, who quickly looked at the floor. "We'll come get you and tell you which door. Did you see the diner across the street? Say to them I sent you."

Frankie's foreman walked through the staging lot sharing jokes with drivers, pointing at men seated in their rigs, indicating door assignments with his fingers. You. Door 3. Hey, you. Door 4. You over there. Door 5. You? Fugetaboutit. He ran over and jumped on my sidestep.

"How you doin'? Frankie says you haven't been here before. Okay, look. The commuters, they hate us. They won't cut you no slack, you start to back up. Use your headlights and four-way flashers. That way, some jackass hits you he can't say he didn't see your truck. We had one tried that. Turn left here, pull all the way out into the far intersection, otherwise you won't have no room. Back straight up across that intersection *and* this one, start your turn, straighten out, push past the wall. Get out, open your doors, bump the dock. Twenty minutes, we'll be done. A word to the wise: Frankie likes drivers who don't make a lot of pull-ups. Nice truck, Idaho."

I pulled into the first intersection, where a commuter refused to yield. He sat at the wheel, arms folded, blocking the way. I smiled, he glared. Perhaps he could see I was not from New York. I put my hands up to say, "Nothing I can do about it," and indicated that he could go ahead. He used sign language too, something to tell the wife. "I flipped off a truck driver this morning. Made my day."

I backed in under the watchful eyes of truck drivers, impatient commuters—and Frankie, who smiled. "Good back-up, Babe," he said, and signed his full name, the name on the big gray building that stood at the corner.

Empty. On the East Coast. Ready for the next dispatch. I was where I wanted to be.

—⚏—

"You're one of our senior drivers," my fleet manager said. "I know you really like your truck, but you should be driving a new one. Take a load to Phoenix, leave 6119 at the shop, and move into 6140. It's a condo with Qualcomm."

Condo, short for condominium. Raised-roof sleeper. Skylight. More windows. You stood up from the seat and the ceiling was still five feet above your head.

Qualcomm. The wireless tether. Messages from the company arrived with an annoying beep. The truck's speed, location, and movements could be tracked. Qualcomm records could be compared with log books by government inspectors; given Line-haul's dispatching practices, that wasn't a good idea.

Beep: *Marc — Enjoy touring the highways and byways.*

Thanks. I think.

—◊◊—

My terminal manager asked if I'd sign up to be a trainer. "Plenty of room for two in that condo. You'll make a ton of money running trainer-team miles and you'll have somebody to talk to. How about it?"

Sleep while a rookie is driving. They couldn't pay me enough. *Give up running alone.* I'd quit first.

Chapter Nine

I am here. I must do the best I can.
ABRAHAM LINCOLN

I-80 westbound near Omaha, on a summer evening.

A Werner Enterprises truck edged slowly past in the hammer lane. The driver waved his mic and held up four fingers: go to channel 4. He wanted to chat about Linehaul, where he'd worked for two years. We talked for 300 miles.

"I did everything they asked," James Boyd said. "Logged it legal, if you know what I mean. No accidents. Never late. When I went to dispatch windows I was polite. Friendly. The dispatchers were rude and hostile, like someone taught them that drivers are the enemy. And I couldn't average more than 2,100 miles a week—not exactly the high miles my recruiter promised. The straw that broke the camel's back? Yelled at. Fontana dispatch window. I took a load to Phoenix and cleaned out my truck. I was going broke anyway."

"James, you'll be pleased to learn that Fontana was voted 'friendliest terminal' in a Linehaul drivers' poll."

"Do you believe it?"

"No. They probably asked three rookies and none of them had ever seen the place."

"I'll tell you about Fontana. They posted a memo there

about a driver who was force-dispatched over the phone. He didn't have enough hours for the load, but a Fontana dispatcher told him to deliver on-time anyway and fudge his log book. The driver refused. The dispatcher threatened him with a write-up. Surprise, surprise, the driver was taping the whole thing and he played the tape for a couple of folks in the safety department. Too bad, so sad."

"I remember. That memo warned office workers to be careful: 'You never know who might have a tape recorder—watch what you say to drivers.'"

"Yeah. Well, I carry a dispatch buster and I use it."

"Welcome to the club."

"I still can't believe they were dumb enough to post the memo where drivers could read it. They even made a copy for me."

"Did you see the 'expendable' memo?"

"I heard about it—*everybody* heard about it. I didn't see it."

Tacked to a bulletin board at the Stockton terminal, the memo looked like what it probably was—last-minute spin control. *From the desk of The Big Guy. I don't want to hear anyone say that drivers at Linehaul are expendable.* Nobody would have dared to say that in his presence if they thought he would disapprove.

"'Expendable' sounds about right," James said. "The Big Guy doesn't give a damn about drivers. He lives off rookies, and they're a dime a dozen. All those new guys are cheap, I guess, but you get what you pay for. I mean, almost every Linehaul truck has some kind of damage. And look at the accident rate—Line-haul gets into more wrecks than anyone else out here."

We drove for twenty minutes without speaking, then James keyed up. "Do you know Trent, the Stockton planner? I had a run-in with him. I refused to make a local delivery without pay. I asked if *he* wanted to work for nothing. Gave me the 'you'll-never-er-pull-freight-in-my-town-again routine.' I laughed in his face."

I did know Trent Potter. He brought a well-honed cruelty to work, barking and snapping from the dispatch window like a mad dog. Drivers talked of fitting up a muzzle. Management ignored co-worker complaints about him. Trent kept on yelling. One day, he forgot himself and yelled at a customer. He was fired.

"That's the kind of person they put behind the window," James said. "And then they wonder why drivers quit and why turnover is sky-high. They never even asked why I was leaving. Assholes."

Linehaul.

Some swore by it, some swore at it.

Linehaul.

By design, a company that lived and breathed trainer teams, sucked in rookies, spit them out, and measured their shelf lives in weeks.

Linehaul.

Its corporate culture came from the heart and soul of The Big Guy, filtering through offices, staining every terminal, darkening every dispatch window. Any interaction with a non-driving employee could be a slap in the face and the message was always the same: *You* just drive. Drivers called it The Treatment. They said, "You stand at the window and the dispatchers ignore you." "The office people treat us like we're pond scum." "Drivers are at the bottom of The Big Guy's hill. Stuff, you know, rolls downhill."

—⚏—

In 1993, 18 years after he founded the company, The Big Guy announced a Total Quality program and opened Linehaul University to train his office workers. Drivers called it dispatcher school. Office employees signed a "pledge of awareness and support" for TQ, but dispatching continued as before, laced with verbal brutality, legal if possible, illegal when necessary.

November 24, 1997. Letter to his drivers from The Big Guy.

We have solicited input from our employees to help us solve our number one problem, driver turnover . . . Our goal is to reduce our turnover by altering the perception of our company from that of a training company to one that not only trains, but also retains and attracts experienced drivers and teams. The Big Guy promised what he called a Whole New Attitude.

May 27, 1998. From The Big Guy.

To all Linehaul drivers . . . All office and shop employees . . . have been instructed to become more involved in your well-being.

Where was the Whole New Attitude, rolled out just six months earlier? Made into paper airplanes, flown into wastebaskets, forgotten. No one had cared about TQ or Linehaul University. Why would anyone care about driver well-being?

At the Greer, SC terminal a rookie said, "They told me I'd be home every weekend. I haven't seen my kids for three weeks. The older boy, he's got trouble at school. I need to get home, but nobody is listening to me. This time next week, I'll be there or I won't be working here, or both."

March, 1999. Memo from The Big Guy.

We have initiated several new programs . . . geared toward the people side of driver retention. We believe we can improve the retention of drivers . . . by showing that we really do care about our drivers and to treat them as we would like to be treated. Drivers should be treated as a human being, not as a truck number or as a unit of Productivity.

I stood, waiting, in front of the Stockton dispatch window, trying to decipher a poster. *We dispatch people, not trucks.* The dispatcher didn't look up from his sports magazine. He said, "Truck number?"

In 2000 The Big Guy unveiled something he called a Quality Assurance Feedback System. No one asked where TQ had been hiding for seven years. No one said a thing about altered perceptions, the Whole New Attitude, driver well-being, the people side of driver retention, or Linehaul University. Nothing changed at dispatch windows. Nothing at all.

At first, I didn't know about driver turnover at Linehaul. My recruiter hadn't said anything about it. No one mentioned it at orientation. I would talk to a Linehaul driver once or twice then never see him again and I thought, Things change, people move on. But only turnover—sky-high turnover—could explain the never-ending stream of new faces, why I heard rookie chatter and little else at Linehaul terminals, why, after six months, I was considered an old hand and, after three years, a prehistoric oddity. I often wondered when I'd get tired of The Treatment, drive to Phoenix like James Boyd, and clean out my truck.

A fleet manager told me, "Respect for drivers isn't very high on the list around here. Every year driver turnover jumps up a notch. One year it's 101 percent, the next year it's 115 percent. This place is a revolving door."

Linehaul's turnover figures shouted what recruiters didn't say, what some managers knew, what reports to stockholders didn't spell out. The Big Guy's company wasn't a good place to work and recruits didn't know enough to ask themselves, "Given the experiences of those who came before me, what are the chances that mine will be different?"

No matter what it cost, high turnover paid. Year after year, quarter after quarter, Linehaul's profits soared. Most of its drivers were rookies—at the bottom of The Big Guy's pay scale—and low retention guaranteed that there would be no collective long-term corporate memory. Newbies heard, "It's just growing pains," and thought they understood, never knowing that their predecessors had heard the same thing from office workers whose predecessors had said the same thing.

A fleet manager in the owner-operator division said, "I was at my desk one morning. A few of my drivers had been clocked at five miles an hour over the company speed limit. The Big Guy walked up behind me and said, 'Slow those trucks down or I'll find someone who can.'"

If The Big Guy had walked up behind his dispatchers, fleet managers, office workers, and shop employees and said, "Treat my drivers like human beings or I'll find someone who can," his number-one problem would have evaporated like spilled diesel on a summer day and perceptions would have changed overnight.

—∿—

Maybe Linehaul's dispatchers were tired of the newly-minted drivers they faced every day and maybe they were just following orders. They used the same stock phrases at every dispatch window. Were they taught these things in dispatcher school? What were they really saying?

"*You* just drive."

Translation: You're expendable.

"I know you'll do your best."

Translation: I know this load is illegal. Don't deliver late.

"Log it legal."

Translation: Run a second log book if you have to.

"I can't sell that load."

Translation: No driver in his right mind will take it.

"Driver, Linehaul is not a travel agency."

Translation: I don't care where you want to go, I don't care what your recruiter promised, I don't care if you need to get home, I don't care, I don't care, I don't care. *You* just drive.

Oklahoma City dispatcher to planner, nodding toward a driver at the window: "This one needs to get home."

Planner: "Tell him to catch a plane."

Company driver at the Gary, IN window: "Do you have anything that's a little more, uh, financially responsible? We've got two kids and bills to pay."

Dispatcher: "What are you talking about? That's a good load, 1,000 miles. That's good money."

"Not over five days, it isn't."

"I'm force-dispatching you. Suck it up."

At 25 cents a mile, 1,000 paid miles over five days came to $50 a day. Before taxes.

Two dispatchers huddled at the Salt Lake City window.

"This load's already late."

"If he takes it, it's out of *our* hands."

They smiled at each other.

Notices at dispatch windows.

The terminal near Portland, OR: *All! Our! Loads! Go! East! No! Loads! South! Don't! Ask! Too bad about the snow and ice in Idaho! Ha! Ha!*

The Phoenix terminal: *Today is not your day. Tomorrow*

doesn't look so good either.

The old Salt Lake City terminal: *Drivers! This is not Burger King! You cannot have it your own way!*

The new Salt Lake City terminal: A drawing of a hand grenade and the words *Driver Complaint Department. Pull Handle.*

—⚋—

Linehaul's recruiters were there to sell the company. They told recruits, "We're proactive." "We're a family-oriented business." "We'll keep you moving." "You'll get consistent high weekly miles with us." "We care about our drivers." They didn't reveal the big secret: once in a while, there's no freight. No freight means no miles. No miles means no pay.

Linehaul wasn't what I had been sold and it wasn't what other drivers had been sold. *Proactive* was just a word. *We're a family-oriented business* meant The Big Guy's family, not yours. *We'll keep you moving* meant freight slows down from time to time. *Consistent high weekly miles* meant you'd run about 2,100 solo miles, on average, every seven days. Translated, *We care about our drivers* became, Our drivers are just hand tools. We can always get a replacement if we break one.

I met half of a Linehaul husband-wife team at a warehouse in St. Cloud, MN. She said, "The recruiter promised us big miles if we ran dedicated, but our runs are short—1,400 miles in three days, 1,100 in two days, 600 in a day-and-a-half. We average 3,100 miles a week. Our best week was 3,900 miles. The recruiter said we'd get at least 20,000 miles a month and we figured our income on that. We want to work. We're talking to other carriers."

At the Reno dispatch window I saw a paper cup half-filled with coffee and cigarette butts. Taped to the cup was a truck key. Taped to the key was a note: *Color me gone.*

I asked a Linehaul recruiter why so many drivers signed on then quickly left the company.

"They don't know what they're getting into," she said. "It's their own fault." She had never driven, "but my ex was a diesel mechanic before he got busted, so I know trucks."

"It must be tough to sell the job," I said. "There's odd hours, uneven paychecks, unpaid delays at docks, drivers are hardly ever home, and they can wait a day or more for a load or a shower."

"I've heard those stories, but they can't be true. Who would keep a job like that? I wouldn't."

—⁂—

Linehaul customer service representatives.

"Don't you *ever* call a customer again," a livid CSR said to me. "You drive! You do *not* call customers!"

There had been no other way. I didn't have directions to any of the consignees—four mom-and-pop upholstery shops in Salt Lake City and another in Idaho Falls—just freight bills and phone numbers, and my Qualcomm requests for instructions had gone unanswered. I sent a message to the CSR, telling her I'd called the customers and pieced together a delivery schedule.

Beep: *I was to pull over right away! And call her immediately!*

She said, "I already have a schedule! Don't you *ever* call a customer again! You drive! You do *not* call customers! Write this down."

I asked if she realized that her unloading times—made up, she admitted, without calling the consignees—wouldn't work. Her first delivery was set for 8 a.m., but that store didn't receive before 10 a.m. Then she had spread all the deliveries out evenly, two neat hours apart, on the same day.

I said, "Idaho Falls is a three-hour drive from Salt Lake. It won't come off until the next day if I don't start until 10 in the morning."

"Don't interfere again! I'll write you up next time! *You* just drive!"

In Greer, SC a dock manager said to me, "We've told your people a hundred times: alloy wheels for Beamers go directly to the plant. We know the directions are wrong in your computers and we don't blame you drivers, but we're tired of it. *Please.* Tell your customer service department to correct the delivery instructions *today*."

I drove to the plant, delivered the wheels—a just-in-time shipment for the assembly line—and called Customer Service.

"Good morning," I said. "BMW has asked me to ask you to change the directions in the computer. Our trucks are going to a warehouse five miles away when they need to go to the factory."

The CSR said, "We don't want to hear about your problems,

driver."

I phoned Customer Service from a loading dock in Colony, WY. "Do you know where the other truck is? The shipper is more than a little ticked off. They've staged two loads and they're expecting two trucks."

"I scheduled one truck," said the CSR. "Why can't you take it?"

"The shipment is 78,000 pounds. It's two 39,000-pound loads."

"You can carry 80,000. Didn't you learn that in school?"

—ɷ—

Linehaul trainers.

At a shipper's drop lot in Cedar City, UT I hooked a loaded trailer and rolled forward, felt a thump and then another, and knew I had at least one flat-spotted tire.

The trailer had come out of Montana and it must have been cold up there, cold enough to freeze brake shoes to brake drums, cold enough for a lazy driver to excuse himself from making sure the wheels turned. Linehaul mechanics painted a big white X on trailer tire sidewalls and drivers were told to look in their mirrors to make sure that every X was rotating, particularly during winter. If they weren't, the tires weren't turning; no matter how cold it was, you shimmied under the axles and pried at the frozen brake shoes with a crowbar or broke them loose by pounding them with a hammer. But it was work and some drivers didn't understand: until brakes released and drums began to turn, tires didn't roll, they dragged. Sections of tread scraped the ground and were rubbed flat. The tires were ruined. Now, the time it would take me to get new tires stood in the way of a delivery appointment. I was mad enough to get the inbound driver's truck number and call his fleet manager.

"He wouldn't do that," she said. "Besides, how would he know?"

"They thump like flat tires. I knew after three feet. He drove through three states. Two tires are worn down to the belts."

"What belts?"

"The steel belts in the tires. They're exposed."

"Exposed his belts? Oh, he wouldn't do that. He's a trainer."

Nine miles south of Grangeville, ID U.S. 95 climbs off the Camas Prairie and onto a wooded ridge. You know there's a nasty downgrade ahead and that truckers lose their lives on it from time to time. Sure enough, warning signs appear while you're still grabbing gears on the upgrade: *Truckers. Steep grade next 8 miles. 7% maximum. Check brakes.* Suddenly, the road and the trees fall away and you're at the top of White Bird Hill, looking out over a jumbled landscape of grass-covered hillsides, narrow canyons and distant mountains. You'll find the Lower Salmon River at the bottom of the grade and drive pleasantly alongside it if you get down alive.

The first time I ran White Bird I parked at the summit, checked my brakes and studied an Idaho Transportation Department billboard: road, curves, three truck escape ramps. On trips after that I parked for the scenery.

The truck pullout atop White Bird. Breakfast with a view.

A Linehaul truck rumbled past, gaining speed. The driver shifted up.

"Linehaul," I said into the mic, "slow down and shift down. This is one long hill."

The driver said, "Mind your own business, peckerhead."

Then, radio silence for about a minute.

"Hey, Linehaul," someone said. "Your brakes are smoking."

"I can't stop! What do I do? I can't stop!"

"Don't panic," someone else said. "Don't panic. Use your service brakes *now* to slow down. Drop as many gears as you can. Snub your brakes! Snub 'em, damnit! Use the ramp! Jesus! Use the next ramp! You'll never get it down!"

But the driver did get it down, somehow, and found a level pullout by the river. I parked behind him, well away, ready to move my truck if his tires caught fire. A short, seriously overweight driver stood on a sidestep watching smoke rise from the trailer tandem. He reached into the cab to set the brakes.

His co-driver ran around from the front of the truck, pointed angrily at the trailer tires and said, "You fool! You idiot! Go ahead, burn 'em up! I told you it was too fast and the driver on the radio told you it was too fast! Are you trying to get us killed?"

I said, "One of you hurry up and put it in gear and shut off the engine. Release the brakes. Let them cool. Hurry! Never set hot brakes."

"That's what I told him," the co-driver said. "That's what I *said* to him! *Never set hot brakes!* He didn't even look at the warning signs up top."

"Hey," said the fat man. "I don't want to tell you again: *I'm* the trainer."

Other Linehaul trainers.

The one who keyed up near the top of Copper Canyon grade, south of Flagstaff. "I've got to get some sleep. Will someone talk my trainee down the hill?"

The one who lectured other drivers on how to back to a tight dock in Falconer, NY, made more corrections than his student, and said, "My mirrors are dirty. I couldn't see."

The one whose trainee told me, "He likes to jump out of the sleeper and yell 'boo!' when I'm driving. Thinks it's funny. I don't know if I should say anything, but he sure passes a lot of gas. I think there's things wrong with him."

The one whose trainee ran off I-5 near Corning, CA. "I woke up just as he left the road. Went right out into a field and I'm damn lucky he didn't flip us over. He'd been with me for three weeks, so I thought it was okay to sleep. If that happens again I'm through with training."

—⁂—

Linehaul rookies.

The one who said, "Ice? I'll drive on ice. Can't be no big deal."

The one who pulled away from a dock in Aurora, CO. A forklift—and the forklift operator—were still inside the trailer.

The one who pulled out from under a loaded trailer in Corsicana, TX before he cranked down the landing gear.

The one who drove out of the shop at the Salt Lake City terminal and didn't look underneath his truck, where a mechanic lay working. The mechanic's legs were broken when four drive tires rolled over them.

The ones who bragged about hard, terrible runs from Phoenix to Tucson (117 miles). Referred to diesel fuel as gas and go-go juice. Called 10-wheel tractors 18-wheelers. Said things like "That's a big 10-4, good buddy," "The Big Guy's wife owns Freightliner. She gives him his trucks for free. I heard he's waiting for her okay to turn them all up to 75 miles an hour," and "The Big Guy is always trying to make things better for his drivers." If asked, most wouldn't admit to less than two years on the road. They wanted to be thought of as soldiers back from the front, but they wore company t-shirts no veteran would ever touch: *80,000 pounds! 18 wheels! 10 gears! 430 horsepower! And you say I just drive a truck? Do the math!* and *Been there! Hauled that!* In time they learned that Linehaul's promises of high miles would turn out to be as thin as their paychecks.

Maybe they'd just survived their first all-nighter and thought it was a rite of passage, over and done with. In January, February, and March they wondered, not why freight slows down after Christmas and often remains slow through the first quarter, but why no one told them before they were hired. Or they'd pulled their first illegal load and were upset about it. Or they'd waited 23 hours for a dispatch and a fleet manager said, "Didn't the recruiter tell you there's no layover pay unless you're laid-over for a full 24 hours?"

Maybe their honeymoons weren't over. They'd been lucky with loads and miles and couldn't understand why other new guys complained. Slow freight, driver unloads, all-night runs, winter driving, and unpaid detention at grocery warehouses hadn't come up yet. They referred to The Big Guy by his first name, as if they were rubbing a rabbit's foot. But if they thought driving trucks would be a nonstop joy ride, they were relieved of that notion the first time they had to get out of a bunk at 1 a.m., punch a starter button, and search for an empty trailer. Short of sleep, they drove on dark highways, backed to a loading dock, and waited for hours. Then they knew there were some long days ahead.

Chapter Ten

*. . . fatigue is the truck driver's biggest enemy. He must
sometimes spend 72 hours at the wheel without prolonged
rest . . . If he trucks between San Antonio and El Paso he may
drive the 1,100-mile round trip practically without stop . . .*

LIFE MAGAZINE, JULY 12, 1937

*The ultimate objective of the safety regulations of the Interstate
Commerce Commission, Bureau of Motor Carriers . . . is to
decrease accidents, save human lives, and reduce property
losses by the following means: every driver mentally and
physically qualified to drive safely; possessed of a driver's license;
subject to rules and regulations relating to qualifications
of drivers and safety of operation; and protected from
hazardous fatigue by limitations in hours of service . . .*

FEDERAL REGISTER, JULY 8, 1936

Log books and the federal Hours of Service regulations, flies
in my trucking ointment. I didn't know whether to laugh, cry, or
get mad. I did all three.

Since March 1, 1939, most truckers who pull freight across
state lines have been required by law to keep daily records of
their driving time, time on duty but not driving, time off duty,

and time spent in the sleeper. In log books, drivers record what they do and where and when, hours worked on each of the previous seven days, and the sum total of those hours. They sign their logs, certifying that entries are true and correct, and present their log books to inspectors, scale masters, or law enforcement personnel upon demand.

In Illinois: "Gimme yer comic book."

In Florida: "Got your joke book handy, driver?"

In Tennessee: "Compliance check! Show me that damn book damn quick!"

In Washington: uplifted hand.

In Georgia, New York, New Mexico, and South Carolina: snapped fingers.

The HOS regulations.

You could legally drive for almost 16 hours in 24.

You were allowed to drive for 10 consecutive hours, take eight off, then drive for 10 more, tumbling through 18-hour work-rest cycles until you couldn't tell the fog line from the center line.

You couldn't legally drive more than 10 hours following eight consecutive hours off duty or after having been on duty for 15 consecutive hours, and you couldn't legally drive or work after you'd been on duty for 70 hours in eight days. So, after a logged eight-hour break, you never logged more than 10 consecutive driving hours. No matter what you did, you never logged more than 70 on-duty hours in eight days or revealed that you drove after 15 consecutive hours on duty. It wasn't hard to beat the system.

You could always legally split your time in the sleeper. If you logged no more than 10 aggregate hours in the seat combined with no less than eight off, and no logged sleeper break was less than two hours—and if you had available hours—you'd be in compliance, at least on paper. If you drove, say, for six hours, logged two in the sleeper, drove four, then logged six more in the sleeper, you accumulated eight hours of recuperative rest, according to the Federal Motor Carrier Safety Administration. Or you could legally drive five hours, sleep four, drive five, then sleep four more and repeat the cycle right on up to burnout, roll-over, or your 70-hour limit, whichever came first; FMCSA used to call this the ideal use of split sleeper time. Drivers called it 'legal but lethal.'

Truck drivers aren't paid for most of their on-duty-not-driving time, but logged on-duty-not-driving hours count, nonetheless, against available driving hours and HOS limits. As defined in the Federal Motor Carrier Safety Regulations, on-duty-not-driving time includes:

"All time inspecting [or servicing] . . . any commercial motor vehicle."

I logged some of it.

"All time waiting to be dispatched, unless the driver has been relieved from duty by the motor carrier."

Relieved from duty or not, I never logged it because no one ever paid me for it.

"All time, other than driving time, in or upon any commercial motor vehicle, except time spent resting in a sleeper berth."

I didn't log it at all. If I was in the passenger seat reading, I was comfortably off duty. If I sat on the sidestep to watch a sunset, I was as off duty as I could be. When asked by inspectors, "Were you in the passenger seat or were you in the sleeper?" or "Were you in the truck? You logged yourself off duty," I lied.

"All time performing compensated work for any non-motor carrier entity."

There isn't enough time to put in 70 hours a week and work a second job.

"All time loading or unloading."

I would show a five-hour driver unload as 30 minutes on the dock and four and a-half hours in the sleeper. If lumpers handled the freight, I logged myself off duty for as long as it took them. If loading or unloading became an all-day affair, I left the trailer at the dock and bobtailed, off duty and on my own, for groceries or a shower. I did what truckers had been doing for 60 years: I practiced creative logging, hoarded hours for seat time (the work that paid), and accepted the risks—fines of $1,000 to $11,000 per violation, state *and* federal prosecution, jail time— of carrying falsified logs.

Portland, OR.

I went back to work after a two-week vacation then waited

five days—Thursday through Monday—for a load assignment.

Beep: *Pick up motor oil Tuesday and take it to Shakopee, MN. Accept? Yes / No.*

Yes.

I logged Thursday through Monday as off duty. I would start my trip with 70 available hours.

I called an FMCSA office, asked an inspector what he thought, and didn't tell him how I'd logged the time.

He said, "You may legally work 15 consecutive hours before you take eight off, right? Monday through Thursday is four days waiting for a dispatch, so you accumulated 60 on-duty hours. You could have worked 10 hours on Friday then enjoyed the weekend. What is the problem?"

The problem was that, according to HOS regulations, my trip to Minnesota was illegal. Technically, I was out of hours and too tired to drive safely. After sitting, unpaid, for five days. On top of 14 days at home.

Flies. Ointment.

I drove when I was rested and out of hours. I drove when I had hours and should have been asleep. Tired has nothing to do with available hours. Legal and compliant don't mean safe. Legal but lethal never appealed to me. Tired or not, I often drove more than 10 consecutive hours because I liked driving and wanted to keep moving; because I hoped to avoid rush-hour traffic or high winds or black ice; because I wasn't ready to sleep every 10 hours or in the middle of the day; because, otherwise, many on-time deliveries would have been impossible.

I ran loads one way and logged them another. I logged loads exactly as I ran them. I accepted illegal dispatches and I refused illegal dispatches. Often, the choice was clear: violate the regulations or violate myself. I violated the rules wholesale and, most of the time, I was a safer driver for it. If I was particularly tired (who knew better?) I said so and tape-recorded dispatchers' threats. I photographed illegal load assignments on my Qualcomm screen, because you never know. I did my best to sleep, if not every night, then at least at night. I fought the HOS, I like to think I won, and I believe that experienced truck drivers who roll with their own biorhythms are safer than those who are in compliance just to be in compliance. I don't know how many truckers are dead because they were tired *and* compliant or who are (as you read this) tired and driving *because* they're compliant. I know that compliance alone will never make a safe trucker. I know that I would rather share the road with drivers who are awake than with drivers who are not, and I know this, having learned it during split-sleeper periods, repeated 18-hour work-sleep cycles, and all-night sessions behind the wheel: a Circadian rhythm beats an HOS regulation hands down, every time. I'd bet my life on it. And yours.

Chapter Eleven

Opportunity makes the thief.

JIMMY BRESLIN

You're at a dock in Tulare, CA. Your load goes to Madison, WI. What is the shortest truck-drivable route? What route promises the fastest transit time? How best to route an eighteen-wheeler from Hopewell, VA to Blue Ridge and La Fayette, GA? From Augusta, KY to Tucson? From Groveton, NH to Buffalo, NY? Is the shortest truck-drivable route always the best route? Best for who? The shipper? The carrier? The driver?

When you pulled a load from Eagan, MN to Pueblo, CO, you knew you'd be paid for 897 HHG miles. The shortest route you could find in your Motor Carrier's Road Atlas ran along slow two-lane highways and through small towns. Figure on 23 driving hours, an average speed of 39 miles an hour, 924 hub miles and a transit time of 44 hours.

An alternate route—1,023 miles on Interstates—required only 17 hours behind the wheel and 25 hours in transit. You could deliver the next day, but Linehaul wouldn't pay for the extra 126 miles.

I knew of two routes from Fort Worth to Scottsdale, AZ. The shortest—973 miles—meant small roads, 38 hours in transit and

22 hours in the driver's seat at an average speed of 44 miles an hour. The alternative—Interstates and Interstate speeds all the way—took only 16 driving hours and 24 hours overall. If you needed to deliver sooner rather than later, The Big Road was the only way to go, but you drove 1,060 miles. Linehaul paid HHG miles, 958 of them.

What *is* HHG? I should have asked at orientation. I learned the hard way.

Household Goods Carriers miles is the trucking industry's primary system for calculating mileage charges and drivers' mileage pay. By definition, HHG miles make up the *shortest* truck-drivable route from one place to another. An HHG route will lead a driver down two-lane roads and through cities and towns, adding hours to cut miles.

Practical miles—again by definition—are the shortest-*quickest* miles between two places. Most of the time, practical routes are longer than HHG routes.

Hub miles? They're the real miles a truck driver drives. We used to put meters on axle hubs to accurately record mileage, but odometer readings these days are close enough for a trucker's work. A hub mile is a mile on the odometer.

Paid miles are the miles a truck driver takes to the bank. Maybe they're the same as HHG miles or practical miles or hub miles. Most of the time they're not.

Sometimes, the shortest and practical routes are one and the same. If you're going from Reno to Sacramento, you drive over the Sierras on I-80, the shortest, fastest, *and* most practical route. But sometimes longer is shorter. The HHG route from Vancouver, WA to Phoenix goes through central Oregon, Reno, and Las Vegas: 1,302 miles, 32 driving hours, at least 53 hours in transit. The practical route runs down I-5 and out I-10: 1,351 miles, 24 driving hours, 44 hours in transit. Des Moines to Salt Lake City is 1,071 practical miles and 17 driving hours or 1,063 HHG miles and 21 driving hours. Seattle to Miami is 3,362 practical miles and 58 driving hours or 3,241 HHG miles and 74 driving hours. What is your time worth?

You could never tell how many miles a load would be off or if the miles would be off at all. Lewiston, ID to Waynesville, NC paid 2,565 miles for 2,550. Salt Lake City to Montgomery, MN paid 1,137 miles—I ran 1,234 on the shortest route I could find. Torrance, CA to Nogales, AZ paid 547 miles for 602. Golden, CO to Elkton, VA paid 1,622 miles—that's exactly how far it was, dock to dock. Sacramento to Louisville and Orlando paid 3,062 miles—I put 3,116 on the hub using a Linehaul routing printout that showed 3,355. I told my dispatcher that the distance to the moon was known with greater precision. He said, "Your odometer is off."

The odometers weren't off on every truck I drove. They weren't off 5 percent on one load and 16 percent on the next. But my paid miles were off, typically, about 6 percent. Driving 120,000 miles a year and giving up 6 percent, a truck driver would donate 72,000 miles in 10 years. Twenty-four trips coast-to-coast. Twenty-four workweeks. Six unpaid months behind the wheel.

Chapter Twelve

Be your own boss.

Linehaul owner-operator recruitment brochure

As I remember it, the full-page advertisement featured a truck stop photographed at daybreak. Saturated hues—yellow, orange and gold—picked up chrome highlights in rows of parked trucks. Backlit and caught in mid-stride by the camera, two drivers ambled across the lot. Western-style hats. Boots. Owner-operators, no doubt—easy-going, confident, experienced. Heirs to the myth of the cowboy.

The ad helped me set my thoughts in order. I lived and breathed the trucking life. I hoped to stay out there for all the time left to me. A true journeyman at last, I felt good about myself for the first time in years, knew what I was doing, and knew that I could make more money with my name on the door. I longed to be one of the men in the picture.

On the way home one night I ran with a Linehaul owner-operator. Six months earlier, he'd been a company driver at the Reno terminal. I asked how it was going.

"Best money move I ever made," he said. "Gave myself a dime-a-mile raise."

Just what I wanted to hear.

"Hi," I said to Gayle when I walked in the door. "We're buying a truck."

She suggested we take a vote first.

I said, "Aye."

"Aye. May I kiss the new owner-operator?"

Owner-operator. I liked the sound of it.

All through the next month I looked at truck leases and purchase agreements, fended off over-eager truck salesmen, and examined new Volvos, used Anteaters and repossessed Macks.

In Denver I walked slow and thoughtful circles around a new Freightliner Classic. Jet black. Owner-operator specs. Loaded with accessories and chicken lights. Nice truck. One hundred and twenty-five thousand dollars.

I sat inside a new teal and gray Classic on a Salt Lake City dealer's lot. Four hundred twenty-five horsepower Caterpillar engine. Thirteen-speed and 3:55 gears. Luxurious diamond-tuck interior. Killer stereo. Full gauge package with chrome bezels. Chrome gearshift. Mirror-shine bumper. Mirror-shine wheels. Mirror-shine fuel tanks. I saw myself stylin' and at $89,500 the price was right—we'd own the truck in three years.

Gayle said, "Do you really want it?"

"Yes and no. It's sweet, but I'm not out here to polish chrome."

"That sounds like 'no.' Keep looking, Puppy. You'll find a truck."

On the road, at truck stops, at loading docks, I tuned in when the topic was carrier lease programs. I listened carefully, knowing that drivers were paid for headhunting.

"You'll like Interstate. Give me your address and they'll send you an application. Be sure to give them my truck number."

"Schneider's absolutely the best. Call them. Here's my name and truck number."

"Well, sure I get $500 if you sign on, but PRIME really *is* a great place to work. I wouldn't tell you they were if they weren't, would I?"

Another driver said, "My lease is okay."

I said, "Just okay?"

"If you'd asked last month, I'd have said I was looking for another company and that would have told you all you needed to know. But freight's picked up and they got rid of shit-for-brains the dispatcher, so I guess I'll stick around for awhile."

"You want to think twice about leasing from a carrier and then back to the same carrier," said a world-wise owner-operator. "They pay you so you can pay them. That's dangerous. Freight will dry up near the end of your lease, you won't be able to make your payments, and they'll repossess the truck. You'll lose every dollar you put into it then they'll come after you for more. Once you sign you're screwed. Good luck."

I met a former PRIME driver who told me about PRIME payments—$700 a week—and short miles. I didn't believe him at first—$700 a week to the company before you even saw your own pay.

"PRIME got its money every week," he said. "Some weeks, I didn't take anything home and I got real sick of that. Drive for them and you'll be working for peanuts, because that's all you'll be eating. They don't advertise the failure rate in their lease program. It's 40 percent. But they do let you pick the truck's color."

Buy, lease. Lease, buy. If you lease, you never own the truck, but so what? You also don't pay federal excise tax on a truck purchase, and the headaches belong to someone else after the warranties expire. If you buy, you enjoy the tax advantage of depreciation, pay the truck off, and say goodbye to payments, but you'll be sitting in an older rig. Either way, you pay close attention to your payments, because payments can make you or break you. I thought that PRIME's $2,800-a-month would be suicide. I was looking for $1,500 or less.

Through Trucklease, his equipment leasing business, The Big Guy had begun to offer new Freightliners to experienced Linehaul drivers. Lease an FLD120 condo from him for four years and make payments of $1,448 a month. It looked like a good way for a man to get into his first tractor and run his own show, and he could pick any color truck he wanted so long as it was white.

There weren't many Linehaul owner-operators in those days, maybe 140 or so, their number and existence almost a corporate secret. I talked to the few I could find and asked about their leases. Did they get more freight or better treatment than company drivers? What was it like? Most were uneasy with Linehaul's heavy-handed accounting and the often painful difference between paid and unpaid miles, but one thing was clear: a leased tractor brought home more money than a company truck.

At a warehouse near Reno.

I backed in next to a truck and looked at the driver's door: *Joe Rodriguez Trucking, Tucson, AZ. Leased to Linehaul, Phoenix, AZ.* Short, wiry, sporting a Willie Nelson ponytail, the lessor stood beside his burnished tractor, a polishing rag in each hand.

While forklift operators loaded wooden crates into our trailers, Joe Rodriguez explained truck leases and showed me settlement statements. Later, over lunch, he freely shared his thoughts about the trucking business—good loads and bad loads, fuel taxes, highway use taxes, self-employment taxes, tire wear, maintenance, the coarse and fine points of life as a Linehaul owner-operator, all of it delivered in a gentle Tex-Mex accent.

"They'll tell you, lease from them and you'll be independent. That is a lie, amigo. It's The Big Guy's truck no matter what happens. He always has his hand on you." He reached across the table to lay a tight grip on my shoulder. "Comprende? For the same work, I make better money than a company driver. I've got a little more freedom and my name is on the door, but I'm not getting rich out here. No one is. You've got to watch the company like a hawk, because they think they own you and they will *mess* with you."

I read and re-read Linehaul's owner-operator recruiting information. No Qualcomm required. Drive five miles an hour faster than company trucks. You had to have at least two years behind the wheel and unimpeachable safety and customer-service histories. Solos would run about 12,000 miles a month, which amounted to almost $50,000 a year after taxes. Not bad for driving a truck in 1994.

Other carriers offered leases on trucks governed at 65 miles an hour, or 75, or not at all. Petes. Volvos. Anteaters. Different specs and different colors. Different down payments and different lease plans. More—or less—pay per mile. More—or less— loading and unloading pay. All permits paid or some permits paid. Tolls paid. Discounts on fuel, parts, and tires. No matter how it was made to appear, it all came out the same on pay day, or pretty close. The carriers were peas in a pod, their promises variations on a theme, and you had no assurances that any of them would keep their word. Everything I learned said the risks for a driver were the same no matter what color his truck was. I decided to lease one of The Big Guy's new Freightliners and sign on as a Linehaul owner-operator.

"You've seen how they treat drivers," a friend said. "Why on earth would you lease to them? There's other outfits."

"Better the devil you know," I said.

He left the company a week later, pushed out the door by low miles, The Treatment, and a mechanic's greasy shoe print on his bunk.

I mailed an application to Linehaul's owner-operator division, waited two weeks, then stopped by the Phoenix terminal to see Tom Kelly, who ran the owner-operator fleet. Tom had been a true old-time owner-operator. He papered the walls of his office with photographs of custom-painted Macks, Kenworths, and long-nose Petes, trucks that evoked speed, elegance, and independent trucking's heyday, trucks that would have been out of place at Linehaul, with its cookie-cutter tractors governed at 57 miles an hour.

He said, "The truck is $78,000, less a $10,000 down payment. You'll be on the hook for 68 grand. Reno tells me you're okay. Do you have ten thousand?"

"Yes."

"You're in. I'll be your fleet manager. I'll send a message when your truck comes to the Wilsonville yard—should be about three weeks. Get there any way you can. Bring a load down here and check in at the prep shop. They'll turn the truck up to 62 and run a full PDI."

"PDI?"

"Pre-delivery inspection. We have to go over the rigs from bumper to bumper because our friends at Freightliner don't finish the job when they build a truck. Drain plugs leak. Doors don't close. Things don't work. Things have been known to fall off. Bring the money when you come back. I'll have your contracts here."

I was rolling toward Phoenix a week later, driving though Goldfield, NV, when a Qualcomm message came in.

Pick up your truck in Wilsonville ASAP.

I pulled a return load to Reno, transferred my gear from 6140 to a rental car, and shook hands with the terminal manager.

He said, "The good ones always leave. Stop by once in awhile."

I drove straight through to Wilsonville and checked into a motel, but not before stopping at the yard and picking up the keys to my new truck, Linehaul power unit 21127. Two. Eleven. Twenty-seven. The next four years of my life and Gayle's were tied to those numbers. I walked around the truck several times. It wasn't a black Classic, but it would do. I adjusted the driver's seat, ran my hands around the wheel, and smiled. I was home. I called Gayle and she said, "Tell me about our new truck. Do you like it? When do I get a ride? I miss you. When are you coming home?" Sam barked.

I went to the truck before sunrise and moved in. I cinched up the fan belts, checked fluid levels and the brakes, tightened loose bolts, vacuumed metal shavings off the floor and policed the cab, picking up dozens of sheet-metal screws left behind by assembly-line workers. I pulled the plastic covers off the seats and the bunk, but left the cover on the floor; when the prep-shop mechanics were finally gone from the truck, I would remove it and the new, clean carpet would be mine alone to enjoy. I started the engine, listening and watching the gauges. I released the brakes, drove around the yard a few times, then bobtailed out to I-5. Everything worked. Nothing fell off.

Linehaul lease trucks came from the factory equipped like company trucks, with the same engines, transmissions, gearing, tires, cloth interiors, and the same cheap AM-FM radios. Until I installed a premium tape deck and high-end speakers, captain's chairs, antennas, and a CB; until the truck was turned up; until my name graced the doors and my graphics dressed the sides, 21127 would be the same as every other Linehaul tractor.

I left the windows open for two nights to clear the cab and sleeper of fumes from the new paint, solvents, and adhesives. On the third day I topped off the tanks with 198 gallons, the first diesel fuel I'd ever paid for, and hooked a load to Phoenix.

—⁂—

Joe Rodriguez had given me copies of his leases, telling me to read them carefully. They leaned heavily toward The Big Guy—all rights were his and all risks and liabilities were the driver's—but who really believed the man's lawyers drafted contracts that didn't favor their client? Forget about being your own boss—you had a truck to drive, a place to sleep, and a chance to earn a living. The Big Guy kept his hand on your shoulder. You'd have been crazy to expect anything else.

Each owner-operator-to-be signed an equipment-leasing agreement and a contractor agreement. With the first, he leased a truck from Trucklease. With the second, he leased the truck and his labor—some said his soul—to Linehaul.

When a driver leased from Trucklease he promised to immediately buy insurance policies covering loss, theft, collision, property damage, and public liability. If he wrecked the truck, he was obligated to pay out all remaining terms of the lease and to cover The Big Guy's losses, without limit. He agreed to make payments of $361.98 a week for 208 weeks. At the end of the lease term a buyout of $13,600 plus $9,360 in federal excise tax would make the truck his if that was what he wanted. Total cost, $108,521.84.

By signing the contractor agreement you promised to make the truck available to Linehaul "continuously and exclusively" and to "perform all work necessary for the transportation of the freight furnished by the company . . . from time to time."

From time to time. What happened to 12,000 miles a month?

Each contractor would be "liable to [the] Company for any damage to any trailers . . . in Contractor's possession."

Any damage? What about *pre-existing* damage?

You agreed to maintain the truck in good repair and to pay for fuel, fuel taxes, the Federal Highway Use Tax, the Arizona Motor Carrier Tax, mileage taxes, registration, permits, tires, maintenance, non-warranty repairs, and tolls.

Owner-operators would be independent contractors, paying their own quarterly taxes, self-employment taxes, and workman's compensation insurance premiums.

The contractor agreement was not "to be construed as the Contractor must accept every load tendered by the Company." At a carrier known for forced-dispatch, then, independent contractors would be turning down loads. Nothing said we had to explain. Nothing said we didn't. Nothing said there would be consequences. Nothing said there wouldn't be.

Pay was 78 cents for each dispatched HHG mile, loaded or empty.

I read through the contracts, twenty pages of boilerplate, take it or leave it. I knew things weren't quite right and that a lot went unsaid. I knew I was leasing from a carrier and back to the same carrier, paying it so it could pay me. But I wanted the truck and I gave Tom Kelly a check for $10,000, signed both agreements, told myself I was an owner-operator, and began sharecropping the highway.

—⁓—

The truck was a business—money flowed in and money flowed out. The leases defined business relationships: who paid for what and when. But many drivers didn't understand. I met lease operators who hadn't read their contracts.

"Read them? Hell, I just walked in and signed the damn things."

"What could go wrong?"

"I trust The Big Guy. Don't you?"

Several believed the truck became theirs at the end of the lease term, that they were getting into it rent-to-own. A few thought they could walk away with a full refund and without further obligation whenever it suited them. Some didn't realize that termination of the contractor agreement also meant the end of the lease agreement. Not one I spoke with fully appreciated the risk he had accepted. Most were naive or willfully ignorant and you couldn't talk business with them. I asked one about his average CPM, a term I thought everyone understood.

He said, "What is CPM?"

"Cost per mile."

"I don't know. I let my accountant worry about that. I'm a businessman."

Another calculated his CPM at 78 cents.

I said, "Your cost is what you're paid?"

Still another volunteered that he was doing "good, real good" after nine months in his own truck, telling me, "I've never made so much money I didn't have to pay taxes on."

What about quarterly income-tax payments?

He said, "What's that?"

"They don't understand much," said a friend who worked in the office. "They sign anyway, then they whine and try to get out of their leases. Or they wreck a truck and they want a new one. Last week, the body shop repaired a driver's tractor. They did a lousy job, so he wants a new truck. The Big Guy said 'no.' The driver's ticked off. He's ready to take a walk. If he does, they'll send it to a collection agency and ruin his credit. He'll never drive again."

"Watch this," I said to a driver who had just picked up his new lease truck. "You'll need to know how to replace the dashboard lamps. There's a trick to it."

"I'm an owner-operator now," he said. "I don't do light bulbs. I don't repair anything. I own a truck."

—ᚾ—

The PDI turned out to be painless. There wasn't much wrong with 21127 and after two days Mayfield Transportation was ready for its first customers. From Phoenix, my loads took me up to the northwest, down to the Bay Area and back to the northwest, all with the same set of pups. After the third live unload in a row, I stopped at the Wilsonville window to ask about freight.

The dispatcher said, "You've got a set . . . I have Stockton for the day after tomorrow. Live load and live unload."

"Well, I'd like to get rid of the pups and step out. Is there anything else?"

"Let's see . . . How about cookies and crackers to New Carrollton and Wheaton, MD? It pays 2,788 miles and picks up tonight in Portland. Shipper load and count, consignees unload, you've got five days to get there. Find a 53 and the load's yours."

I called in from Wheaton when the forklift driver lifted the last pallet.

"There's no more freight today," said the east-coast dispatcher. "Check back with me in the morning. You can probably find a place to park at that old truck hotel between D.C. and Baltimore. It's on I-95 at the Jessup exit. Expect to be entertained."

At the TA truck stop, Jessup, MD.

I found a space opposite the main driveway and put the trailer between the lines on the first dig. By mid-afternoon each of the TA's 650 parking spaces sheltered a truck and a steady parade of rigs circled the lot—drivers on the prowl for a place to park, CB mics at the ready.

"I'm out of hours and I've got to park my yacht. Somebody

move."

"I'm burnt, man, burnt to a crisp. Got hours up the wazoo but I am *toast* and that's no lie. I'll pay twenty dollars green cash money for a parking place."

"Anybody leaving soon? Got to take me a nap . . . Hey! Yellow Freightliner in the back row! You going out?"

"Yeah. Just a minute and you can have it . . . There. I look legal."

Those of us in the front row watched from our trucks while a hooker and a TA security guard slugged it out. He dodged a kick to his groin, wrestled her to the ground, planted a knee on her chest and called for back-up.

Someone on channel 19 said, "Hey, I know her. I *know* her."

"How well do you *know* the lady, driver?"

"Anybody want to talk about the Bible?"

"Aw, shut up, preacher man."

"Oh, well . . . any other Commercial here tonight?"

"Right here, honey. Whatever you want to do. But no handcuffs."

"Where you at, girl? Go to 23."

"Don't do it, driver. It's a sin. Now, the Bible is God's word and He . . ."

"Shut up, preacher man."

"damns all fornicators to eternal hellfire and . . ."

"Shut *up*, preacher man. You're a fornicator yourself, I'll bet, every chance you get. Live and let live."

Drivers keyed up to hawk tools, videos, CB radios, televisions, a portable refrigerator, prepaid phone cards, and CB noise toys—aggravation toys, some call them. Echo and reverb. Microchip repeaters. Sound effects: Tarzan; railroad air horns; Daffy Duck and Woody Woodpecker; myriad varieties of intestinal gas; James Brown shouting that he feels good; a certain scene from *When Harry Met Sally*.

"She sure is doing a good job of faking it."

"Reminds me of home."

"You wish."

"Anybody want to borrow my girlfriend? I ain't let the air out of her yet."

"Who wants to run up to Chicago?"

"Hey, if I've got it does that mean I brought it?"

"No. If *you've* got it, *I* brought it."

"What do they call you, sweetheart?"

"They call me 'After Midnight.'"

"Can I call you before?"

"I'm working a crossword puzzle. Anybody know Smokey the Bear's middle name?"

"The."

"Oh . . . Yeah, that fits. Thanks."

"Say, that's a fine sounding radio you got there. What do they call you when they ain't mad at you?"

"They call me Easy Rider."

"C'mon. Who wants to run up to Chicago with me?"

"Copy that, Easy. They call us Mongoose and Cow Pie. What type of radio is that?"

"The wages of sin is death! You are all sinners!"

"Preacher man, don't make me come over there."

"Mongoose, I got me a Galaxy 88 with a 400-watt kicker. I'm running two Wilson 5000 antennas through number 8 co-ax, all tuned by that kid in Amarillo. I've got fire in my wire and I can talk to a man on the moon with this set-up."

"Damnit, driver. With a radio like that you could talk to Elvis."

Out of the ether, The King spoke. "Wha' d' y'all wauna tawk t' me fo?"

The earth stood still. For a full minute no one on the channel said a word. Then somebody whistled softly.

"Whoa. Maybe he ain't left the building after all."

"Chicago. Last call for Chicago."

"What the hell kind of handle is 'Cow Pie'?"

When Harry Met Sally met Tarzan.

When Harry Met Sally met James Brown.

When Harry Met Sally met a freight train.

"Thank ya very much," said Elvis.

I called Tom Kelly to ask about a payroll problem. Someone answered his phone and said, "Tom's not around anymore. They put him out to pasture. I'm your new fleet manager."

"What's your name?"

"Peter French."

Phoenix, September 17, 1994. The first-ever meeting for

Linehaul owner-operators.

After welcoming everyone, The Big Guy announced a decrease in our deadhead rate, from 78 cents a mile to 61. The reaction—shouts of protest—was predictable, but he seemed surprised and annoyed.

He said, "Oh, what are you complaining about? You're *still* making money."

On 100,000 annual miles and 6 percent annual deadhead, The Big Guy had just slipped us a $1,000 pay cut.

"I signed on three days ago," said the man behind me. "They didn't say anything about plans to lower deadhead pay."

The driver sitting next to me leaned over and said, "I'll give him this: he knows how to squeeze you once he's got you in a lease."

Someone asked The Big Guy if he made more on company equipment or owner-operator trucks. "I make about the same," he said, but he waited a few seconds before he answered. He began to talk about opportunities for owner-operator teams and trainer teams on a new national account, dedicated runs for a department store chain; drop and hook; no doubles; pull only high-cube trailers, drive only low-rider tractors; miles, lots of miles. "You'll need 19.5 rubber to go east with the high cubes. We'll offer good trade-ins on low-rider trucks if you sign up for the account and want to get out of your current Trucklease equipment."

The low-riders were, he said, new and completely different.

A driver asked, "It's really the same truck, though, isn't it?"

The Big Guy hesitated before he said, "No. It's a completely different truck."

The driver next to me leaned over again and whispered, "Did you notice? There's always a *deelay* when he stretches the truth."

"But those 19.5 tires," another driver said. "They don't last very long. We'd have to replace them more often. They're not free."

The Big Guy hesitated. "We think you'll make it up on mileage."

I didn't hear most of the next question—it was about interest rates on lease trucks—but I caught The Big Guy's swift answer: "I'm going to make money on my money!"

"What's mine is mine and what's yours is mine," someone said. "Doesn't he have enough?"

"You never have enough if you want to be as big as he wants to be," said another driver, "and you have to be willing to steal. That means, my friend, that you have to be willing to steal from somebody. Just look around this room. There's a somebody in every chair."

From the desk of The Big Guy, January 30, 1995.

In the past twelve months . . . our profits nearly doubled, increasing from $12.3 million in 1993 to $22.6 million in 1994.

From the Linehaul Transportation 1995 Report to Stockholders.

We have been able to maintain our low operating ratio by

implementing strict cost controls . . . and shifting our fleet growth strategy to utilize more owner-operators. Indeed, the shift to more owner-operators in 1995 reduced the Company's capital expenditures by nearly $20 million. More than 60 percent of our fleet growth in 1995 was achieved with owner-operators.

More than 60 percent fleet growth due to owner-operators.

Doubled profits.

A $20 million saving.

A pay cut.

—⁂—

It was a good trip offer, Oregon to the southern tip of Texas, 2,450 miles over four days, and the best time of year—early autumn—to go. Then I learned the shipper's name.

I said, "What else do you have? I won't cross a picket line."

In a non-union company this amounted to heresy, but the dispatcher said, "I'll see what else there is."

A voice slithered over an office partition. "I would make you sit until you took that load. Wouldn't give you one little thing more until you took it."

The speaker came to the window, fists clenched, his ruddy complexion darkened by anger. Known for yelling at drivers and lording it over them, he was rumored to have married into the founder's family—a little big guy.

"I would make you go out there and sit and rot until you took the load!"

"Well, you can't," I said. "If you want a scab, do it yourself."

"You can't turn down freight! This is a forced-dispatch company!"

"Not for owner-operators. Have you read our contract?"

"What contract? You think you're some kind of goddamn Teamster?"

The Denver planner asked me to make a live-unload local delivery that would take at least half a day.

"Glad to help out," I said. "Our contract gets us $18 an hour for local work. What can I do for you?"

"I'll pay you nine."

"The contract says 18."

"I don't care about *your* contract. Nine."

"Actually, it's The Big Guy's contract. Eighteen."

"I'll get someone else. You owner-operators think you're God's gift to trucking."

A weekend dispatcher at the Reno window told me to take what he gave me—288 paid miles over three days—and to get my butt moving. I said 'no.'

"Sonny," he said, "if I tell you to move out, that's what you do."

I said, "You'll pull that load before I will. There's no forced dispatch for the owner-operator division. Didn't they tell you?"

"You don't know much about Linehaul, do you?"

Still, my name was on the door, my revenue was up, and my net income—that most important number—was also up. It did indeed look like a dime-a-mile raise. In just three months Gayle and I saw the return of our $10,000 investment. We looked forward to returns on it. I looked forward to more time alone. The road went on forever.

Chapter Thirteen

Get home when you want, get home when you need.

Linehaul recruiting slogan

Phoenix, March 19, 1996.

I'd been awake since 6 a.m., ready to roll, calling dispatchers throughout the day for a load. They told me, "Check back in an hour." "Call after lunch." "Call after 4 p.m."

"I'll take anything that lets me sleep," I said when I called at 4:30. "No all-nighters."

"Got one," a dispatcher said. "Picks up here in Phoenix at 8 p.m. and delivers in Los Angeles at 8 a.m. It's 380 miles."

Drive until midnight, sleep four hours, drive four more, deliver on time. Not much of a load, but doable. And Los Angeles was a trucker's gold mine—freight to Florida, Virginia, New York, and New Jersey came out of there every day.

Except . . . the shipper's office didn't open until 8:30 and the papers showed two deliveries, 3 a.m. and 9 a.m., both driver unloads, no lumpers allowed.

Stay up all day, drive 6 hours, hand stack for three, drive one, sleep two, hand stack for three. I'd done it before and I would probably do it again, but not when I'd said no all-nighters and not when the first delivery was already late.

I called Dispatch, explained why the load wouldn't work,

waited on hold for 25 minutes, then explained to a second dispatcher, who put me back on hold. Fifteen minutes later another dispatcher said, "You accepted a two-dropper and now you won't do it. I'll take the load off your hands, but I have to charge the owner-operator drop fee. It's $185."

"You can forget about that," I said. "Dispatch got it wrong, not me. Repower or reschedule and notify the consignees. It's done all the time."

"Well, bring the papers to the window and talk to Logan. He's the planner and he's head honcho."

Back at the yard Logan asked why his dispatchers were biting their nails. I explained a third time, point by weary point.

"You'll have to talk to my boss," he said. He looked at his computer screen, frowned, and picked up a phone. A woman's voice rose through the headset while I unpacked my dispatch buster. Logan said, "Careful. He's got a tape recorder." He handed the phone to me and I attached the mic.

"Good evening," I said. "Who is this?"

"*I* am Monica Peyton. *I* am in charge of customer service. I already know who *you* are."

Indeed, I was one of those lazy, useless owner-operators. We had no respect for customers. We weren't team players. She didn't know why The Big Guy kept us around. She was ordering me to take the load. *Ordering me*. Did I understand?

I tried a fourth explanation, adding that the dispatch violated company policy and federal safety regulations. Did Ms. Peyton know of Federal Motor Carrier Safety Regulation 393.2, which prohibited the dispatch of tired drivers? No, she didn't. Was the freight worth more on a dock or driven into a ditch by a guy who fell asleep behind the wheel? What nerve! How dare I ask a question like that? Was she aware of a recent Linehaul memo that said there were to be no trade-offs between safety and customer service? No, she wasn't. I reminded her of the tape we were making together. Did she want me to play it at a DOT hearing? For starters, she could listen to it in the office of Linehaul's Vice President of Safety.

I said, "See you soon."

She was screaming when I put the phone down.

A driver came to the window and a dispatcher pointed at him, at the door into Dispatch, then at the planner. The driver yawned and rubbed his eyes, leaned on Logan's desk, and stared at the paperwork I had just turned in.

He said, "I should be asleep. I don't want to do this. It's an all-nighter and I'm gonna be late—what if they won't take them?"

"They'll take them," said the planner. "We'll make it up to you with a really good load. You can sleep tomorrow."

In the morning I showered early and called the Vice President of Safety.

"Come right over," said his secretary. "They're expecting you."

Ms. Peyton, my fleet manager, and the terminal manager lined the office walls in high-back chairs. The VP delivered a stern lecture from behind his desk. His voice trailed off when I opened the office door. "I don't want him to call anyone . . ."

The meeting I had just asked for was already in progress.

Only Ms. Peyton smiled. Glancing from man to man, crossing and uncrossing legs under a skirt much too short for the office, she took the lead.

"*He* accepted a load then refused to deliver it! They called me at home last night to straighten him out. At home! We had to wake up a driver in another truck to cover the load!"

She repeated her evening rant, skipping over the botched dispatch and her efforts to shout me into a burnout. Customer service *always* came first, she said; there were no trade-offs, no matter what *some* people thought. Owner-operators were known for making trouble and *this* one had created a logistics nightmare last night. He was *too* independent. Linehaul didn't need people like *him*.

The VP looked up from his desk calendar.

He said, "Driver?"

Driver. My name and rank.

As I saw it, we had a dispatcher's error and an attempt to force me to drive tired. I explained for the fifth time. Ms. Peyton interrupted, gasped and guffawed, raged against the owner-operator division, and flirted until the VP mentioned tape recorders. Her smile fell away. The terminal manager sucked in his breath.

"The planner told me he *called* you," the VP said to Ms. Peyton. "You had the duty. Was your computer on at home?"

"I was in bed."

"Was. Your. Computer. On. At. Home."

"I was in bed. I was—*you* know—*in bed.*"

The terminal manager, linked to her by corporate gossip, squirmed in his chair and blushed.

I asked Ms. Peyton how she would view a fatigue-related crash on the dispatch in question. The Linehaul University cheerleader tugged at her skirt and recited the textbook answer. "Driver's fault. Preventable accident. Termination."

The terminal manager said, "You should have slept!"

"He *said* he had to sleep," the VP said. "Dispatch ignored that and didn't tell him about the first stop. Monica tried to force the issue. They found another driver. Why are we here this morning, Monica?"

He turned to me. "Do you still intend to call DOT?"

"Not if this goes away."

"Done deal." He didn't offer his hand.

My fleet manager ushered me from the office, closing the door on raised voices.

"You did good," he said. "You stayed calm."

"Did you expect a threat to kill someone?"

"It's happened. I've got a Bay Area load for you. It's on a set, but you'll be rolling."

—⁓—

Check-call the following morning at Cabazon, CA.

Peter said, "Call your wife."

"Sam," Gayle said, crying. "Tumor . . . shots for pain . . .

the vet gives him a day, maybe two. Sam keeps looking for you. Come home today."

Home. Northern California. Four hundred and seventy-five miles away, a full day of trucking in a 55 mile-an-hour state, but I'd be there before noon if I caught a plane and if the nearest terminal repowered the load. Another driver could easily run up to the Bay Area for tomorrow's delivery.

I called Fontana. A man answered and said, "Yeah?"

"Hello," I said. "Who am I talking to?"

"Dominic. Who wants to know?"

"Dominic. Mayfield here, 21127. I've got a family emergency. I need a repower."

"Aw. Another dwiver with a pwoblem. What is it *this* time?"

"Imminent death in the family."

I didn't think to mention the dog, but Sam was as much a part of our lives and family as any close relative.

"Oh really? I've heard that one before. Talk to Bruno."

Bruno said, "I ain't gonna help *you*."

"Ah . . . I don't know," Peter said after I called him and he called Bruno. "Can't you deliver tomorrow, spot the trailers for us, and then go home? Fontana won't repower. It's a money thing."

Gayle took Sam to the vet for another shot. She didn't think he felt much after the injection, but he whimpered and looked around, she said, when the needle slid in. He probably wondered where I was.

March 22, 1996.

The consignee's crew took half a day to sort, stack, count, lose count, and re-count. I drove home with the empty trailers, thinking about my wife's grief, our years with Sam, and the company's response to our needs.

I parked at the foot of our driveway. Sam barked and rose to greet me when he heard the air brakes then he dropped to the ground. He didn't understand his agony, or that his life would soon be over, or why, for a change, he was allowed to eat all the corn bread he wanted. Sam always liked corn bread. That evening, we took him to the vet for the final shot, his death shadowed by three company men.

I stayed home for a few days, manufacturing chores to fill the hours. I touched Sam's leash and Frisbee every morning and thought I heard him by the back door several times. At night, I put my hand out for his warmth. I felt his tail thump the blanket.

Peter called and said, "They want the trailers."

"Send Bruno to get them. My wife wants to meet him."

I went back to the road and Gayle mourned alone in a cold, quiet house.

Get home when you want, get home when you need.

I ain't gonna help you.

A money thing.

Sons of bitches.

The company never paid for the trip from Phoenix to the Bay Area. Payback from Ms. Peyton? An under-the-table extraction of the owner-operator drop fee? What prompted Bruno's rancor? How did a carrier lose a trip?

The year before, Linehaul had paid me for a vacation and a loss prevention bonus. Owner-operators weren't eligible for either and I'd asked the accounting department to deduct those items from a settlement statement. "Let it go," Peter had said. "They'll never find it."

I bought new steer tires from the company and wasn't charged for them because Accounting had no record of the purchase. I just wanted to pay for the tires. Peter said, "They'll never find it."

An unpaid trip. Unearned vacation pay. A bonus. Free steer tires. A death in the family. I owed the company about what it owed me and I figured we were even.

—ᴍ—

I called Peter one morning to give him my hours and someone else answered his phone. "Peter's been promoted. He's now Director of the owner-operator division. I'm your new fleet manager. My name's Jack. Call me anytime about anything. I'm here to help."

—ᴍ—

June 4, 1996.

The Stockton planner offered me a California run, Vacaville down to Buena Park. I wasn't interested in a short trip and the

7 a.m. delivery appointment meant I'd be fighting Los Angeles' long rush hour. Not good. Not good at all.

"We've got tons of freight in Southern California," he said. "We need trucks down there."

If freight is at the other end of a state, that's where you go.

In Vacaville, a forklift operator drove out of the shipper's warehouse and brought the papers to my truck. He shut off the forklift motor, handed me a clip- board, and turned his head, listening.

He said, "Hear that? Those scratching sounds?"

Three crows balanced on the leading edge of the trailer's roof.

The forklift operator whispered, "An omen."

"Good or bad?"

"You never know with crows."

He crossed himself, gave me a look that said, "I don't want what you've got," and held still for a moment when I gave back his clipboard, as if he didn't want to be close to anything I'd touched.

I drove south through the Central Valley and across the Wheeler Ridge scale then up the Grapevine to the Flying J, where I planned to stay for eight hours. I'd get moving by 3 a.m., early enough to avoid most of the morning's heavy traffic. The J's half-empty parking lot guaranteed that there'd be no waiting for a shower, washing machines, or clothes dryers. I backed into an isolated parking place.

The sun had gone down by the time I carried my laundry

to the truck. I puttered in the cab then sat in the passenger seat reading and thinking about crows. *An omen.* That was the fork-lift driver's thing, not mine.

Nobody bothered with the parking spaces on either side of me until a truck quickly turned, headed in at an angle, and stopped, taking up two spots on my right. The driver cut his wheels to the left and started to back up. He didn't get out to look. He hadn't allowed himself room to maneuver. He'd lined himself up perfectly to hit a truck in the row behind him.

I turned on the marker lights, slipped into my moccasins, and opened the door—maybe I could help. The side of his trailer swung slowly toward my rig, closer, closer, then closer and faster. I tugged at the lanyard. This guy didn't know what he was doing! He didn't even have his lights on after dark. He pulled forward again and backed up again. I was blowing the air horn a second time when his trailer slammed into my tractor.

He'll stop, I thought. But he rolled forward and, his wheels still turned hard to the left, rolled back. His trailer hit 21127 again, harder, almost knocking the hood off. He pulled up a third time, turned his wheels to the right, cleared my truck, and nearly backed into an Anteater. Air horns blared. Drivers turned their headlamps on. CB radios were suddenly alive.

"You hit a truck, stupid."

"Idiot."

"*Stupid* idiot."

"*Completely* stupid idiot."

I was out of the cab, standing to one side, waiting for the

driver to tell me why he'd hit my truck twice, watching him drive away.

A woman ran over to me. She said, "Are you all right? I'm a nurse."

"Yeah. I'm not hurt."

"My husband and I saw what happened. We got his truck number and his company. It's Southern Shippers."

"Thanks. I got that."

"He almost hit our KW. Drivers like that—they get me on the warpath. Anyway, here's our names and phone number. Call us if you need witnesses. Are you sure you're not hurt?"

Drivers crowded around the damaged tractor.

"I didn't know Southern Shippers hired scumbags like that."

"He was breathing, so they hired him. Driver shortage, you know."

"Damn near hit my truck."

"Mine too."

"Anybody call the sheriff or the highway patrol?"

"They won't come out—this is private property."

"We got us a truck-stop lawyer here. So, if there's a murder they won't come out?"

"I'm telling you, it's private property. They won't come."

I left them to their argument, walked to the phone room, and called the California Highway Patrol. Fifteen minutes later, two officers showed up to take my statement. After they left, I called Linehaul: I couldn't make the delivery, they needed to notify the customer, they needed to find another truck, they needed to repower the load. Then I called Gayle. "The truck's been smacked. Hit and run. Don't worry, I'm not hurt. I've taken lots of pictures, you'll see it's not that bad."

The next morning.

"I appreciate your call," said Southern Shippers' safety director. "The California Highway Patrol phoned last night. Our driver hasn't checked in. I've sent three Qualcomm messages but he doesn't answer. I want to talk to him. The highway patrol wants to talk to him. I expect you want to talk to him. It sounds like it was our fault. We apologize and we'll pay for your repairs."

"And my down time. Are you going to fire the guy?"

"He's already out the door. This wasn't his first rodeo."

Dispatch assured me several times that someone would be along sooner or later to swap trailers. I waited for hours, looking at the hood all smashed on one side, dragged forward off the hood straps and away from the latches. I took out my tools, removed the torn air dam and threw it away—I could drive without it, but if I couldn't close and latch the hood, I'd be calling a tow truck.

A Linehaul driver finally appeared with an empty trailer and I guided him slowly back against the hood, just enough to hold it in place while I snapped the latches. Then I headed north to Stockton, dropped the empty at the terminal, and drove to the local Freightliner dealer. The shop foreman said, "It's a simple job. New hood, new grill, new headlight bezels, full air dam. We'll have you back on the road in three days." He kept his promise.

Five weeks later a California Highway Patrol officer called me at home and said, "Can you *positively* identify the driver?"

"No. It was dark inside his cab."

"We can't proceed if you can't prove it was him."

"The man drove solo. The truck was equipped with Qualcomm and he probably had to log on to use it. Who else could have been driving?"

"He's denying it."

"I've got witnesses."

"No one saw him in the cab. I'm sorry. There's nothing more we can do."

Southern Shippers paid for the repairs in full and covered my lost revenue; it probably didn't hurt that the CHP phoned them before I did. The preventable part of the collision—I wouldn't call it an accident—was on someone else's driving record. He'd skated on a charge of misdemeanor hit-and-run and cost his former employer $6,400. On my side, there'd been no harm done and no hard feelings.

I never saw another crow on a trailer.

—⁂—

July 5, 1996. A Friday.

The Stockton planner said, "Call your fleet manager."

"You're one of the last drivers without Qualcomm," Jack said. "I know you don't want it, but The Big Guy says now everybody has to have one. I'd like you to come to Phoenix so the shop can put it in."

"All right, but Gayle and I are moving to Oregon next week. I've got to be home by Thursday. Not *headed* home. *At* home."

"We can do that. I'll tell Stockton we need a Phoenix load and set you up at the shop for Monday. They're closed weekends."

The Stockton planner said, "All I've got for Arizona is on a reefer. Imported chocolates. High-dollar stuff. Two drops—Phoenix on Sunday at 8 a.m. and Tucson Monday at noon. I can't change the appointments."

I called the Tucson consignee and arranged a Sunday afternoon delivery.

Phoenix. Monday.

The shop took just three hours to install, program, and test the Qualcomm. A dispatcher said, "There's no more freight going your way today." I told Jack that the company wasn't meeting my needs and started for home, 700 miles away, bobtail.

Interstates 10, 5, and 80 made the fastest route, but in Southern California I-15 beckoned, and U. S. 395, and the Owens Valley. I would sneak another look at the east side of the Sierras. Make another pilgrimage to Bishop. Drive up to Convict Lake for lunch. Stay pissed off for awhile and see what The Director did.

Lone Pine, CA. Tuesday.

Beep: *Please call me—Peter.*

He said, "I know you're pissed off. What can we do?"

"Right now, nothing. Right now, I'm just driving home. You

and Jack knew I had to get to the house. You could have pulled a string or two. Maybe I'll start looking for another carrier."

He said, "This won't happen again. I'll take care of it," and I believed him. But then I realized that he was just tracking The Big Guy's truck by satellite.

Chapter Fourteen

Keep It Between The Lines
RICKY VAN SHELTON

In the restaurant at Rip Griffin's truck stop, Tonopah, AZ.

An overweight trucker asked a waitress about the daily specials. "What's good?"

"The road kill is good. The barbecued chicken buffalo wings are good. What would you like, sweetie?"

"Well, my doctor says I've got to watch what I eat and road kill's got too much fat on it. What part of the buffalo did them wings come from?"

Somewhere in Kentucky.

It wasn't a truck stop at all, just a gravel lot, one gas pump, and a small grocery run by two *old* ladies. Several trailers, probably dropped by drivers home for the weekend, made a back row. I purchased a few sundries and asked if I could park overnight.

"Why, of course you can, hon. Make yourself comfortable. And come back early tomorrow for biscuits. We'll be here."

In the morning, a black and tan Collie lay motionless near the front door and at first I thought he was dead.

"Hey, boy," I said. "How are you?"

He groaned and stretched. His tail flopped once in the dirt.

He looked tired, hungry, and thirsty. I bought biscuits, a gallon of water, and four packages of lunch meat.

"You're not going to eat all that today, hon," said the cashier.

"No, it's for that dog. He looks hungry."

"He's going to feed you-know-who," she said to the woman breading chicken for the fryer, and they followed me outside.

The Collie knew we were coming. Sitting at attention, he watched closely as I cut open the jug and spread his food on the ground. He slurped some of the water and gulped down the meat. The biscuits went untouched. He gave me a short salute—one tail wag—and padded off to mark a truck tire, but he ran back a moment later, grinning, coming at me fake-and-dodge, a healthy, playful dog. After he paused to anoint a garbage can and send me another solitary tail wag, he was gone, racing off behind a trailer.

I said, "I feel used."

"Oh, don't, hon. He does that to all you truckers. He eats your food then he pees on your tires. That dog sure knows how to panhandle."

Leave your tractor at the Stockton terminal, go home for a few days, and see what happens. You get a cracked fender, a broken headlight bezel, a smashed headlight and a nicked grill. You get a gash across the front of your new hood and holes gouged into your new air dam level-on with an ICC bumper. You don't get a sorry-I-did-it note on your windshield.

Someone—a rookie, probably—had spun a trailer around in

the tight yard. My second hit-and-run, maybe his first, maybe his careless seventeenth. I used up two disposable cameras from my accident kit and went inside to find Darrel Davis, the terminal manager.

He said, "Your truck got hit in my yard? That's not my problem. That's why you have insurance."

"Wrong. That's why the company has insurance."

"How do I know it happened here?"

"There's plastic and broken glass under the truck. Let's go look."

"Why? Do you think I'm going to fix it for you?"

"I think the company's going to fix it. I want you to call the owner-operator division. Then I'll report the damage to Claims."

He scowled and picked up the phone.

"Hey, hey, Peter French, my main man . . . I'm doing great. Got this manager gig now. I'm the big guy around here."

The buddy-buddy conversation lasted several minutes.

"Oh. Almost forgot. I have one of your, uh, operators in my office. He *says* one of my drivers hit his truck. Talk to the boy. Make a few things clear to him." He laid the phone on his desk, just beyond my reach.

"I'll take care of it," Peter said. "Put Darrel back on."

"For you," I said.

Darrel snapped his fingers and extended a hand for the phone. I held it in the air for a moment then set it on a corner of an in-bin, far from his chair. He frowned, shook his head, leaned forward in his chair, leaned back, and lunged.

"Yeah . . . No, I said . . . I know, but . . . *Why*? He took pictures. He can make prints for us . . . Okay."

Darrel pitched an accident kit to a mechanic. "Take pictures of Mr. Operator's bad-ass truck. Bring me the camera." He pushed his chair away from the desk and stood up. "My lot's not very big. Maybe you shouldn't park here."

In the hallway outside Darrell's office, I stood under a banner that stretched the length of one wall. *Support our drivers! Every day! In every way!*

Yuma, AZ. A truck stop parking lot. Five a.m.

A decrepit camper van shook as I walked by. Inside, an excited coyote leaped back and forth between the front seats. Wire-thin, sunburned, and bent at the waist, a leathery old-timer in threadbare cut-offs limped from the C-store, whistling happily to himself. He carried groceries and a six-pack. The coyote howled.

"I give her a hamburger and a few hot dogs every morning before I open my own breakfast. She's partial to chocolate cupcakes for dessert. You're hungry today, aren't you, Natalie? That's her name. Natalie."

He popped a top, turned his gap-toothed smile to me, and patted the camper.

"We live in here. Kind of adopted each other. Ahh . . . I love a cold breakfast."

Somebody was pounding on a shower-room door at the old

Union 76 truck stop in Ontario, CA.

"Eddy! Eddy! Your truck's on fire!"

"Yeah, yeah. You're just trying to get me to run outside in my underwear again."

"I'm not fooling *this* time, man! It's really burning!"

"Yeah, yeah."

After my shower, I walked toward a crowd in the parking lot. Smoke poured through the open doors of a tractor and drivers stood by with fire extinguishers.

Old Glory rippled in an air-brushed breeze on the side of a white Freightliner Classic XL near Ocala, FL. Drivers keyed up to tell the owner, "Nice truck."

Two spit-shined Peterbilt 379s—one violet, the other shocking pink, and each with a trailer painted to match—rolled east out of Mojave one night, chicken lights blazing. Probably show trucks.

A teal Kenworth W900L pulled the Tehachapi grade, two surfboards and a mountain bike strapped behind the sleeper, a beautiful young woman at the wheel, delicate lettering on the driver's door: *Sweet Dream.*

Warning, taped to a Louisiana scale-house window: "Next time you wave, use all five fingers."

Custom lettering.

On refrigerated doubles in Idaho: *Reefer Madness.*

On a yellow Peterbilt 379 blowing railroad air horns at four-wheelers in Ohio: *Attila The Horn.*

On a green Kenworth T2000 near Rapid City, SD: *You can have this truck when you pry my cold, dead fingers from the wheel.*

In Virginia, truckers running I-81 talked about a larger-than-life Powerball jackpot, almost $50 million after taxes if you took the cash option.

"I'd buy me a new Pete and gold plate the sucker."

"I'd weld the doors shut and tell my boss to come get his truck."

"I'd get hold of a trucking company and make me some *real* money."

Every phone was in use at the Union 76 truck stop in Wheatridge, CO. Drivers on hold looked at the floor, the walls, the ceiling, each other.

"I didn't get any sleep last night," the driver on the phone next to me said. "I just hand-stacked and fingerprinted a 42,000-pound floor load, I'm out of hours, and you're telling me to deliver in Kansas City this evening. That's 600 miles. I quit."

He hung up quietly. Pale, sweaty, his eyes red and sunken, he had surely missed more than one night's sleep. He sighed, leaned against the wall, and slowly, wearily, punched in a number. "I apologize," he said. "I'll take it."

I turned on the CB late one afternoon and heard a driver say he was due in Gresham, OR at 6 a.m.

"Bud," said the trucker he was talking to, "how are you going to do that?"

"Pedal to the metal all night, I guess. I'll make it if I don't fall asleep."

We were westbound on I-84, near Devil's Slide, UT. He had 740 miles to go—about 12 hours of driving—and maybe 30 minutes to spare. He'd already been in the seat, he said, for nine hours.

South Pass, WY, just after 3 a.m.

A white W900L pulling a spread-axle reefer passed me and I flicked the lights. The driver flashed his marker lamps.

He said, "Hey, Linehaul. You copy?"

"Yeah. What's up?"

"Nothing but the sky and the stars. Where's everybody hiding? There's no one out here but you and me. It's dark as a gopher hole, too."

"It sure is. I was thinking it'd be easy for a man to fall asleep, drive off the road, and not even know it."

"I did that once."

"Around here?"

"Down on I-10 near Las Cruces. It was a blackout night like this."

"Damn."

"I nodded off and ran out of highway. They said my truck peeled away from the Interstate and headed into the sagebrush, hit a sand dune or something and went up in the air. It came down, hit a rock pile, and broke all apart. I sort of woke up when I went through the windshield, then the lights went out. I opened my eyes two weeks later in the hospital. Everything hurt. I asked my wife why she was crying."

He didn't say anything for a few minutes and I tried to imagine what it must have been like—the sounds of the crash he didn't hear, waking up in a hospital bed, the pain, his wife's worry and anguish, the what ifs, the financial crunch, a trucker's true horror story.

"I don't remember falling asleep. I'd been running hard for days and I'll admit I was burnt out, but I never thought I'd total my rig. I've had seven surgeries and a lot of physical therapy. Now, my legs hurt when it gets cold and I rest when I feel like it and to hell with shippers and my company. I get goose bumps every time I drive by the place where it happened. I thought I'd never be able to get into a truck again, but driving's in my blood, I guess. I just can't give it up."

Bend, OR. Gridlocked summer traffic. Channel 17.

1st driver: "This town's a parking lot today. What's the hang-up?"

2nd driver: "Road construction. They're only letting a few vehicles through at a time."

1st driver: "Shoot. It's probably one guy leaning on a shovel."

2nd driver: "Nah, I heard they got equipment there and everything."

3rd driver: "You're not going to believe this. It *is* one guy leaning on a shovel."

Hammond, LA.

Rubber spiders and bats hung from a low ceiling over the fuel desk. Shelves and aisles were jam-packed with Halloween candy, plastic pumpkins, laughing ghosts, cackling witches, and talking skulls.

"Hey," said the skulls. "Where you going? I see you. Hey. Where you going? I see you."

Deep in thought, a driver walked by the skull display.

"Hey. Where you going? I see you."

His head came up, he looked around, and his eyes focused on mine.

"Please, mister," he said. "Go easy on me. I'm just going to my truck."

Eight p.m., December 18, 1996, near Crowley's Ridge, AR.

Black ice on I-40 slowed traffic to 10 miles an hour, not fast enough for one trucker, and he keyed up. "If you people don't know how to drive on a little bit of ice, get the hell off the road and let a *real* winter driver from Minnesota through."

"Good buddy," said another trucker, "if you don't like it, just pass us."

"I ain't your good buddy, scumbag."

"Well, I know you're somebody's. But I'll let that go. I'll call you Super Trucker."

The two men taunted each other for an hour, threatening to stop and kick each other's asses, urged on by a few drivers, reminded by others that stopping on ice was a bad idea.

"Why don't you two kiss and make up?"

"Yeah. Make up and *shut* up."

"Y'all keep out of this! I'm having a *good* time arguing with good buddy. Excuse me, *pardon* me, I am *so* sorry, I mean Super Trucker. The man from Minny-so-tah."

"Well, one thing's for certain. You and Super Balls and your big radios will keep us all from knowing if something happens on this ice tonight."

They thought about that for awhile, in silence. Then someone was laughing.

"Y'all are just going to *love* this. Super Trucker is in the median. That's right. How you doin' in there, winter driver from Minny-so-tah? Just had to pass, didn't you? Oh, yah. Talk to me, *good buddy*. Tell me how we don't know how to drive on ice and how we should all get the hell out of *your* way. Have yourself a pleasant evening spun out in the co-median."

San Jon, NM.

The eastbound scale on I-40 was open late and they were checking every log book. Drivers pulled off at the truck stops to wait and talk on the CB.

"Man, I took two white ones and my eyes are *wide* open. I look like the Cookie Monster! *Why'd* they have to unlock the coop *tonight*? I got to *move*. My deliveries are so tight I don't even have time to *pee*."

Ten minutes later.

"Cookie Monster? Cookie Monster! You awake?"

"Man, I ain't gonna sleep *now*."

"They just closed. You're out of jail."

"Yeehaw! I'm on and I'm gone!"

San Francisco, CA. A mid-day delivery to a grocery outlet in a neighborhood shopping district.

The customer's docking instructions called for a blind-side off a busy street and through a crowded parking lot, the perfect setup for a backing accident and out of the question unless someone stopped traffic while I maneuvered. The store manager laughed at my request. The receiving clerk said I should have brought a shorter trailer. The forklift driver said, "UPS comes in here all the time. They don't ask for help."

I drove around the block for an approach from the opposite direction and a sight-side across oncoming traffic. Four-ways flashing, ready to blow the air horn, I slowly angled left into the opposing lane, then right, then left again to set up. My tractor and trailer formed an arc that blocked the street.

I made three corrections. Each time, a teenager in a low-slung coupe revved his engine to the red line, let the pipes back off, and inched closer to the passenger side of the truck. I set the brakes and climbed down from the cab. Didn't he see that my tractor tires could not clear his car? Would he please back up?

He said, "*You* back up."

"I *am* backing up. We'll all just sit here until *you* do."

He shifted into reverse and shot backward, stopped only by the long, angry blast of a German horn. "The truck driver told me to back into the car behind me" would have been a dandy excuse for his flattened rear bumper and a smashed BMW grille.

I started backing again, closing the gap between the rear of the trailer and the driveway. An impatient four-wheeler squeezed by, his right-side front and rear tires riding the curb. The trailer underride guard almost creased his new Buick. When the tandems crossed the sidewalk I straightened out and slowly backed the trailer through the parking lot. I opened and latched the trailer doors, bumped the dock, and shut off the engine.

"Young man? I say, young man!"

A little old lady—black hat, black overcoat, and pink sneakers—waved a walking stick and hobbled toward me.

"That *horrid* boy," she said. "He would *not* get out of your way."

Her cane rapped the ground and she smiled.

"But I *watched* you, young man. Oh, yes, I *watched* you. You were magnificent. You were just . . . *magnificent.*"

I locked myself out of 21127 at the Gearjammer Truck Plaza in Union Gap, WA, walked toward the shop to ask about lockout service, and noticed a tow-truck driver waiting at the fuel island.

I said, "Do you have a Slim Jim?"

"Yes I do," he said, grinning. "And I know why you asked. I'll be with you in a minute."

"Thanks," I said when he tripped the lock. "What do I owe you?"

"Oh, nothing. My brother's a truck driver. He's locked himself out so many times, I gave him a Slim Jim for his birthday. He called me last night—yup, locked it in his rig. Have a good one. Nice truck."

Near Tumwater, WA a flatbed passed a line of trucks traveling in the slow lane. The driver held a white Miniature Poodle on a lap pillow. He was talking to the dog and petting it. Someone keyed up.

"Lord, lord. That flatbed driver has got him a Poodle on his lap and he's a stroking it."

"Driver, just what exactly is he stroking?"

"His Poodle, son."

"Oh. Ten-four on the southbound flatbedder strokin' his Poodle."

An owner-operator transferred tools and bedding from his rig to a rental tractor at the Freightliner dealer near Indianapolis. A jagged crack stretched across the front of the sleeper. The skylight had been smashed.

He said, "I followed a day cab into a pipe yard without even thinking, right under a low-clearance utility bridge. Wham! Had to back out. Never been so professionally embarrassed. My truck will be in the shop for three weeks and it'll be something like $3,900. I hate to think what this loaner truck will cost. I haven't told my wife yet."

Portland, OR.

Impatient for their morning espressos, annoyed with a drag queen at the head of the line, drivers in the upstairs coffee bar at Jubitz truck stop exchanged grins and knowing looks. An uneasy hostess behind the counter recited the list of coffee condiments for her out-of-place customer and asked for his selections. With each question, he placed a forefinger to one rouged cheek, tilted his head, and thought at length.

Would he like whipped cream?

"Oh . . . *whipped* cream," he shrieked. "Oh . . . *yes.*"

Cocoa powder? Chocolate sprinkles?

Forefinger. Cheek.

"Oh . . . okay . . . I *suppose.*"

Cinnamon stick?

"Oh . . . well . . . I *think* so."

He slowly lifted quarters and dimes from a sequined purse, examining both sides of each coin. He set them in a careful row near the cash register. The room watched and waited. The young man sucked hard on a straw, gathered and inspected his change, batted mascara-thickened eyelashes, and pranced into the hall. His high heels clicked down the stairs in tiny, mincing steps.

"Oh . . . this is *so* good . . . oh . . . *oh my God.*"

A burly, unshaven trucker who looked like he had driven straight through from New Jersey stepped to the bar.

"Give me a fast cup of *coffee*," he said. "Without any of that *sheeyit* in it."

A Linehaul driver and a forklift operator were shouting at each other inside an auto parts warehouse.

Driver: "Your directions suck!"

Forklift operator: "Someone in our *office* wrote the directions! I already told you that! You got here, didn't you?"

The driver turned to me. He wore a faded work shirt from a pest exterminator company. "Curly" was written in orange thread above a torn, ink-stained pocket.

"I had to call Dispatch *and* my fleet manager for directions," he said. "How'd you ever find this damn place?"

"There's a phone number on the freight bill and the words 'Call toll-free for directions.' See? You found the address and you're in a door. Why pick on the forklift guy?"

"*Nobody* could find this rat's nest with *his* lousy instructions."

"Just go outside," I said. "I'll bring the paperwork when you're empty."

Curly didn't wait in his truck for the papers, so I jammed them against a mirror bracket and went back to the dock, where the forklift operator shucked pallets from my trailer two at a time and set them gently on the floor in perfect rows.

He said, "I don't get it. What did *I* do?"

"Don't mind him. Probably had a fight with his wife."

"Oh . . . ah . . . Do you know how to cook?"

"A little. Why?"

"I promised my new girlfriend I'd make dinner Saturday night. Problem is, I can't cook."

"Well . . . How about baked chicken breasts, baked red potatoes, and sautéed zucchini with tomatoes, garlic, onions, and Italian spices?"

"Man, I couldn't come close to that."

"It's easy. I'll give you the recipes. She'll be impressed."

I wrote everything down and we went over it until I was sure he understood.

"This is bizarre," he said. "I'm taking cooking lessons from a truck driver. Say, how come it's always a different Linehaul driver and they can't back up? It took our friend 20 minutes to hit the dock. You slid right in."

"Linehaul hires new drivers by the trainload. Most of them don't stay long enough to learn much. But don't worry—you'll never see Curly again. He'll probably go back to squirting bugs."

"Ah . . . What's for dessert?"

"Get a can of whipped cream."

"Huh? . . . *oh* . . . She'll like that."

Neat white lettering on a jet-black W900L said it all: "Owner-Operator: William Arnold, Fargo, ND. Owner of the Operator: Mrs. William Arnold."

"Bring it back, Mrs. Arnold," I said. "Nice truck."

"Thank you, Mr. Mayfield. Aren't the wildflowers beautiful this year?"

A friend taught his wife to drive. They teamed, ran hard, loved each other, and loved the road. One night in west Texas she woke him for his stint behind the wheel. Five hours later he called to her, but she didn't answer. He pulled over, went into the sleeper, and touched her. She was cold, he told me, so cold. Massive heart attack, the doctors said. He couldn't understand. She was only 27 years of age.

It was one of those long-distance phone calls from a truck stop. If the wrong thing is said, if either party hangs up, that's the tipping point and you go your separate ways. Maybe Gayle and I were tired of each other, maybe living apart most of the time had killed the friendship and the love. Maybe, without words, the big question had been asked and answered—I loved trucking more. We talked for two hours and agreed on only one thing: our marriage was worth saving.

"Well, that's that," Gayle said. "Are you ready to come home?"

"No."

"Then I'm going with you."

"No you're not."

"I am going with you."

No. You're not getting in the way of my solitude. I won't give that up.

Gayle said, "What about running local?"

Running local wasn't for me—you *had* to go home every night.

Chapter Fifteen

Let there be spaces in your togetherness.
KAHLIL GIBRAN

"I'm going with you."

No. You're not getting in the way of my solitude.

"I'm going with you."

"You, ah, don't want to drive? I mean . . . "

It was a plea, not a question.

"I just want to be with my husband. I love him."

I did my best work when I ran solo and I had tried, many times, to explain. I didn't want to explain again that I wasn't ready to give up driving, that I didn't want company, that there were still too many sunsets and still too much new country that I just had to see on my own. There was—always—my need for isolation. So what if I skipped my daily shower once in a while and got mad about no sleep, no freight, Linehaul, or the HOS regulations? Anger and frustration came with the job. They were easier to handle alone.

Alone.

It's just you and the truck. Flop a jacket over the Qualcomm. Turn off your CB and your CD player. Solve the world's problems or solve your own. Laugh, sing, cry, say anything—who's going to know? You're your own audience.

Alone.

Book pages turn quietly. You thump your pillow and roll over in the bunk. Your blanket moves with you. You breathe. You get up from the driver's seat and step into the sleeper. You don't notice the creaking of the seat frame or the rustle of your clothing. It's all barely audible when you're by yourself. Put someone else in the truck and everything changes.

"I'm going with you."

Nothing she ever said frightened me as much.

Gayle knew that you could be less than comfortable on the road. That there wasn't always a clean restroom nearby when you needed one. That the food often wasn't worth eating. That you were too cold one day and too hot the next. That the truck, the trips, and the loads came first, came before sleep and meals and showers and time off.

To say no and hold to it would have been a declaration that I wanted to spend the rest of my life running free. Gayle wouldn't be a part of it. Neither would anyone else. I'd name each new truck *Solitaire* and, most days, I wouldn't have to talk to a soul.

"I'm going with you."

"No. For the last time."

"What's your problem?"

My problem? I wasn't thinking about anyone but the man in the mirror. Gayle knew this—she lived it—but I couldn't see. I didn't sleep at home a lot and I never gave a thought to what my absences said to her or about me. The whole thing was wrong. Once again, I hadn't been paying attention.

A man can't be a hermit all his married life.

"Okay," I said. "You can come with me."

On the day she moved in, Gayle kept asking nervously where she could put her things, afraid that she was intruding. "You live here, too," I said. "Put your stuff where you want and I'll work around it," and I tried hard to smile. But I had given away the isolation I cherished above everything else.

I knew that we'd have fun together, take time off, bobtail around or snap up rental cars, behave like tourists and normal married people who see each other every day. For years I'd been on the phone saying "You've got to see this," and more than once Gayle had said that she wished she was going with me. Now, she would. Perhaps we could close the gap between us. Maybe she'd embrace trucking, as I had. Or maybe she'd fly home and we'd never see each other again. I wasn't looking forward to on-road arguments and the long silences that would follow. A truck cab can be a very small place if the two people in it aren't talking.

Chapter Sixteen

In exchange for free transportation, the undersigned do hereby remise, release, forever discharge, and covenant to hold harmless the involved motor carrier and its employees from any and all actions, causes of actions or damages as a result of the free transportation.

<small>LINEHAUL SPOUSE-RIDER AGREEMENT</small>

Beep: *If you are driving a Freightliner Century Class truck, stop! The steering wheel may fall off!*

"They mean the wheels on the steering axle," a Linehaul shop foreman told me. "It seems that Freightliner went stupid and forgot how to install front wheel bearings—they don't torque 'em right, so they come loose, front wheels fall off, and there's wrecks. Every Century Class tractor has to be checked. Every one."

I said, "I didn't know we had Centuries."

"We've got a few and more are on the way. New lease trucks for the owner-operators. They're always in the shop for wheel bearings or electrical problems or some pesky thing. Two caught fire. Trust me, you don't want one."

You don't want one.
Maybe, maybe not.

I stole away, sat in a Century Class tractor built to owner-operator specs, and fell desperately in love. The dash curved smoothly around me and held enough gauges, controls, and rocker switches to keep me happy. The driver's seat and its twin armrests felt right. My hand belonged on the gearshift lever. From the outside, the truck looked sleek, euro-styled, and smart. It only needed a CB, a high-end CD player, Gayle, and me.

I told her, "You've got to see this."

She said, laughing, "Stop that. I've seen new-truck fever before and I know what's going on here. Do we need to talk or do you want to vote right now?"

—⁂—

We seesawed. Should we buy 21127, put payments behind us, and shoulder increased maintenance costs after the warranty expired? Should we finance a new truck, make payments, and take comfort in a curved dashboard and warranty protection?

If we kept 21127, we'd have to sell it sooner or later, but what if there were no buyers? We couldn't just park it somewhere and walk off. I asked long-time owner-operators about keeping an old truck, buying new, and selling used.

"I advertised. Put up for-sale signs. Waited for phone calls. Got *one*. A fellow drove it, said 'Okay,' didn't call me back."

"A driver wanted me to take $250 down and carry the note for five years. Told him to get lost. No one else ever called."

"Couldn't even give it away. Damn thing's been sitting behind my barn for two years."

"I always liked my Anteater and the way it looks, but it started looking better the day I paid it off. If something goes wrong, I've got the money to get it fixed. I sure don't miss those $1,800 payments. Now, I put that money in the bank every month. Got me a nice bundle."

"I trade 'em in every four years—it works for the big guys. I like warranty coverage and that new-truck smell."

For weeks while I drove, Gayle and I talked about our trucking possibilities, looking at all the angles. Should we team in an expediter straight truck? Should I stay in 18-wheelers but switch carriers? Spec a Century Class truck or buy one ready-made off a dealer's lot? Haul refrigerated freight? Trade for a new Truck-lease tractor? If short-term lease cycles worked for the big guys and they laughed all the way to the bank protected by warranties, maybe we should follow their lead. Get some of that new-truck smell for ourselves.

One night in De Soto, TX Gayle looked up from our stack of sales and recruiting brochures, financial statements, and business plans and said, "Time to vote."

We would turn in 21127 and lease a new Century Class tractor from The Big Guy for 36 months. When the music stopped three years down the line we wouldn't be sitting in a used truck decorated with for-sale signs. Maybe then I'd go with another carrier. Maybe then I'd spec a truck, buy a trailer, get my own authority, and find my own freight. Maybe then my roads would go on forever.

—∾—

From the Trucklease Equipment Leasing Agreement.

"Upon the expiration or termination of the lease term, Lessee, at its own expense, will return [the] equipment in . . . as good order and condition as when delivered to Lessee, ordinary wear and tear . . . excepted."

At the Phoenix prep shop, mechanics swarmed over 21127. What should they replace to ready the truck for trade-in and resale? What should they repair? They put together an estimate of my costs, then Allen Dobbs—the Trucklease-Linehaul go-between—and I went over the findings.

It was too easy. After $1,700 in prep charges, Gayle and I were due $10,740. Allen cut a check for $740 and applied $10,000—our intact deposit from 21127—to the new truck. Trucklease took 21127 off our hands and Freightliner bought it back for a pre-arranged price. Volume buybacks, driven by high demand for used late-model tractors, Allen told us, made The Big Guy's leasing agreements possible and profitable.

"We'd be dead without buybacks," he said. "Still, your deal is really a favor."

It wasn't a favor at all. The Big Guy would have never considered an early lease termination and a new lease if it hadn't penciled out for him.

If we wanted the new truck three years on, a $35,600 balloon payment plus federal excise tax—a little more than $10,000—would make it ours. Total price, $121,488. Until then, we were renters at $418 a week.

Allen said, "You know the drill. I'll send a message when everything's ready. Turn in 21127 here, pick up your new truck at Troutdale, come back for a PDI and Qualcomm installation."

There were rumors of optional colors and thirteen speed transmissions for Trucklease tractors, but I took the new truck as it was offered: metallic blue paint, 70-inch raised-roof sleeper, 239-inch wheelbase, 430-horsepower Detroit. Two-stage Jake brake. Dual chrome exhaust stacks mounted behind the sleeper. Cruise control, anti-lock brakes, 3.90 rear-axle, 10-speed transmission with one overdrive gear. Sliding fifth-wheel. Air-suspension dump. Power-divider axle. Ten aluminum wheels, Michelin low-profile 22.5 tires, full-length side fairings, and sidesteps. Roof fairings. Fog lamps and daytime running lights. Pneumatic spray-washers for the headlights. Electric intermittent windshield wipers. Motorized and heated outside mirrors. Tilt-and-telescoping steering wheel. Outside-temperature gauge. An imitation wood-grain dash that looked like real wood. Plush interior (gray and navy blue) and captain's chairs finished in thick, patterned fabric. Carpeted sleeper. Electric refrigerator. Skylight. Power windows and power door locks. Slide-out desk. Separate cab-and-sleeper heating and cooling. Upper and lower bunks. Cabinets with real doors. On each side of the sleeper, slide-up windows and mesh screens let air in and kept bugs out. If you had a good parking place and a gentle breeze, you raised the curtains and opened the windows and you were at home in your mobile home.

Century Class trucks came with something else I knew I'd appreciate: a short, sloped hood, aerodynamic and fuel-efficient. It allowed better visibility than the longer hood on the FLD model, which was fine with me—the less hood the better, in my view.

We pulled our last load in 21127, parked it at the Phoenix terminal, and caught a night flight to Oregon. At the Troutdale yard we picked up keys, a permit book, and the driver's manual, and took our first look at Linehaul power unit 22247.

Gayle said, "Nice truck."

We gave a day to the tractor, tightening bolts and screws, vacuum-cleaning metal shavings and assembly-line debris from the floor. We adjusted our seats, the steering column, and the mirrors. I checked the oil and coolant levels before I flipped the ignition switch and stood with the hood open, listening to the tight clatter of a new diesel engine. Once again, I was home. Time would tell if Gayle felt the same way.

—∞—

Phoenix, a Tuesday morning, 7 a.m.

I parked in front of the prep shop and Gayle asked, "How long will the PDI take?"

"We'll be out of here tonight."

Wednesday evening.

A PDI tech said, "We've got your repair list. It's long and

we're only halfway through it."

Adjust hood and hood stops. Fix leaks at front axle hubs. Fix wire bundle caught in the hood springs. Fix loose axle vents. Adjust clutch. Adjust brakes. Adjust air governor. Tighten axle flange nuts. Tighten loose fuel lines and fittings. Tighten loose brake-hose fittings. And on and on.

The tech said, "Those people in Portland sure build a sloppy truck. Yours is pretty good compared to some, but you need parts that we don't stock. It'll take another day to get it all together. Nothing to worry about—everything's covered by the warranty. We'll bill Freightliner."

Warranty kickbacks for Linehaul didn't help us when we weren't loaded and rolling.

Thursday afternoon.

"You're almost done," said the PDI foreman. "The driver's door rubs the frame and you've got peeling paint up by the skylight. We don't fix doors or paint. You need to see Doug, down at the body shop. A bit of advice: get there early."

The Linehaul body shop.

A dirt lot five miles from the terminal, ringed with barbed wire and crammed with dust-covered wrecks and piles of truck components—axles, drive shafts, radiators, rusted springs and shackles, seats, doors, engines, hoods. Trucks were repaired outside, rain or shine. The paint booth stood open to the elements and the air-borne sand of south Phoenix.

We met Doug when he opened the gate at 5 a.m.

He said, "My best men will take care of you. You'll be out of here in two hours."

Four hours later a shop worker knocked on the door. Would I mind if he raised the hood and looked under the truck to see how the front end, air lines, and electrical wiring were laid out? Century Class trucks were new and no one at Linehaul understood how they were put together.

I said, "Doesn't Freightliner train you?"

"Nope. We learn as we go. We haven't had to repair a Century Class sleeper box yet, so we don't know sleepers. We know hoods real good." He nodded toward the truck he was working on. "That's my first Century Class front end. Hit a deer. The truck is just a few weeks old and Doug gave me used parts. The driver's gonna scream if he finds out."

Late that afternoon Doug's men fixed the door then primed and sanded the roof before they brought out their spray guns. They resealed the skylight.

"Most of them leak," one said. "Yours won't."

While we waited for the paint to set up, Doug talked of offering body-shop services to other carriers. "My plan's simple. We'll do fast turnarounds and quality work. I'll put my best men on the tough jobs."

Saturday morning.

A dispatcher asked what I wanted and I said, "Miles."

Beep: *Load assignment. Phoenix to Mt. Pleasant, IA, 1,476 paid miles. Deliver ASAP. Hot load.*

Miles. From Mt. Pleasant to Muscatine, Il, to Billings, to Elbert, CO, to Pueblo, to Oklahoma City, to Tulsa, to St. Louis, to Hannibal, MO, to Forest Park, GA, to Opelika, AL, to Laval, PQ, to Edison, NJ, to Memphis, to Dallas. We were off to a good start.

—⁓—

Portland, OR.

The Jakes wouldn't shut off. We took the truck to a Detroit Diesel repair shop, where the foreman said, "I know what's wrong. Won't take but a day to fix it." Four days after that he said, "We're finishing up. You'll be rolling in an hour." I called Dispatch, asked for miles, accepted a load to Ohio, and drove two blocks. The Jakes still wouldn't shut off.

We went back and the foreman said, "Hmm . . . Well, it's warranty. Won't cost you a penny. You ain't lost nothing."

It cost us four days' revenue and we lost the Ohio load.

Vancouver, WA.

Beep: *We were to go to the Troutdale terminal immediately, drop our loaded trailer, and wait for a wheel-bearing check. Every Century Class truck had to be checked. Every one.*

Two days later the shop manager said, "You're a free man again. You only had one bad bearing."

"*Only* one?"

"Yeah, but if you're doing 65 and you lose the one, you probably lose everything."

"I thought Freightliner had fixed this problem."

"That's what we thought. Oh, well. We'll bill them for warranty repairs. No harm done."

Just downtime and another lost load.

The air conditioning unit began to blow hot air. Freightliner charged the A/C system then repaired it again because it had been overcharged. More downtime.

The Century Class heating-ventilating-air conditioning system didn't maintain the constant cab and sleeper temperatures promised in the sales literature and there was no bi-level heat in the cab unless you ran the defroster. In winter, your feet froze and your head and shoulders cooked while you drove, or your feet roasted and you wore a jacket.

"Can't fix it," said a Freightliner mechanic. "They're all like that."

Mansfield, LA.

It began to rain. I switched on the windshield wipers. The passenger-side wiper arm fell off. A service manager at the Freightliner dealer in Shreveport shook his head and said, "They only break when you use them. We'll have a new one on in 10 minutes. There's no charge, it's warranty."

West Plains, MO.

It began to rain. I switched on the windshield wipers. The wiper arm on the driver's side fell off. We waited 20 minutes for the rain to stop and drove under clearing skies to Springfield, MO, where Freightliner replaced the arm. "It's warranty," said the shop foreman. "We do see a lot of these."

At a Freightliner parts counter I remarked that there were more than 50 light bulbs in the Century Class dash and two bulbs in every switch.

"My FLD had fiber optics," I said, "and one bulb for six or eight lights."

"Ah," said the counter man. "Now that was a good idea."

"Yes it was. What happened?"

"It was *too* good. You guys didn't buy enough bulbs." He checked his computer screen. "The old bulbs were 45 cents, the new ones retail for $2.23—we only charge $1.75. The switch you asked about? They're very proud of it. That switch retails for $91.35. I can let you have one for $15.98."

The new truck wasn't a quiet truck. Sound levels inside—from wind, the road, the turbo, and the engine—were the same as any old FLD, more industrial noise to chip away at your hearing. On mornings when the truck warmed in the sun, something always popped inside the sleeper walls—probably defective fasteners or misapplied beads of adhesive. The clutch linkage rattled, just like an FLD. Wind whistled through the door seals, just like an FLD. Dash and interior materials, engineered to feel "soft," were too easily scratched. Long-life light bulbs didn't live long. Plastic rocker switches wore out; I replaced them on my own, learning switch by switch the intricacies of dashboard construction and wiring.

Gayle said, "At least the skylight doesn't leak."

Signs and graphics for 22247.

We chose a two-tone color scheme—cranberry and cream—to set off the metallic blue paint. A design store put our signs on the doors, fenders, and sleeper sides, and gave the truck a personality. Drivers keyed up.

"Damnit, Mayfield, damn*it*. You're lookin' *good*. For a Linehaul truck, that is. Ha ha. Just kidding."

"Nice truck, Mayfield. Nice graphics."

"Mayfield, that's a 100-percent sign job. You and your seat cover be *stylin'*."

—⁂—

Gayle and I fought. At times, there were such distances between us it didn't seem we were married.

On I-82, near Sunnyside, WA, I said the wrong thing. She reached over and ripped a toothpick from my mouth. I told her, "You can get out any time you like. You don't have to ask me."

Near Sturgis, SD.

Gayle said, "You've changed a lot out here. You're more cheerful and more confident than I've ever seen you, and I'm happy for you, but all you want to do is drive trucks. What kind of life is this for us?"

"It works for yours truly."

She turned to the window and didn't say anything for the rest of the day.

At a truck stop in Ardmore, OK.

I said, "There's a phone in the C-store."

Those were the first words either of us had spoken for two days. I could no longer remember what started the fight, but the arguments—long and fierce—had raged across three states.

"There's a phone in the C-store. Call a cab. Leave." I wanted to be mad and for her to go and for us to split up and settle everything long-distance. I enjoyed my anger. Like solitude, it was an old, close friend, always calling me back.

She said, "Where will I go?"

I didn't know and at that moment I didn't care and I said so. Then we sat in silence for the better part of an hour.

Gayle said, "Truce?"

We shook hands without any real enthusiasm and she stayed in the truck. Things gradually got better between us.

—ᴡᴡ—

Beep: *You have a new fleet manager.*

Tyler Sanderson appeared without fanfare or greeting. Arrogant, disinterested, and short-tempered, he knew next to nothing about trucking and even less about working with people.

In Dallas we accepted our first dispatch from him, drove to the shipper, and waited two hours for beeps and load information. Tyler sent everything but a pick-up number—"No number, no load," the shipping clerk said—and didn't answer Qualcomm messages. I called him.

He said, "You probably thought I was sitting here fucking off."

"Nothing like that. You're new to the job and I understand, but I'm due in Denver tomorrow and I'd like to get moving. I just need the pick-up number."

"I fucking sent you the thing. Oh, fuck. I pushed the wrong fucking button. Here you go."

I agreed to a two-drop run after Tyler promised $180 unload pay. My settlement came out $120 short.

"I meant to tell you," he said when I called to ask about it. "I made a mistake. It was $60 for both drops."

"I hand-stacked and fingerprinted at two consignees on your say-so. Anyone else would make it right."

"I'm not anyone else."

I put new batteries in my dispatch buster.

Gayle and I had an appointment in the Bay Area, one we couldn't miss. I reminded Tyler again and again. The fourth time I mentioned it he said, "I'll put a note in the computer. Then you'll stop bugging me."

In Phoenix a dispatcher said, "There's nothing about your appointment on the screen. I'd have preplanned you on a Bay Area load if I'd known. Sorry, there's no more westbound freight today."

I sent Tyler a message that we were heading west and that I'd call him in a couple of days.

Beep: *You should have waited for a load.*

Couldn't. Would have missed an important meeting.

Beep: *Why didn't you take a load?*

No answer was possible. No answer was necessary.

Detroit, MI.

"We need a favor," Tyler said. "There's no freight today. If you help us tonight, I'll work with the planner to get you a good load tomorrow."

I helped out, picked up the good load in the morning, and looked at the shipper's sign-in sheet. Nineteen Linehaul drivers had picked up trailers the day before, and there'd been 24 loads, most of them going where I was going. My trailer had been sitting, loaded, for two days.

The favor would pay $34.93, less a $3 wire transfer fee for a Comchek to pay a lumper. Gross revenue for 24 hours came to $31.93. I hung a sign on the favor store: *Closed*.

—⚎—

Denver.

We asked Dispatch for miles and accepted the first offer, picked up our loaded trailer, took it to Linehaul's terminal for safekeeping, and spent the evening at a bookstore where I could park, bobtail, right outside.

Early the next morning we headed east with our freight,

ice-making machines for bars and restaurants in Columbus and Cleveland, OH, Rochester, NY, and Woburn, MA.

The Columbus consignee didn't have a dock. I blocked a busy downtown street and hefted boxes onto pallets held up by a forklift on the sidewalk.

In Cleveland the only approach to a narrow dock forced drivers to roll their tractors over a well-groomed lawn. I wasn't going to do that.

The receiver said, "I can get a forklift into your trailer if you bump the dock. If we unload on the street, you tailgate."

I said, "Tailgating's cheaper than buying a new lawn."

"Well, that's true. I can't tell you how many drivers have paid for grass over there. The guy watches. He's watching now. He'll be disappointed if you don't give him a chance to come over and get in your face."

In Rochester, you faced the dock entrance as soon as you drove onto the customer's property, there was no room to turn around, and you couldn't see the dock, which was more than a trailer length inside an unlit shed.

"I'm sorry our parking lot is full today," the proprietor said. "Do you think you can get in?"

"Piece of cake."

Gayle said to him, "He loves this sort of thing."

I backed out of the lot and down a block, sight-sided into an intersection, pulled out, backed along the block again, and threaded the trailer between parked cars then into the shed.

The proprietor clapped his hands, said, "Bravo! Interesting

solution to my dock problem," and invited us to his office for bagels and coffee. He wanted to hear trucker tales. We wanted to hear about life during the last ice storm.

"I walked to work," he said. "Couldn't drive."

Gayle asked, "Why did you even come in?"

"We sell machines *and* service, so someone is here all the time—that's how we built up our business. I live just a few streets away."

I said, "I'll bet you didn't sell many ice makers."

"Not a one. You know, I never thought of it that way."

In Woburn the next day, we drove a mile off I-95 to the consignee and passed a supermarket and a motel.

Gayle said, "That looks like a decent market. Can you get in there?"

"Piece of cake, bobtail."

"And that motel looks okay."

"Another piece of cake."

The dock was easy, the forklift operators fast, and our next load—computer parts for North Carolina—waited just half a mile away. The shipper had a huge lot and a row of Linehaul empties and didn't mind if you dropped a trailer and went off to buy groceries. You don't forget a customer like that, or a store you can bobtail to, or a convenient, tractor-friendly motel.

Three weeks later we were back in Denver, hoping for another run east. That's what we asked for and that's what we got.

The load:

Boxed vitamin supplements on pallets, 18,455 pounds, shipper load and count, consignees to unload, 2,072 paid miles, two and a-half days.

The trip:

Forty-two hours after leaving Denver on a Friday night, the driver had to deliver 1,742 miles away in Sharon Hill, PA, just south of Philadelphia. He would push on to Elizabeth, NJ and Lawrence, NY, then drive straight through to Chelsea, MA for Monday morning. Late was not an option. Vitamin loads were hot.

The dispatch:

Illegal and a violation of company policy—the planner shouldn't have offered team miles and a team's schedule to a solo driver. Tyler shouldn't have passed the load assignment to me. I shouldn't have accepted it.

"You're crazy," Gayle said. "What's the plan?"

"Standard blitz. Woburn's not far from Chelsea. When we're empty on Monday, we can drop the trailer at the customer with the big yard and get a room at that motel."

"And we'll sleep and take long showers and make love, and then, husband, you're not going to pull blitz loads anymore."

I was already tired, thinking of what I'd have to do to be in the Philadelphia area by 4 o'clock Sunday afternoon. I ran it the way I had to run it. I logged it legal. Forty-one hours and forty minutes after leaving the shipper's dock, I rang the doorbell at a Sharon Hill warehouse.

"On time," the receiver said. "That's a first for Linehaul. Did you fly?"

In Elizabeth, I found a note and a phone number taped to the dock plate. I called. A forklift operator showed up 15 minutes later. "Your drivers are *always* late, so I quit waiting here. They call, I come down and unload them. They don't call, I watch TV at home. They show up Monday, I slept good, I didn't sit here twiddling my thumbs. You called, you're on time, what do you have for me?"

It was 42 truck-route miles from Elizabeth to Lawrence, but we crawled along in traffic for two-and-a-half hours. The receiver came to work an hour and 45 minutes late and took two full hours to unload—the delays came out of my bunk time—and we didn't leave his dock until 1 a.m. Gayle asked how I felt.

"I'm tired," I said. "You get some sleep."

Sleep.

In Connecticut, I tried a rest area and two service areas. All full. I pulled into a Massachusetts service area without any real hope, but found three parking places to choose from, set the brakes, and leaned over the steering wheel. I'd been up and driving for 21 hours. I slept for three and felt worse when I woke up than I would have if I'd stayed awake.

In Chelsea, the dock manager said, "I used to drive solo. I know when you left Denver. I know what you did. You're crazy. Nice truck."

I drove to Woburn, asked to drop the trailer, and said we'd be back for it in a day or two, if that would be all right. The dock foreman said, "Better make it three days, buddy. You look like you should sleep at least that long."

In the motel room I promised that we'd come back to Boston as tourists someday, on our own lazy schedule. Before we fell asleep Gayle said, "I'm glad we're together. I really like it out here."

Chapter Seventeen

*What we call each other ultimately becomes what
we think of each other, and it matters.*

JEANNE J. KIRKPATRICK

Laredo, TX. December 1, 1998. Late afternoon at the Pilot truck stop.

I was sure no one with a long trailer would tackle the narrow parking place on our left. A driver would have to angle back over landscaping and a high curb along his left side and squirm back and forth to get in, then he wouldn't have room to pull out unless I dropped my trailer and I wouldn't have room to pull out unless he dropped his. Any experienced trucker would see that and park somewhere else. I expected to wake up next to a straight truck, a bobtail, or a still-empty space.

Drivers rolled by, shook their heads, and moved on.

A flatbedder pulling an empty decided to try. He backed in fast, banging his tractor and trailer tandems through the landscaping and across the curb. The front corner of his trailer swung close to my fender. I blew the air horn, squeezed the mic hard, and yelled, "Stop, flatbed! Stop!" He pulled up and came back to the same place and at the same angle, did it three more times, corrected, then almost hit my mirror. Four pull-ups, four key-ups, and four horn blasts later he was wedged in, his mirror inches from mine, leaving neither of us room to move.

"Don't take my hood off when you leave," I said to him when he climbed down from his cab. "Come get me, okay? I don't care what time it is. I'll drop my trailer."

He hitched his pants up under his fat gut, and, without a word, marched toward the restaurant.

The tires on both sides of his tractor and trailer were bruised and scuffed—this man hit a lot of curbs—and two were worn down close to the legal tread limits. Tie-downs hung from the chain bar, ready to fall off, forgotten since his last delivery. The steps and the fiberglass fairing on the driver's side had been crushed recently—this man hit things that were right under his nose. His truck signs—uneven lettering on squares of wrinkled vinyl— told me that he worked for a building supply outfit in El Paso, a regional brick and steel hauler operating on a shoe-string budget. Safety and maintenance probably took a back seat to hauling cheap freight. The flatbedder drove a dented truck, earned a modest living, and stopped at home once or twice a week. Driving was just a job. Pride had nothing to do with it.

Our neighbor wasn't back from the restaurant by the time we went to bed and I hoped he'd be up when we were ready to roll. If not, I'd hammer on his door.

December 2, 1998, 5:30 a.m.

Darkness. A deep rumble. Violent shaking. Our truck was suddenly lifted, rocked from side to side, and dropped. We braced ourselves against the cabinets and sleeper walls before we were fully awake and I shouted up to Gayle, "Hold on!" Something crumpled and snapped. Something heavy hit the ground. A truck engine revved and faded, leaving only the steady drone of idling diesels. An earthquake? Unlikely in Laredo. Wind or a tornado, maybe, but the CB's NOAA weather alert hadn't gone off. I ripped the sleeper curtain aside.

Our hood leaned up at a crazy angle. I stared down into the engine compartment, out to the pre-dawn parking lot, and over to the empty space on our left. "That damn flatbedder! Gayle! He's leaving! Call the police!" I slid into my moccasins, pushed open the door, and staggered down the steps, pulling up my jeans. I started running.

The flatbed gained speed and crossed the lot behind a row of trucks, heading, I knew, for the exit driveway. I cut between two parked rigs, burst through a group of surprised drivers, and squeezed by a bull hauler inching into a tight spot. The flatbedder edged around trucks queued for the scale and turned his lights on. I bolted past two bobtails to stand—breathing hard, waving and shouting—in his path. I caught the grab handle and pounded the door window with my fist. "Stop! You hit my truck! Stop, damnit! Stop!"

The man who backed over curbs and landscaping rolled his window down and stared straight ahead.

"I didn't know," he said, flat as paint.

I should have grabbed his keys and I should have broken his jaw and I should have forced him to stay where he was—proof he'd left the scene—but he drove back and parked in front of our truck. Arms crossed, silent, expressionless, he leaned against his trailer and gazed at his handiwork: our hood, forced up against the windshield and knocked to one side like a boxer's bruised and overpunched nose; our grill, reduced to strips of bent aluminum; a smashed fog lamp hanging from its electrical cord, an eyeball knocked from a socket. One section of the three-piece air dam lay on the ground, coated with fiberglass dust, slivers of glass, and jagged pieces of plastic. A deep gouge high on the left fender marked the point where the trailer had chewed into our hood. The flatbedder felt the bite and knew he'd hit us. He put the pedal down. His tandems rode up and over our steer tire, dragged the hood from its hinges, and dropped to the pavement. He felt all that, too, and he heard it—any truck driver would—but he kept going.

Drivers gathered to sympathize and comment. A blue-eyed Texan—big hat, big shirt, big jeans, big boots—eyed our hood and the flatbedder.

"What the hell happened here?"

"Ask him," I said. "He tried to get away. I chased him down on foot. Says he didn't know."

"I *didn't* know."

"Bullshit, Pancho," said the Texan. "Thought you'd scoot back across the border, didn't you?"

I asked the flatbedder how long he had been on the road.

"Fifteen years."

"You don't drive like you've been out here that long. You made a lot of pull-ups trying to back in last night, you almost took my mirror off, and you ran over someone else's landscaping."

"Fifteen years, my butt," said the Texan. "You can't back up and you can't drive forward, Pancho. Wetback jackass. How the hell did you get a CDL? Do you even have one?"

"You were moving pretty damn fast to get out of here," I said. "With your lights off. I think you knew. I think you've done this before. Yeah, I think you knew."

I stopped thinking, walked back to our truck, and grabbed the small baseball bat I used for a tire thumper.

"Don't," Gayle said, her hand on my arm. "We aren't hurt."

I pictured her thrown out of the upper bunk, falling six feet to the sleeper floor, breaking ribs, a shoulder, or her neck. There would have been no one to restrain me.

Truck hit at Pilot, Laredo. No injuries. Other driver responsible. Police on the way. You will have to re-power the load.

Two nice trucks. Two good, honest parking places in truck stops and one at a Linehaul yard, and three men who didn't know how to drive. What were the odds? The first hit had been painless. The second one stung a bit. This one hurt. What would the fourth be like? The fifth?

Two Laredo police officers arrived, one for me and one for the flatbed driver, who suddenly had a lot to say, in Spanish. He liked the word *gringo*. He liked it so much he smiled every time he said it.

They say you should take photos of the people after an accident so no one can claim later that they were hurt when they weren't and to carefully document the scene, the striking vehicle, and the struck vehicle. I took pictures of the flatbedder looking away, unwilling to face the camera, his hands stuffed into his pants pockets below that beer gut. I photographed his fancy cowboy boots and held the lens inches from his chin just to see what he would do.

"Smile," I said, "Say *gringo*."

I took pictures of his abused tractor, our blue paint on his trailer tires, our fiberglass embedded in his chain bar and winches. I shot panoramas of our truck and his empty parking place and close-ups of the damage.

The flatbedder drove away as soon as the police were through with him. The whole time, he spoke five words in English: "fifteen," "years," "I," "didn't," "know." One officer watched him leave and shook his head.

"There's many drivers like that," he said. "Too bad you met one. He's 100 percent at fault. Said he didn't know, but I told him to save it—we hear that all the time. You can pick up a copy of my accident report at city hall tomorrow morning. I cited him for inattention and an improper start from a parked position."

"What about leaving the scene of an accident? I had to run after him."

"There's no place on our reports for that. What are you hauling? I need it for my paperwork."

"Truck hoods for a body shop in Montana."

"Truck hoods. Like yours?"

"Not exactly."

Mechanics at Linehaul's Laredo terminal wired the hood shut. I called Doug, the Linehaul body shop manager. His work had been good before and I didn't know where else to go.

"If you can get your truck to me," he said, "I'll take care of you. I'll put my best men on it."

Then Gayle and I sat in the cab for a day—full of anger, waiting for a load to Phoenix.

The clerk at the Laredo city hall barely spoke English, I didn't speak Spanish, and we had a *hard* time understanding each other. But I understood enough—the accident report wouldn't be available for two or three weeks. I needed that report. Without it, I wouldn't have a chance of filing an insurance claim. I saw myself burning up a lot of time in Texas courtrooms. Saw the flatbedder and his employer playing games. Saw myself not thinking and doing something I'd regret. It took awhile before I calmed down enough to realize the clerk was also telling me that they would mail a copy of the report, that I wouldn't have to visit city hall again.

On the way back to the yard a mud-covered mini van with a Coahuila license plate cut in front of us as I slowed for a red light. The driver peeled out before the light changed to green, and the spinning tires shot rocks at our truck. Two hit the windshield.

We should have been on our way to Montana. Instead, we were in Laredo chasing a police report that wouldn't be ready for weeks, looking through newly-cracked glass, and waiting for a load to Phoenix that might or might not turn up, all because a man with a CDL couldn't drive. I watched the van speed off and said, "Damn Mexicans."

"We've been together eighteen years," Gayle said, "and I have never heard you talk that way."

My father taught me that hating people for their skin color, ethnic background, or native country made as much sense as hating them for the color of their eyes. "Everyone is the same color inside," he used to say. "There's just one race, the human race, and we're all in it. Some people don't like that, so there are problems." I followed his teaching, or at least I thought I did. But after one Mexican truck driver, a language barrier at a city hall in the country of my birth, a broken windshield, and a little crazy thinking, I struggled to believe what I had always accepted.

Back at the Linehaul terminal, an owner-operator—he happened to be black—backed in next to us and took a long look at the truck.

He said, "Mexican done that, I'll bet."

I nodded. I didn't want this conversation.

"They always drive off. Did he drive off?"

"He did, but I caught him."

"They come here, they want what we have, then they drive like that. I've tried to like those people. I can't say I will ever get there."

For all I knew, the flatbedder had been born in the United States.

Still . . . in my experience, the meanest guys at Linehaul, those with the big-man attitude and the heavy, threatening manner, were Mexicans, often as not. On docks and in warehouses, Mexican truckers spoke only Spanish and glared at other drivers. Maybe it was cultural. Maybe they were trying to prove something. Maybe they were unsure about *us*. Maybe I just didn't understand.

And . . . the man who hit our truck was a Mexican. The men—uncle and nephew—who robbed and savagely raped a girlfriend of mine years before were Mexicans. Hadn't Gayle and I seen a Mexican trucker speeding on the wrong side of a Laredo street, flashing his headlights and waving a fist at oncoming traffic? Didn't rocks from a Mexican's tires crack our windshield?

Then again . . . I once ran from California to Texas with a Mexican driver named Roberto—I'd have been proud to call him a friend. Joe Rodriguez—salt of the earth—shared his settlement sheets with me in Reno. Ernesto Martinez was a friendly Linehaul trainer who I first met at a dock near Seattle and ran into at company terminals across the country. His students had only good things to say about him. Not one of them ever said *Mexican* trainer and that was what I needed to remember—the flatbedder's Mexican-ness or Mexican-American-ness made no difference. He couldn't drive and he didn't care. Things didn't have to go farther than that.

I called his company and asked for his name.

"He didn't tell you? He's supposed to tell you. Garcia. Javier Garcia. Now call my insurance company, *hombre*. Don't bother us again."

I inked the hood with large, black letters: "Hit and run courtesy of Javier Garcia, truck #15, F & F Building Supplies, El Paso," and kept channel 19 open all the way to Phoenix.

"Hit in a truck stop, right?"

We heard that eleven times.

"Hit-and-run. It happened to me."

Ten times.

"Did it happen at a Pilot?"

Seven times.

"The Pilot in Laredo?"

Three times.

"Mexican?"

Twice.

"Mexican hit you and ran? That's just like them."

Once.

In Phoenix we took everything out of the truck, down to the last toothpick. Pens. Pencils. Pads of paper. Stapler and staples. Permits and truck papers. Accounting files. Note books, log books, check books, bank statements, settlement statements, everything with our names and address. All clothing and bedding. CD player. CD collection. CB and antenna. Scanner. Cameras. Binoculars. Books. All food. All tools. Maps. Paper towels. Trash bags. Cleaning supplies. Oil. Coolant. Windshield washer fluid. Storage bins. Fire extinguisher. Hazard triangles. Spare parts. Anything that might catch a body-shop employee's eye. Personal property walked away from trucks in the Phoenix shops and drivers were told that the company wasn't responsible. There were sting operations and mechanics had been fired for stealing, but if you wanted to say goodbye to something you only had to leave it in your truck.

I taped plastic sheeting to the dash, the floor, the carpet and the door panels, and wrapped the seats and the bunks. We expected to be out of the truck for two weeks.

At the body shop, we met Dave Lancaster, a claims adjuster.

"The shop's good," he said. "Real good. Fix you right up. Doug knows what he's doing and I want you to be satisfied. There won't be any problems, but if there are call me right away. Doug will be here in a few minutes. He's in the bone yard."

"Bone yard?"

"Out back. Where he keeps old parts and wrecks. Ah, there he is."

Doug and I talked about the job. I specified a new hood and three new, matching air dams.

"You're in luck," he said. "I've got a new hood and new dams in stock. Give me three days and you'll never know your truck was hit. I'll put my best men on it. I'll paint it personally."

We shook hands and I began to relax. When I went to pick up the truck, I couldn't believe what I saw.

Doug had pawed through the bone yard, picked out a mangled hood, and patched it with gobs of epoxy and body filler. Both wheel wells were caked with dirt from someone else's miles. A smashed fender had been puttied and crudely reshaped. The new paint might have been smeared on by children playing with brushes—before it dried, one of Doug's best men had signed his work in blue fingerprints. In places smooth, in places pitted and rough with what felt like embedded grit, the dull finish didn't match the original clear-coat on the rest of the truck.

I released the latches and tugged at the hood. I tugged again and one side popped loose. I lifted the other side, walked back to the front, and pulled the hood open. Behind the radiator, tangled knots of misrouted air lines and electrical wiring were bundled together with gray duct tape.

Doug had sprayed paint on the windshield, door glass, mirrors, hood latches, the new grill, the sidesteps, the air dams, the splash guards, a kick plate, the steer tires and rims, the radiator, and the license plates. I could see and feel the spattered droplets. Apparently, he hadn't noticed.

I drew up a list of what was wrong, what had been promised, what had been done and what hadn't. The grill sat unevenly in its opening. The headlight bezels were loose. A mix of fasteners— some too big, some too small, some with fender washers, some without—had been used on the grill and the wheel-well splash guards. A fog lamp and wiring harness were missing. The hood gaskets were torn. The original paint had been sandpapered off the sidesteps. A headlight pointed almost straight down. Only one piece of the air dam had been replaced—it didn't fit properly and wasn't even the right color. Old parts and rusted bolts, screws, clips, and washers—whatever lay on the shop floor—were used without disguise or apology. I called the claims adjuster and asked him to come look at the truck. In the body shop's parking lot he said, "This is not good."

"I know that, Dave. Would you say they lowered the truck's value?"

"Definitely. By at least $5,000. This is not good."

"This is the worst. I'll go find Doug."

I walked through the body shop, where a fog of paint fumes and resin hung in the air. Across the floor, wrecked trucks were painted and pieced together by trainee teams, body-shop hopefuls who worked without respirators in the cancerous haze. Those who didn't quit after a week or two became Doug's best men. Above his desk, a banner set the tone for the workplace: *Beware of The Doug.*

"Hey," he said, "What do you think?"

"I think you raped our truck. You put on an old hood and sprayed paint everywhere. Don't you use masking paper? Are you too busy for prep work? And what about new air dams?"

"Well, I don't have any."

"You told me you did. You also said you had a new hood. I don't know who did more damage, you or the guy who hit us. Your work is shit. Let's take a close look at it."

Doug's foreman walked around the truck, glanced at me, and half hid behind his boss. I gave copies of my list to Doug and the claims adjuster. Doug wadded his up then passed the wad to the foreman.

"Dave," I said, "I'm not paying for this garbage. Neither are you."

"Linehaul is our biggest customer. We have to pay them. What the shop says, well, that's the way it is."

"*I* am your customer. *I* pay the premiums every week. *I* am not satisfied."

The shop foreman studied the list and flipped the hood latches.

"I'll help you open that," I said. "This hood feels like it's nailed down. Would you do this kind of work on your own car?"

A snarl from The Doug cut off his answer.

I said, "The truck is a mess. Dave thinks you guys dropped its value by five grand."

"I didn't say that," Dave said quickly. "Doug . . . is there something we can work out?"

"I won't charge him as long as I get my parts back. Marc, Gayle, give us another chance and you can have your truck back tomorrow. I'll put my best men on it."

Gayle said, "That's what you told us three days ago."

Doug shuffled back to his bone yard and I drove across town to the Freightliner dealer.

"The dealer's body shop is good," Dave said. "Real good. Fix you right up. They know what they're doing." After that, he didn't return my phone calls.

"That is the nastiest body work I've ever seen," said the manager at Freightliner. "Who did it, school kids?"

"Linehaul's body shop."

"Like I said. School kids."

We talked about the job. I ordered a new hood and three new air dam pieces.

"I'm paying," I said. "I'm your customer."

"Well, Linehaul's our *biggest* customer, so I'll have to talk to Doug. If I know him, he'll want his parts back. I'll let you know when to bring the truck in. It'll take about two weeks to stockpile everything."

I went back to work, driving a truck that looked like it had been hit twice. Fasteners came loose and dropped off. Air lines leaked. Doug's hood cracked open. The original hood—I thought of it as ours—lay in the bone yard. Doug would glue it together, slop paint over it, then palm it off on someone.

Beep: *Freightliner called. They're ready for you.*

At Freightliner the shop foreman told us, "We'll need the truck for about three weeks."

"About three weeks" meant taking everything out and finding a place to store it all, again. It meant more unwelcome workers inside the truck and taping the interior, again. It meant no miles and no revenue until the truck was fixed. Javier Garcia was probably loaded and rolling.

Three weeks.

We rented an SUV and drove out to California. Visited friends. Visited my mother but didn't tell her about the truck.

Drove down to Carmel and along the coast to Big Sur and San Simeon. Walked on beaches. Drove from the coast to Williams, AZ in one day—Gayle said, "Lemmee see yer log book." Went to Meteor Crater. Stayed at the Grand Canyon for a few days. Saw dropped trailers at the park entrance and bobtail tractors at scenic view points—drivers on mini-vacations. I got up early and hiked alone along the canyon rim before dawn, inhaled the dark morning air, and thought about shooting a few people.

I remembered Jennie, a Linehaul lease operator. She picked up her new truck in Oregon, took a load to California, parked in the old Stockton yard, and went home for a weekend. She came back to find the hood shattered and hanging from its hinges. Doug and his best men replaced it, but the paint didn't match and he'd said nothing to her about putting an old, beat-up hood on a brand-new tractor. She made herself unwelcome in company offices by loudly saying "No!" to anything but a new hood and matching paint. The owner-operator division dragged its feet. Doug refused to square things. Jennie insisted. After all, her name was on the door. She held on for three months, until a Linehaul fleet manager took Doug aside and told him to do the right thing.

Freightliner, March 18, 1999.

We accepted the work and paid our bill—$4,603. I sent a demand for reimbursement to F & F's insurance company, called Doug, and reminded him of our agreement: no charges.

"That's right," he said. "No charges. I've got my parts. Johnnie knows all about it."

I said, "Who's Johnnie?"

"My bookkeeper."

El Paso, March 31, 1999.

Tyler—There's a $1,541.20 charge from the body shop that just showed up on a settlement. Doug said no charges. He has to keep his word.

Beep: *Don't know about it.*

Find out, please.

Beep: *Just talked to Johnnie . . . he is going to give you a credit for the parts they received back . . . talk to him . . . be nice.*

Nice, hell.

I called Johnnie. "What do you mean credit only for the parts? Doug and I had an understanding. He said you knew about it. The shop's lousy work forced me to go to Freightliner, remember?"

"Yeah, yeah. I saw your squawk sheet. You didn't give us a chance to make it right. You took your ass somewhere else."

"Johnnie. Listen to me. I can be in your office tomorrow morning if you want to talk that way."

"Wait a minute. Let me think."

"I'll do it for you. The Big Guy's chop shop won't get a penny from me. Your guys lowered the truck's value by $5,000. Do you have $5,000 for me? Do you want to pay for my downtime?"

"Wait a minute, wait a minute. Maybe I can work something out."

"Time's up. Doug gets a free hood, I get a 100-percent credit. That was the deal. And what kind of voodoo bookkeeping is this, anyway? Shouldn't you bill the insurance company? Are you double billing?"

"I can't say nothing about that."

"Yeah. I'll bet you can't."

Beep: *Johnnie . . . will credit you the full amount they charged for the repair.*

Damn right.

"This Garcia thing," Gayle said. "Will it ever be over?"

That night in a dream a cokehead parrot named Johnnie bobbed and screeched, "You took your ass somewhere else! You took your ass somewhere else!" Javier Garcia and The Doug laughed and juggled buckets of blue plaint. I was headed for the parrot with my bat when a reefer kicked over and woke me up.

The Texas Department of Public Safety sent me copies of files on F & F and its drivers, who ran around on tires worn below legal limits and drove with cracked windshields, brakes out of adjustment, engine oil leaks, worn air hoses, bare electrical wires, defective stop lamps, and bundles of bricks that weren't tied down. F & F consistently ignored annual equipment inspection requirements. DPS had visited their offices and cited them for failing to inquire into a driver's safety records. I could guess who that driver was.

I called the New Mexico Driver Services Bureau—Javier Garcia lived in Las Cruces—and a clerk recited his driving record. Nine hours after he hit our truck, Texas inspectors stopped him on a scale. They found improperly installed wiring on his trailer and an inoperative tractor turn-signal. He probably said he didn't know. He was 1,700 pounds over on his drives. He knew, I am sure of it. A flat tire—he didn't know—put him out of service. Four months later he received a speeding ticket. Two months after that he was fined for a log-book violation and for failure to stop at a scale. He didn't know it was open.

"Oh, no," said the clerk. "This man had an accident in Texas last December."

"I know," I said. "I was there."

I called F & F's insurance adjuster. "Javier Garcia has a history. He's working his way up to a major accident. He'll kill a few people and claim he didn't know. It will cost you millions. Millions."

"Why are you telling me this? We've already paid to fix your truck."

"It's not enough. If we can't come to terms, I'm going to sue your client and his driver for lost revenue, travel expenses, attorneys' fees, court costs, and the headache. I'll tell F & F that their insurance carrier let them down. Remember, the police report states that Mr. Garcia was 100 percent at fault. And it *was* hit-and- run. A jury's going to love that."

"How much more do you want?"

When all was said and done, Javier Garcia's improper start from a stopped position cost his employer's insurer almost $12,000.

After the collision I stayed as far away from other parked trucks as possible, even farther than I had before, and I worried every time I left the cab for coffee, a shower, or an unload. I wrote down the company names and truck numbers of rigs parked on either side. When I slept, I still kept a pair of jeans and my moccasins within reach. On the floor, between the seats, I placed a flashlight, a camera, and the bat. I thought seriously about carrying a pistol again. The next guy to hit my truck—whether he drove off or not—would be sorry he was number four.

Chapter Eighteen

Nobody Said That It Would Be Easy

Robert Lee Castleman

June 25, 1999. Three hours northeast of Denver.

Late-afternoon thunderheads formed over I-76, billowing first into one cell and then another and another until white anvil clouds towered above the Interstate in a late-afternoon squall line. A dark wall cloud streaked with lightning promised heavy rain, strong winds and white-knuckle driving.

"Westbound," I said. "What's it like in there?"

"Eastbound, be afraid. Be very afraid. Wind, rain, lightning like you've never seen, idiot four-wheelers driving without headlights. You can't see but a few feet in front of your hood. I heard a motor home and an eighteen got blown over near Ogallala. This thing is kicking butt."

"What he said, Eastbound. It's big, dark, and wet. Did I say dark? Did I say wet? You're gonna get your truck washed. I hope you're loaded heavy, man, I hope you've got some real weight in your box so you don't go flyin' off like Dorothy and Toto."

Gayle said, "Is 43,000 pounds enough to hold us down?"

"I hope so," I said. "Maybe. I don't know."

"What can we do?"

"Nothing. Here it is. Hang on!"

The first hard gusts hit the truck, one-two punches that shook the trailer and knocked us toward the shoulder. Then rain pelted the cab like hail on a tin roof, streaked across the windshield in sheets, and blew through gaskets on the driver's door. Silent lightning split the darkness. Four-wheelers pulled over or crept along at 15 miles an hour.

One hell of a truck wash. It seemed to go on forever.

The rain stopped and left us with nothing but wind, wind that swirled around the rig and pushed the trailer halfway into the hammer lane. Then more rain. Then more wind, buffeting us back to the shoulder.

Suddenly, we were out on the other side looking at stars in a clear sky, Gayle was saying, "I just lived the longest 20 minutes of my life," and westbound drivers were asking what it was like in there.

—◊—

I thought about mounting a video camera on the dash to capture four-wheeler antics and impending collisions, because accidents often result in lawsuits, and truck drivers get blamed and sued a lot. One flick of a switch and a jury would see what I had seen and tried to avoid: a car in my lap. Short of driving as if our lives depended on it, that was the only defense I could think of.

Near Temple, GA. Mid-afternoon, July 11, 1999.

A dashboard cam that day would have recorded rain-dampened pavement and a pale-blue Corvette ascending a curved on-ramp about 100 yards ahead of us. The driver looked over her shoulder, decided she had to get in front of our truck, forgot she was rounding a turn, and ignored the wet road surface. She opened the secondaries. Her fuel-injected torque went to the rear wheels and they broke loose, coursing arcs of white spray as the 'Vette spun around twice then stalled across the eastbound lanes of I-20.

Car.

Car in the lap of everyone on that highway.

Yelling and swearing weren't going to help, but Gayle and I did our best. I tugged on the four-way lever and steered to the right, aiming to squeeze the truck between the Corvette and an overpass railing. All I could do was slow the rig—we were too close to stop without locking the brakes and jackknifing the trailer. If the driver started up and shifted into gear, she'd likely shoot straight across our lane, right into our path and die t-boned. If she rolled forward as we passed, she'd wedge her car under the tandem and die crushed in a flattened sports car.

I put my arm out the window and motioned to anyone who might notice to slow down, slow down, slow down. Four-wheelers behind us braked and swerved.

Car.

Car in the middle of the Interstate.

I eased by, still slowing, shifting down. Other drivers would have to figure out for themselves how to avoid hitting her. I heard "Look out!" on the CB and glanced at my mirror. The Corvette was moving, lost in a cloud of spray and smoking tires. It disappeared behind our trailer, fishtailed out, then sped up alongside—burning rubber, throwing spray, gone in seconds.

Two four-wheelers blew their horns. A hand waved from a window. A passenger fake-wiped sweat from her brow and mouthed a thank you. I looked at my mirror again. A van full of kids, laughing and unaware, was coming up to pass.

—⚂—

Ogden, UT.

"I did it," I said.

Gayle said, "Did what?"

"I've driven one million accident-free hub miles. I've earned an award. I'm going to put decals on the doors."

I had never seen a million-mile decal on a Linehaul company truck or, for that matter, on a Linehaul owner-operator's. The corporate newsletter might announce a million-miler once in awhile, but Linehaul's focus on rookies worked against safe-driving awards. I called the safety department.

"Let's see, 22247, how long have you been driving?"

"Eight years and seven months."

"We give the award at 10 years."

"It's based on miles, not time."

"We won't even consider it until your tenth year."

"Drivers make their own perks at Linehaul," Gayle said, and I ordered lettering for the doors: "One million miles—no accident, no incident."

Four-wheelers noticed and waved. Truck drivers grinned

and saluted. Other million-milers keyed up to talk. A scale master in Cortez, CO pointed at the door then offered two thumbs-up and a smile. Rookies at Linehaul terminals gaped. I was uncomfortable with the attention, but never took the decals off. I guess I needed to show the world that I knew what I was doing and that no one had to worry when Mayfield backed a trailer. Every time I walked to the truck, the signs—they weren't for other people at all—reminded me of my small achievement.

Then, someone at Linehaul noticed. The award package was a jacket, a wall plaque, a belt buckle, and a wallet-sized card. I just had to wait for the company to order them.

—⁓—

Memo from The Director of the owner-operator division, one of many on refusing loads.

We now have Owner Operators that consistently turn down freight for any number of reasons: too many stops, not enough miles, wrong direction, wanted to be home this weekend . . . and it has affected . . . the miles the Owner Operators are getting. I have written a memo to the Terminal Managers requesting Owner Operator miles improve and to ensure equitable miles between company drivers and Owner Operators.

He didn't say he'd written a memo reminding terminal managers that owner-operators could refuse loads without apology or explanation, and that Linehaul policy forbade reprisals.

The uproar about running your own business but never turning down freight! Didn't the company turn down freight that barely met expenses, freight that would have a truck running at a loss? Refusing a bad load was simply a calculated investment in the possibility of a good one. Memos weren't going to change anything.

We turned down a trip from Denver to Idaho Falls, 592 paid miles over three days. The planner didn't understand my refusal. I told him that short miles didn't cover our day-to-day expenses and that we'd be out-of-pocket if we accepted. I was about to bring up the independent contractor agreement, but he said, "Now I know why owner-operators turn down small stuff. No one's ever explained it to me," and gave us a load to New Hampshire.

In Cleveland, NC we were offered a long deadhead and a short run to a 2 a.m. delivery at a grocery warehouse in Cincinnati. We refused. The next day we accepted a load to Utah. In Utah we accepted a hot load to Ohio. In Ohio we accepted an immediate return load to Utah. From there, dispatchers sent us to Texas and on to Florida, then up to Pennsylvania, then out to Colorado. Who said you never turn down freight?

Loads from an Addison, TX distribution center came out four, five, or six hours late, but drop-off schedules were based on the original pick-up times. This guaranteed illegal runs, doctored logbooks, and a store manager in Orlando who asked me, "Why aren't my Addison loads ever on time?"

"They always ship late. Always."

"But you're on time. You were here at 7 a.m., clean and ready, before my crew."

I didn't tell her that I'd just driven 922 miles nonstop from Shreveport—running a second log book—or that I'd waited six hours for my trailer and had to choose: sleep and be charged with a service failure or deliver on time. I didn't tell her that I'd splashed my face with cold water, brushed my teeth, and pulled on a fresh shirt minutes earlier. I didn't tell her that I'd slept two-and-a-half hours in the last 24 or that I had three more deliveries after hers and a 9 p.m. live-load in Ft. Lauderdale and that it would be close to midnight before I'd have a chance to rest. I didn't tell her that I would never pull freight for her company again and that I didn't care what The Director or anyone else might say.

—⚍—

Beep: *Tyler's leaving. My name is Annie. I'll be your new fleet manager.*

Hi.

Beep: *Hi, you two.*

"She answered right away," Gayle said. "That's a good sign."

—⚍—

By early 2000 Gayle had grown tired of truck stops, the paired smells of urine and diesel fuel in parking lots, showers and laundromats that were less than clean, and living small in a truck.

One morning she said, "Two years is enough. I'm going home and I'm going back to work. What will you do when the lease is up?"

"I don't know. Get another truck, I guess."

"Then we're back where we were two years ago."

In East Liberty, OH the Qualcomm beeped and she said, "What's next?"

"We deadhead about 90 miles to Clyde—nice little town—and pick up preloaded washers and dryers for Laredo. Fifteen hundred miles. We're moving you closer to home."

"Speaking of home, husband . . ."

I said, just to be saying something and because I didn't want to fight, that I would think about looking for a job that would get me home every night, but I couldn't promise.

"I wouldn't know how to live a normal life."

She said, "You could try. Sooner or later you'll have to choose: me or trucks and this life you live out here."

Laredo, three days later.

The Qualcomm beeped and Gayle said, "What's next this time?"

"Preloaded washers and dryers again. For Los Angeles. Fourteen hundred miles. Then I'll get you home. We'll have to wait until the trailer comes across the border."

We waited 27 hours.

Beep: *Trailer 63553 is at the Laredo yard. It's yours.*

Trailer 63553 bore enough rust, dents, and tarnished aluminum for two trailers, but it had eight good tires, all the lights worked, and someone had adjusted the brakes. A small elongate hole, its edges tarnished and spattered with mud and rust, pierced the aluminum skin above the tandem on the driver's side. I usually carried adhesive-backed aluminum tape to patch holes in trailers, but I had used my last roll and I knew that the trailer shop in Phoenix would make the repair. All I could do was note the damage in my log book.

Phoenix, two days later.

I filled out and signed a bright-red damage tag and asked the shop foreman if he was going to tape the hole.

"Sure," he said. "We do it all the time."

Then, before he looked at the damage, he decided to take 63553 out of service and transfer the freight. Odd, but so what?

My curiosity got the better of me and I watched as two day-laborers sweated the washers and dryers into another trailer. The yard boss stood inside 63553 and shouted orders.

"Are you the driver who did it? Hey, you! Careful with those!"

"Did what? I'm the driver who filed the red-tag."

I climbed into 63553 and stood beside him.

He said, "I don't see no destruction in here."

"There isn't any to see. The other box doesn't look too good, though."

"No. You could drive a truck through those holes. Why'd the shop call for a transfer? Hey! I told you to be careful!"

"Beats me. Judgment call, I guess."

"Weird."

No internal damage. A small, easily repaired puncture. Freight shifted to a trailer that looked like someone had used it for target practice. Weird.

Annie found us another load, one going to Portland.

"Looks like your last trip is right to our front door," I said to Gayle.

"Piece of cake," she said, and we laughed.

Beep: *Why haven't you reported your accident?*

No accident to report. Message sent to wrong truck?

Las Vegas, the following morning.

Beep: *Looks like they are trying to charge you for trailer damage and a transfer. Annie.*

Beep: *Trailer had structural damage and cargo was jeopardized. No report by you. Submit documentation on your behalf through driver manager. John Cadger, Claims Department.*

Beep: *Oh, no! John Cadger put your truck on the daily owner-operator accident report! Call me! Annie!*

"Annie, I have not had an accident. The yard boss and I inspected 63553 inside and out. There's no 'structural damage.' Who's John Cadger?"

Beep: *Took photos of trailer. We'll get this farce corrected. Unbelievable . . . Don't worry too much. Will fight this. Annie.*

I called John Cadger.

"You poked a hole in one of our trailers," he said. "That puts a preventable accident on your record. I will add to your file that you failed to report it and attempted to conceal the damage. We could have lost the entire load! I'm going to charge you $1,500 for repairs and the transfer. We have to recover our losses."

"Whoa, John. There haven't been any losses. There hasn't been an accident. You aren't going to charge me for anything. You're going to keep your hands off my driving record."

"You picked up that trailer in Mexico and gouged a hole in it between Laredo and Phoenix. I don't know where, but I'll find out."

"John, are you aware that we don't pick up trailers across the border?"

"You didn't even care enough to inspect the trailer or file a report! If we can't recover from the Mexicans we have to recover from you."

"Think. The hole is old. There's mud and rust around the edges. How could rust develop in 45 hours? That's how long I had the trailer. By the way, we don't report old damage. It's company policy."

"*I* know policy! *You* just drive! You tried to conceal your damage!"

"It's not *my* damage!"

"You failed to report an accident!"

"There was no accident to report!"

We went on and on, louder and angrier. John said I was negligent. Inattentive. A liar. I called him an idiot, a jackass, and a coward, then a jackass once more because he didn't like hearing it the first time, and an idiot twice more because he didn't like that either. I was in high gear for someone who doesn't like to argue, yell, and trade insults.

I said, "What about the pretrip inspection in my log book? I'm looking right at it. You want me to read it to you?"

"You snuck that in after the trailer was red-tagged by the shop! We're talking about new damage."

"What about the rust?"

"Rust doesn't mean a thing! You owe us $1,500."

"No, I don't. I'm coming to Phoenix."

"Are you threatening me?"

"I am coming to Phoenix. We'll talk."

"First the body shop," Gayle said. "Now this. Annie's right. It *is* unbelievable. Why do you stay with these people?"

She knew the answer. We were two years into a three-year lease without a reasonable way out. Financial reality aside, I still loved driving, I wasn't ready to quit, and I had a record to be proud of. John Cadger wasn't going to change any of that.

Beep: *Marc—please call me. Annie.*

"Damnit," she said. "You shouldn't have called him. John doesn't like drivers and he doesn't like to talk to them. He'll be weeks getting over it."

"This isn't about him."

"John thinks it is. He's in shock. He's a mean little guy, and you didn't roll over like he expected. Ha! I could have told him that! Anyway, we can't talk to him unless he's in a good mood, and even then it's almost impossible. We've had a lot of trouble with John, but don't worry, we believe you and we know he's wrong. We've got the photographs as proof, so just send me your documentation. This kind of injustice goes on around here all the time. People have left the company over John's stuff because there are no appeals from his decisions."

"And it all comes from the top, right?"

"Straight on down, every bit of it."

So. John Cadger had played this game before. Hanging judge, revenue officer, and surrogate bully for The Big Guy, he beat up drivers for a living. People rolled over, they quit, and you couldn't talk to the man unless you caught him on a good day. Now his feelings were hurt and the issue was no longer a hole in a trailer, but his quick trip from confident accusations to a bruised ego.

When we left Reno early the next morning, Gayle said, "I'm sad *and* angry." I felt the same way, but I trotted out my best Humphrey Bogart imitation to cheer her up. "Look on the bright side, sweetheart. It's a beautiful day for a ride in the country, you've taken your last truck-stop shower, and you'll be home tonight, see?" It fell flat.

We didn't laugh on Gayle's final day in the truck. We didn't sum up her time out there. We didn't remind each other of the people and places we'd seen, or the good times. We didn't talk about when—or if—I'd get off the road. We talked, instead, about

John Cadger, his announced intention to steal $1,500 from us ("For nothing," Gayle kept saying. "For *nothing*."), and his threat to smear my driving record.

She said, "Trucking isn't difficult. Why do they make it so hard?"

"It'll be okay," I said. "I'm going to Phoenix. I'll clear this up."

I wanted to kick John Cadger's ass.

I mailed my notes to Annie and waited a few days before calling her.

"I'm sorry," she said. "I'm no longer in the picture. I can't even talk to you about it. You have to get with Jeff, the new owner-operator liaison."

"I've got to wait two or three weeks for John to calm down," Jeff said, "but he's the company's ultimate authority on trailer damage. You should talk to The Director."

Peter said, "Be patient. These things take six or seven months."

"You don't have six or seven months. I want a meeting with you and John Cadger. In your office. As soon as I can get to Phoenix. And no more funny business."

Chapter Nineteen

Nearly every crisis seems to be the worst one,
but after it's over it isn't so bad.
HARRY TRUMAN

I stayed home for two weeks, looking forward to more seat time, worried that the coming separation would be difficult for Gayle because I couldn't decide between life out there and life with her. One thing was certain: I wouldn't sign a third lease at Linehaul. The place was a minefield and I'd just have to pick my way through it for another year. I'd turn the truck in at the Phoenix terminal by mid-April, 2001 and walk away. After that, who knew?

I packed my bags on our last morning together and Gayle drove me to the Troutdale yard. She handed up the duffles, climbed in after them, and sat on the edge of the passenger seat looking around the cab. Then she stared out the window while I stowed clothing, gear, and supplies. Once everything was in place I fine-tuned the driver's seat and started the engine. I said, as much to her as to myself, "It's time, kid." She held me close. "Come back to me, husband. I'll miss you."

And I would miss her, now that I'd learned to share the truck. But I still longed for solitude, thought about it night and day, and wasn't sure I'd be willing to give it up again.

Twelve months and counting, as far as Linehaul was concerned.

Four solo seasons out there.

Maybe 120,000 hub miles.

First, I would go to Phoenix and teach John Cadger a lesson.

There was, every Oregon dispatcher insisted, no freight headed south.

Annie said, "I'm not supposed to tell you this, but they won't help you with a load to Phoenix. Peter's scared. He knows you're ticked off and he doesn't want you in the same room with John. You'll have to get down here on your own."

If that's what I had to do . . . But I wasn't driving to Phoenix on my own nickel. Paid miles would get me there one way or another.

My first load took me to Colorado. I stayed at the Denver yard for a day and saw what I'd been seeing since I'd started driving: rust on trailers, holes in trailers, trailers that had been taped, puttied, and patched, and loaded trailers that should have been inspected, red-tagged, and repaired before they were sent to customers. I saw enough damage and blame to keep John Cadger busy for years. I photographed all of it.

There was, the Colorado dispatchers said, no freight to Arizona.

I took a load to Southern California, conned a rookie dispatcher into a next-day Phoenix delivery, and called Peter.

"It's time for our meeting. Nothing to worry about."

He said, "Give me your word on that and I'll set it up."

In Phoenix.

Beep: *Fleet Safety Message . . . pretrip protects you from having to pay for old trailer damage caused by someone else's poor judgment or bad driving.*

There it was: extortion, straight from the top. What's yours is mine.

Beep: *Call fleet manager re: your accident. Safety Department.*

If John Cadger's trumped-up accusation was now officially an accident, he had that much farther to back down. Tomorrow, the mean little guy who didn't like to talk to drivers would talk to me. I had some things I wanted to show him.

I went to the owner-operator division and asked to see my personnel file, because you never know. The clerk at the window asked a secretary, "Do they get to see their files?"

"*They* are not allowed in the vault."

I said, "Get Tom, will you?"

Tom, the division's second-in-command, said, "Oh, yes. We encourage our drivers to look at their files."

That was a lie. Linehaul drivers had never been encouraged to look at their personnel files. A peek at the file was my own idea. I needed to know if John Cadger had slipped an accident report into it.

Tom stepped out of the vault. "I can't seem to find your file. Maybe some other time?"

I said, "Let's ask The Director."

Tom shook his head. He opened the steel door that shielded office workers, dispatchers, and fleet managers from drivers, and I passed through a metal detector into the division's small city of cubicles. Tom reached toward a shelf just inside the vault entrance. He grabbed a thick folder, dropped it on a desk, and walked off. I began to read. *Driver threatened security guard. Driver ran trailer over customer's fence. Driver hit car in parking lot and left scene. Driver insulted dock personnel. Driver drove over stop sign. Driver hit truck in rest area. Driver service failure. Insubordination. Load refusal.*

Nine negative reports.

Nine negative reports for nine different drivers.

I handed them to the division's file clerk and said, "These were in my folder. They're not about me." She shrugged. A small radio played softly on her desk. She hummed along. She said, "It's just paper."

John Cadger hadn't placed anything in my file. Yet.

The next day.

Steel door again. Metal detector again. Security guard. The Director, safely behind his desk, talking with Jeff. John Cadger, sitting in a straight-back chair staring at his knees. He was short. Thin. A little guy. Colorless and stiff, he might have been cut from sheetrock. He didn't look mean. He looked scared.

"I told you I would come to Phoenix," I said, and slapped my Denver photographs onto his lap. "Look at these. Look at them, John. You'll never know who, when, or where. Look. Rust. *Surface* rust. It isn't new. Do we have to debate the meaning of rust?"

John Cadger didn't move or say a word. The Director glanced at the security guard.

"It's okay, Peter," I said. "Really."

He pointed to a chair, waited until I sat down, and began our meeting. "We haven't always gotten along, John. We're all here to work together, aren't we? We need to communicate better."

If John Cadger heard, if he was even listening, I couldn't tell. Thumbing through the photographs, he spoke of policy and procedure, an epidemic of unreported trailer damage, his need to make an example of a driver, and recovery, recovery, recovery. The Director brought up my driving history and my years with the company and the division. He and I went back to the early days, he said.

"Many of our guys don't bother with the rules. Marc does things by the book and you slap him. That's not right."

"I intend to charge him for repairs and the transfer," John said and returned to the photos, but he looked up when I said that my wife and I, speaking as Linehaul stockholders, were angered by his waste of company time and resources. "Gayle is worried sick over this. She was with me. If I had damaged 63553 she would have known." I thought, Say anything about her, you little toad, anything at all, and I'll get to you before that security guard gets to me. "As a driver, I don't appreciate pulling short miles to come here and deal with you—that's money out of my pocket. And I'm not happy about your sneak attack on my driving record. We're going to fix that before I leave today."

John Cadger sat quiet and still, an unrepentant schoolboy.

"We'll never know what hit 63553," I said. "The only evidence we have—rust—says the hole was there before I was. Does anyone in this room think I'm going to shell out for old damage or an unnecessary transfer?"

"We recover from the Mexicans or we recover from you," John said.

"That's crazy. I'm the man who red-tagged the trailer, not the one who punched a hole in it, and you're the only guy around here who doesn't get it. You can't make rust in 45 hours."

I handed out copies of John's accident report. "This shows an accident at 8 a.m. I didn't get under the trailer until mid-afternoon."

John Cadger leaned forward. "I want to know who gave you that!"

I said, "You falsified an accident report. Should we discuss it with The Big Guy?"

"Well, the trailer was all smashed up inside!"

"No, it wasn't. I walked around in there with the yard boss during the transfer. And if it had been damaged, what would that have to do with me? I hooked a sealed trailer in Laredo, Texas, *USA*, remember?"

I flashed a photograph of a Qualcomm message. *Structural*

damage . . . Cargo jeopardized. "Did you even look at 63553 before you sent that, John?"

"The hole was six feet long!"

"The hole was six *inches* long—I measured it. Do we have the photos taken at the shop?"

Jeff cleared his throat and said, "Our photographs seem to have gone south."

I said, "South . . . Alright, that's enough. It comes down to policy and rust. If there's rust, drivers don't call."

John Cadger stood up. "Who told you that? You are to call me or send me a message!"

"Wrong. Listen to this. 'You must call the Safety Department to report any damage. If you feel the damage is old, if it has rust on it, you do not have to call.' That's right out of our latest operations handbook. I made a copy of the page for you."

John Cadger bit his lip and sank back onto the chair a smaller little guy.

"We'll change it to a preventable incident," Jeff said. "No money."

"*Incident?* What incident? Nothing happened on my end and nothing, absolutely nothing, goes in my file. Ever. I should be driving, not sitting here telling you that."

The Director nodded. "You're right. I'll take care of it."

"I know you did it," said the company's ultimate authority on trailer damage.

I said, "Rust and policy, John. Keep the photos."

And keep away from me.

"I heard you did good," Annie said.

"Let's just say that John Cadger stepped on a rusty nail. Got freight?"

"Ten-four, Rusty. Where do you want to go?"

Where did I want to go? Away from Phoenix. Away from funny business.

—⁊⁊⁊—

At a shipper in Fort Worth.

I said, "I'm here for a load of golf carts. Goes to Scottsdale, AZ."

The foreman said, "Back in and my loader will put five new ones in your old box."

The loader drove the first vehicle into the trailer, grinned, and said, "*Four* wheels—count 'em yourself, driver, don't take my word for it—on *two* axles, one in front and one *in your rear*. You can place *your* butt on *our* seat for just pennies a day. And please allow me to point out the futuristic design of our bright and shiny thermoplastic body panels *and* fenders."

Workers braced the front axles with scrapwood blocks nailed loosely to the trailer floor. The blocks didn't look like they would hold. The first stretch of bad road was sure to shake them loose and, free to move, the carts would grind against each other, reducing the shiny thermoplastic fenders to worthless powder. There had to be a better way, one that didn't invite a cargo claim.

"Don't worry about it," said the loader.

I worried about it, took photographs of the carts and the

bracing and wrote "shipper load, count, and brace" on the bill
of lading. The dock manager signed, accepting all responsibility.

And I worried all the way to Big Spring—265 miles west of
Fort Worth—where I stopped for the night. I grabbed my flashlight and a camera and opened the trailer doors. Three carts had
jumped their chocks and were braced only by each other. Fenders scraped against fenders, sifting plastic dust onto the floor.

In the morning, Linehaul authorized payment for wood,
nails, and labor. A truck-stop mechanic and I separated the vehicles, built new braces, and braced every wheel. I took more
photographs, thinking ahead to the rough sections of I-10 east
of El Paso.

The new braces held. The consignee said, "These are the best
I've ever seen. Who built them?" He accepted his freight and
my explanation for the damage. "Don't worry about it," he said.
"This happens once in awhile."

Linehaul charged me $101.60 for the mechanic's services.
The claims department said that owner-operators had to pay for
their own repairs, refused my requests for reimbursement, and
told me to take it to The Director, who dallied for three months
then fabricated 297 deadhead miles, $185.62. I kept the change.

Linehaul's yard near Inver Grove Heights, MN.

Here we go again, I thought. Here's another unscaled heavy
load and they've asked me to run with it. I called the regional
planner and said, "This should have been scaled at the shipper in

Green Bay. That's in Wisconsin. We can't legal it now."

"I want you to take it anyway. I'll pay for any scale tickets."

"Send me a Qualcomm message that says that."

"Oh, you know I can't. I said I'd cover your tickets, didn't I?"

"Whose driving record will they be on?"

"I want you to take this load."

"It'll have to cross scales in Minnesota, Iowa, Nebraska, Colorado, New Mexico, and Arizona. Any one of them could shut me down. The fines will be more than the company earns on the freight."

"That's the company's business, not yours. You can go around."

"My driving record is my business. I'm not going around scales for you."

"I'll write you up."

I didn't have to mention the owner-operator contract. I played his voice back on my dispatch buster. "You can go around."

I said, "Recognize anyone?"

"I won't forget this."

"Neither will I. My memory's longer than yours."

I went back to the vault in Phoenix to see if John Cadger had swept any dirt into my file. A secretary said, "Talk to Jim Barnes. He handles driver files now."

Jim Barnes met me at the steel door and escorted me to his desk. "We moved the files upstairs for security reasons—too many nosy people poking around in them. I'll have to take the elevator. Sit here. *Stay* here. Give me 10 minutes."

Jim brought my file and said, "Don't take too long."

Inside the folder I found, this time, an old commendation for an illegal delivery, two printouts—one that reported a load refusal, another complaining that I had turned down a long deadhead—and a penciled note: "Customer called. Driver is on drugs."

I said, "Look at this, Jim. No one ever told me about this."

—⁓—

Friday, March 10, 1995.

A Fontana dispatcher said, "There's not much freight today. Oh. Here's a good one. Picks up at Shannon Transport in Pico Rivera. The appointment's for 6 p.m. You'll need a set." The load went to Spokane for Monday and paid 1,200 miles, not a bad weekend trip when freight was slow.

I arrived at 5:30, broke my set down, and backed both pups in for loading.

"You Linehaul boys are usually late for these runs," the owner said. "It's about time one of you showed up early." He pointed to a James Dean look-alike. "That's my son, a Marlboro Man just like his dad. He'll load you personally and seal the trailers. Leave everything to him. It should take about an hour."

I walked into the warehouse at 11:30. One trailer stood empty. The other was loaded front-to-back with palletized cases of swimming pool shocker, enough chlorine for all the pools in southern California. Each case bore a yellow, diamond-shaped label: *Oxidizer 5.1.* I counted the pallets and calculated the weight, checked my Hazardous Materials Compliance Handbook, peeked over the forklift operator's shoulder at the manifest, and asked Marlboro Man, Jr. about his freight. He stubbed out a cigarette, quickly lit another, and said, "It's not hazardous materials."

"Yeah, it is. Placard weight for Class 5 is 1,001 pounds. You have 12,000 and you're not done loading. We need placards. We need shipping papers that show hazardous materials classes, quantities, identification numbers, and emergency response information. Your paperwork doesn't even come close to what's required by law."

"What is all that supposed to mean?"

"Without placards and the proper shipping papers this load can't leave the dock."

"You're on drugs."

"Let's start again. By law, the shipper notifies the carrier in advance of a hazardous materials shipment and issues placards and documents."

"We don't do that legal shit here. Get your own placards."

"And you're smoking. That's prohibited when loading or unloading oxidizer. Would you like to see the hazmat handbook?"

The young Marlboro Man pointed a gun-like finger at my chest. "For the record, dude, my father *owns* this dock and I smoke here if I want to. You're on drugs. Your other driver had the same problem. We called your company."

I made the call for him.

Our local dispatcher said, "It doesn't show as hazmat. 'Pick-up by appointment only. Cannot deliver late.' That's all it says."

I called the Linehaul safety department in Phoenix. For the record.

"It's up to you," said the leader of the after-hours safety team. "Do what you think is best."

"They do this all the time," whispered the forklift operator, and I went out to my truck for a camera and my dispatch buster. Marlboro Man, Jr. followed me, a cigarette dangling from his lips.

"Hook up," he said. "We're almost done."

"I won't touch a thing until you supply placards and legal paperwork."

"Drugs. You *must* be on drugs. Okay, okay, I'll get you some placards. There's a truck stop around here somewhere."

The nearest truck stops were 30 miles away.

He jumped into his Camaro, peeled out, came back in 15 minutes, and pulled up next to my tractor.

"They're closed," he said. "You'll have to do it."

"I'm not going to violate the law for you. I thought I made that clear."

He tried to stare me down from the seat of his car. "Hook up."

"Look, we can't do this. The law . . ."

"Fuck the law! I told you to hook up!" He started to get out, fast, face contorted, fists clenched. As his feet touched the ground, I caught the car door by reflex and leaned on it.

"Hey," he said. "Hey! My leg! That hurts!"

"Are you going to hit me?"

"That hurts!"

"Are you going to hit me?"

I bounced the door against his leg.

"No! Hey! That hurts!"

"No placards, no papers, no trucking. Do you understand now?"

His shaking hands ripped the filter off a cigarette.

"You're on drugs! I'm calling your company!"

I phoned Linehaul, left the trailers at Shannon's dock, and bobtailed to the yard. Net income for the day, less than zero. I hooked the only available load and my 1,200-mile weekend became 387 paid miles over three days. I slept more than I drove.

Check-call, Monday morning.

"I've got a note here says you're on drugs," Peter said. "What's going on?"

I told him.

He said, "I'll take care of it."

On drugs? I phoned the California Highway Patrol and said, "Talk to the forklift operator." The CHP did. They also talked to Marlboro Man, Jr. and Marlboro Man, Sr. Then they audited Shannon's business records and learned that the company had been shipping hazardous materials—without placards or paperwork—for years. The fines, an officer told me, were substantial.

I'll never know how many Linehaul drivers were pressured

into pulling Shannon's freight. If I hadn't seen the cargo—if the trailers had been sealed—I would have hauled un-placarded and undocumented dangerous goods through three states. Emergency personnel responding to an accident or spill wouldn't have known they were dealing with the potential hazards of fire, explosion, inhalation, or skin contact, because the Marlboro men didn't do legal shit. It never occurred to me that a dispatcher's unofficial memo would officially sum up the affair and come to rest in my personnel file.

"'On drugs' is serious," Jim Barnes said. "That little piece of paper can keep you from getting another job. Your fleet manager is supposed to give you a chance to rebut negative reports in writing—it's always been company policy. Who was it?"

"Peter. Before he made Director."

Jim Barnes shrank inside his starched shirt. "I wouldn't touch it with a 10-foot pole."

There was still nothing from John Cadger in my file.

Nine months and counting.

—ᴍ—

August and September.

Slow freight and just 17,130 paid miles. Home for a few days, eager to get back on the road, conflicted as always. Not good. Not good at all.

But then came October and thirty-one days on the road. Easy freight, easy weather, 13,358 paid miles, hardly any deadhead. Good runs and good money. Driving, just driving, as free out there as I was ever going to be.

—∾—

In the check-out line at Sapp's truck stop, Sidney, NE.

Behind me, a familiar voice said, "Snickers and coffee. Great dinner, Marc."

I looked around. "Oh, jeez," I said. "They'll let anybody in here."

Eric Le Clare laughed and held up his own supper: two Hershey bars, an ice-cream sandwich, spearmint gum, a fried pie, coffee.

"Pie and gum for dessert," he said. "Just like always."

We sat in his cab eating, drinking our coffee, catching up on the miles and the years. Eric worked for a small Minnesota contract carrier, drove 3,200 paid miles each week on a dedicated loop, and owned his truck free and clear. He said, "I'm living in a no-payment paradise." He stopped by his house every weekend. He still loved the road. He'd remarried.

"Her father and brothers all drive and she used to. It's made things easier on the home front."

I said, "'Home front.' That's one way to put it," and told him about my own opt-in, opt-out battleground.

He said, "It's rough, I know. You'll have to choose. Local? I might go local in a year or two. Home every night might not be so bad. Never thought I'd say such a thing. It *would* take some getting used to . . . Hey, million-mile man, you're an owner-operator now."

"*Lease* operator. 'Hey' yourself, mister. You disappeared. No word from you, nothing. I thought you died. I expected to see you with the deer and elk at Cabella's, stuffed."

"Had to get away from Linehaul and training. Needed some peace and quiet after the divorce. Got into a spat with The Big Guy. He couldn't care less about his drivers, as you know. I told him to pack sand."

"It's good to see you."

"Same here. Headed east?"

"West."

"Too bad. We could have run together. Picked a channel and gabbed all night."

"I'd have liked that."

—⚟—

At a warehouse in Ft. Lauderdale.

I hooked a preloaded trailer then donated 25 minutes to document rust and old damage. A Linehaul owner-operator backed under a nearby trailer, looked at my door, and caught me looking at his: *Ruben Escalante, Miami.*

"I'm going to Jacksonville," he said. "And you?"

"Little Rock."

"Got a few minutes?"

We parked our trucks on a side street and talked about the company.

"I commit to them, they should commit to me," Ruben said. "When freight slows down, company trucks keep moving. Owner-operators sit. And the way they treat us! You know Dominic at Fontana? That's a rude little man. I told him once, 'Don't talk to me that way. I'm old enough to be your father.' Just because I speak with an accent they think I don't know anything. I take every load and I still don't get the miles they promised." He was looking for another carrier. "One that keeps their word. What about you?"

"I'm running out the clock on my lease. Six months, then I'll be gone. My wife wants me to get off the road."

"Mine too. But I don't know."

"Neither do I."

"I watched you pretrip—there's a lot wrong with your trailer. I had one like that, holes and rust, you could see it was all old, but they said I did it. They came after me for $2,900."

"What did you do?"

"I got a lawyer and they backed down. You have to stand up to them or they walk all over you. They've got a little *gusano* in the office who goes after drivers, that's all he does. He lies. He has no honor. He'll say anything to stick you. John Cadger. Ever heard of him?"

—∞—

The first load in my November log book was cardboard boxes from a paper mill in Longview, WA to a vegetable packing shed in Santa Maria, CA, 927 paid miles, Friday afternoon to Monday morning. It came with the standard West Coast problem, one day too many for the miles. I spent most of Sunday at a

Santa Maria truck stop, reading.

Monday morning. Empty.

Beep: *Deadhead to East Los Angeles for a midnight pick-up. It goes to Portland, OR for Wednesday. It's a drop.*

Annie said, "There's nothing else. I don't know when we'll get you out of there if you don't take it."

I took it to keep moving. I took it for the drive down the coast and the views of the Pacific Ocean past Santa Barbara and Malibu. I took it because there was nothing else. When I dropped in Portland, I'd have racked up less than 2,000 paid miles for the first eight days of the month. I wasn't even running for payments. Five-and-a-half months and counting.

I went back to look at my file again. Jim Barnes said that I'd already looked at it once, wasn't that enough? That he had stacks of folders on his desk and a lot of work to do. That he'd have to stop and go upstairs to Personnel.

I said, "Come on, Jim. You won't have to *walk*. There's an elevator."

He came back fifteen minutes later. "They're busy."

Jim talked about himself for awhile then he said, "I'll try once more." He was smiling when he stepped off the elevator. "Your file is missing. Could be weeks or months before it turns up. Weeks or months."

Fontana, December 21.

Beep: *Preplan. Swap out in Rialto, CA for Coos Bay, Tuala-*

tin, and McMinnville, OR, 1,142 paid miles.

And get home two days early for Christmas.

Lewiston, December 29.

Beep: *Preplan. Deliver in Chicago 01/02/01. Accept? Yes/No. Yes.*

Fargo, New Years Day.

Seventeen degrees below zero, the lowest temperature I have ever experienced. A driver at a truck stop said, "This ain't cold. I heard it's 32 below in Minot. Now *that's* cold."

Twenty minutes after I was empty in Chicago I had a preplan for Atlanta. I'd expected to sit for a day or two. And I thought I'd have to sit in Atlanta, but the Qualcomm beeped before I bumped the consignee's dock. *Deadhead to Corinth, MS, swap out, drop in Ogden, UT ASAP, 277 empty miles, 1,602 loaded miles.* I sat in Ogden for two days and two nights then hooked a 48-hour run to Phoenix. I heard, "That's all there is" from Salt Lake Dispatch, "We don't receive early!" from the consignee when I called to ask, and "We don't expect any freight for at least four days" from a Phoenix dispatcher when I was empty. Delivering early wouldn't have made any difference.

"There's *nothing* happening," Annie said. "This is the slowest I've ever seen it."

It stayed slow, slower than any January I could remember. I ran just 8,007 paid miles during the month, but I wasn't alone—the company's terminals were full of trucks that weren't moving and drivers who weren't making a dime.

Ten weeks and counting.

Denver, late on a Friday afternoon.

Annie said, "There's no freight."

I didn't believe her. Something told me to call local dispatch.

"'No freight'? We've got so much freight we don't know what to do. Where do you want to go?"

"East. As far east as you can get me."

"I have Elkton, VA for Monday. I grew up there and I'm here to tell you, John Denver had it right. You live-load tomorrow morning in Golden. Happy trails."

Sunday evening at the Elkton consignee.

I told the security guard I'd never been there before and asked if I could sleep on the property.

He said, "Yessir. All night and all day, if you like. Just park over where they is waitin' for loads, won't no one bother you. And if they does, that's what my shotgun is for."

I was awake at first light, drinking coffee, watching an off-duty sunrise from the passenger seat, fully taken by a peaceful countryside, shadowed mountains, and echoes of history.

Beep: *Hook an empty and deadhead to Sportsdrink, in Winchester. They'll load you . Drop at Sportsdrink in Norcross, GA tomorrow night, 70 empty miles, 559 loaded miles.*

From Winchester I drove south through the Shenandoah Valley, in awe once more and maybe for the last time at the day-lit beauty of the place. Almost heaven.

There was no freight in or near Atlanta. "Man," said a dispatcher, "there ain't no freight in the whole *world!*" I waited two days for a load then blitzed out to Nogales, AZ—drive, sleep, drive, sleep, drive—delivered a day early, and sat at a truck stop for 24 hours. "Freight's slow in the west," Annie said. "No one's having any fun."

From Nogales, she deadheaded me to Tucson. I took toys to Yuma, AZ, deadheaded to Calexico, CA, hauled a trailer full of taco shells from there to Vancouver, WA, and deadheaded to Lewiston, where I lobbied for another load to Chicago. But Lewiston only had freight for San Jose, CA, and the only freight out of San Jose was a 32-mile hop to Gilroy tied to a next-day delivery in San Jose—64 paid miles in 24 hours wasn't better than nothing. But San Jose got me to Oregon. I went back to Lewiston and back to the Bay Area and picked up a multi-drop load for Tacoma, Silverdale, and Sequim, WA. Not much driving, really. Not much at all.

I called Annie from Silverdale and said, "You know, girl, slow or not, there are 44 states east of California, Oregon, Washington, and Idaho. And what about Quebec or Alberta, eh?"

She laughed and said, "I'll see what I can do."

Sequim.

I parked, empty, in a corner of the consignee's lot and waited a day for my next load assignment. Slow freight was becoming a way of life.

Beep: *Deadhead 98 miles to Sumner, WA. Pick up in the morning for Greenfield, IN, 2,191 paid miles. Deliver ASAP. Enjoy. Annie.*

I felt the old long-haul magic, felt like I'd always felt when there was nothing but good miles and good weather ahead. Maybe freight would carry me east from Indiana, down to Florida, or up into Canada. I still wanted to see as much country as I could and to drive, just drive.

Three weeks and counting.

In Greenfield.

Beep: *Deadhead to Bloomington, IN—44 miles—and swap out for Olive Branch, MS.*

Annie said, "That's all there is."

Olive Branch wasn't far—just 411 loaded miles—and south by southwest wasn't the direction I'd had in mind, but why not? You never know.

I delivered the next day and sat for 20 hours. Then two pre-plans came in, a long one and a short one. The short one—cotton seed for farmers in the Mississippi delta—went just 138 miles, from Linehaul's Memphis yard to Stoneville, MS. After a 180-mile deadhead to Meridian, MS, the long one—paper towels—would take me to Grand Junction, CO, 1,439 paid miles away.

Beep: *Accept both? Yes / No.*

Of course.

I drove south out of Memphis, past the casinos on Highway

61 and down through the delta, listening to live gospel music on the radio. It was the real thing—sweet, sweaty, transcendent, with a message, a beat, and a rocking choir.

In Stoneville the next morning a Linehaul driver had trouble backing into the dock area, a wide, fully-lit space inside a warehouse. There was room to line up and back straight in, but he tried—several times—to back at an angle then correct at the last moment. Another driver sat on a bench outside, watching.

I said, "Trainee?"

"*I'm* the trainee. God help me."

Three days later in Grand Junction.

Beep: *Pick up in Fruita, CO. Deliver to a construction project—a dam—in northern Idaho. Good load!*

Well, construction projects are always interesting, but the load only paid 786 miles and wasn't due at the job site for four days. If somebody else wanted to drive less than 200 miles a day and call it a good load, that was his affair. I pulled the trailer to the Salt Lake City yard and asked to swap for a load east.

The dispatcher said, "How about Old Fort, OH for Monday morning? It's hot."

Sold.

A hot Ohio load would give me a 3,551-mile paycheck and more than cover my last truck payment.

Ten days and counting.

Chapter Twenty

What does a man need—really need?
STERLING HAYDEN, WANDERER

In Old Fort.

Beep: *There's not much freight. Deadhead to Defiance, IN and pick up for Muscatine, IA, 72 empty miles, 374 loaded miles. Deliver tomorrow.*

Not what I'd hoped for, but better than sitting still.

I called Annie and said, "It's time to pull the plug."

"Right. I'll start moving you more or less toward Phoenix. Come see me when you get down here. I have your million-mile awards."

Nothing like waiting until the last minute. Million-mile lettering had been on my doors for almost two years.

In Muscatine, I accepted the next preplan—office furniture to La Vergne, TN, just south of Nashville, 544 paid miles and a next-day delivery. Why not? Maybe there was freight in Tennessee. Maybe I could keep moving right up until the end.

A second preplan for a load from Nashville to Pennsylvania and the planner's promise of a flip to Denver, Phoenix, or the West Coast meant that I'd be going out the right and proper way: on a cross-country run. Think of it! Driving through Tennessee, into Virginia and up through the Shenandoah Valley to Pennsylvania, going east to go west, continental drifting, taking the long way home. (If I treasured the ride that much, why was I jumping off? Why was I hanging up my keys?)

Oh, the route west out of Pennsylvania to Denver! Cross the Ohio River at Wheeling. Roll through the Buckeye and the Hoosier—I preferred them dressed in fall colors, but they'd be fine now, they'd be perfect. Rumble along the ill-constructed, potholed excuses for Interstates in Illinois—as bad as anything Arkansas ever threw at travelers. Rubberneck over the Mississippi at St. Louis. Listen on the CB while drivers groused about The Show Me State's highways. Run Kansas at night just to do it. Then I'd be back in the arid west with the Rocky Mountains rising, rose-colored at dawn, from the plains.

Maybe I'd get lucky and hook a load from Denver to Los Angeles. Transit the Rockies again. Top Loveland Pass just for old time's sake. Stop in Grand Junction, gaze up at Colorado National Monument and the Uncompahgre Plateau and remember. Climb the San Rafael Swell. Descend the Virgin River canyon. Slip through Las Vegas at night, when it's bright as day. Sleep in Baker, CA under the world's tallest thermometer. By Barstow, the trip and my years at Linehaul would be over except for Southern California's smog and a grungy desert hop to Phoenix, but I'd have had one last fling. (Maybe I'd go *east* from Denver—it didn't all have to end so quickly, did it? Next week, the week after, or the week after that would be soon enough.)

I was a run junkie looking for his last big score and it didn't take much to set me up, just a good preplan. Ah, if only there could have been more of the long trips, trips where a few unpaid miles didn't matter, trips where you really made it up on volume, trips top to bottom or side to side, trips where the distance more than matched the money. I checked a newspaper weather map—apart from a chance of wind in Missouri, I'd be okay.

At the dock in La Vergne.

Beep: *Un-preplan.*

What the hell? I called Annie. There'd been a mistake, she said. The planner had shopped the load to another driver. He was already on his way to Pennsylvania.

Sucker-punched. Let down. Dash-pounding mad. I drove two miles to a truck stop on I-24, found the tightest parking place in the lot, and fought with it just to let off steam. Somebody keyed up.

"Mayfield, if you're good enough to get into that hole, why are you driving for a rookie mill like Linehaul?"

It was the driver parked next to me. I asked about her carrier. She asked about mine. I told her about Bruno, Peter, and Sam.

"If they did that to me," she said, "I'd kill somebody. They'd deserve it, too." She choked up and hugged her dog close. "I'd go crazy."

An alternate load paid 419 miles and went, Annie said, to Chicago for the next day. I'd heard "That's all there is" so many times I said it before she did. She wouldn't tell me the planner's name. Afraid I'd go crazy.

I accepted. Why not? Chicago was good for freight. From there, I'd take almost anything—New Jersey, Florida, Maine. I thought about asking for a load to Alaska. You never know.

In Chicago I waited, empty, for a preplan. When it came, I was boiling mad all over again. If I would make a local delivery in the morning—as a favor—they'd book me on a Phoenix load that picked up in the afternoon. I came close to telling them to shove it, that I was tired of Linehaul's favor game, that my time was worth more to me than straight mileage pay in a city, that I'd bobtail down to Phoenix on my own.

Annie said, "That's all there is."

I accepted both loads, going out on the indignity of a favor.

"Your appointment's at 8 a.m.," the Chicago dispatcher said. "They're jerks. Get through the gate half-an-hour early or they'll refuse the load."

I pulled up at the consignee's gate an hour before my appointment. I waited two hours for a door then four hours for the unload and the paperwork, the consignee another appointments-only distribution center where appointments didn't mean anything. Drivers were told to drop their trailers, bobtail half a block away, and wait with the CB on. Those who fell asleep in their trucks were out of luck—a sign above the receiving window said, "Truckers! Snooze and you lose! No wake up calls!"

The deadhead—to Chicago's south side—paid 41 miles.

I drove 48 hub miles along gridlocked highways, almost three hours of stop-and-go seat time logged as 45 minutes. I signed for my load, backed under a trailer, and began the trip to end all trips.

Will be in Phoenix Monday morning @8:30.

Annie knew I didn't mean 8:31.

Three days and counting.

One thousand, seven hundred and fifty-five miles to go.

Then what? Life on the road or life with Gayle?

I couldn't decide.

I didn't need a map for my last blitz. I'd cut my own grooves in the big and little roads between Chicago and Phoenix, and, blindfolded, I could find every on-ramp, truck stop, and secluded parking place along the way. My truckers' road atlas went into a duffel bag.

I turned south onto I-57 and waited to merge into slow-moving traffic. A truck driver said, "Come on over, Mayfield, join the herd of turtles."

I said, "Thanks, big truck. Getting out of town for the weekend?"

"No. Been here two days. I'm paid by the mile, I ain't made a cent, and I ain't never coming back. I've got The Windy City in my rear-view mirror."

"That's what *I* like to see," said another driver. "Chicago in my rear-view mirror."

I drove for five hours, pulled into a rest area, and fell onto the bunk, mad at myself, mad at the world, worn out. Three hours later I was awake with a pounding headache, up against the reasons to stay in trucking and the reasons to leave it behind.

Stay. Keep on seeing the country.

Get out. Be home every night. Be fully committed to marriage.

Stay. Revel in the pleasures of competence and solitude. Listen to my own wheels turning, all issues resolved, free at last.

Beep: *Won't you miss it? Annie.*

I'll miss the whole shebang.

I would. Ah, I surely always would. I'd lived many of my life's finest hours on the road and trucking had turned out to be my deliverance.

"Then stay out here," a voice said. "Don't go home. Call her from Albuquerque. The truck wins. The road wins. Give yourself to the only work you've ever loved. Go mobile, drive for 10 more years, and retire with a *two*-million mile award. What's one million? *Nothing.* You've run solo through most of your life anyway. Find another carrier and punch your own ticket."

Gayle had worried that I would not—could not—quit and she'd said that she loved me, she would understand, but it meant a divorce. She'd had enough of being married and living by herself. I'd be on my own if I stayed out there, without a home base or a lifeline—like many expatriate drivers I'd met—and I knew the Albuquerque truck stop where I'd call my soon-to-be ex-wife to tell her that I'd decided to live on the highway, I loved and hated trucking too much to give it up.

Saturday.

Two days and counting.

My last view through a windshield of the Gateway Arch (maybe). My last crossing of the Mississippi (maybe). My last run through Missouri (maybe, maybe not), cursing every miserable inch of I-44. I bought fuel in Joplin—184 gallons, enough to get to Phoenix. Maybe it was my last-ever diesel purchase, maybe it wasn't.

The truck stops in Sayre and Erick, OK were full. Wide awake, restless, and illegal again, I drove on to Amarillo, closing out an 814-mile day. I woke up early Sunday craving fresh pastry and hot coffee. Pick a truck stop, any truck stop, there's no shortage in Amarillo. I chose the new Williams.

I have never seen a travel plaza go down hill so fast. The lot stank of piss, the trash barrels and dumpsters overflowed, and you walked around pools of spilled diesel at the fuel islands. Inside, drivers waited in long lines to buy stale doughnuts and lukewarm coffee from cashiers less interested in customers than boy talk.

"When that guy's in town my horns are out."

"Like a horse, I heard."

"Umm. I couldn't believe it."

A driver said, "Do you two mind? I'd like to get out of here today."

The cashier who couldn't believe it sighed. She slid his change across the counter but didn't even look at him. She said, "There you go."

He said, "'There you go.' What happened to 'Thank you'?"

Then Amarillo, the first Texas town I'd ever seen, was in my rear-view mirror. I turned on the CB just to listen.

"Westbound, how's it look over your shoulder?"

"Haven't seen a thing since Okie City. It's a beautiful day in the neighborhood."

"Four. I ain't seen nothin' since Flag. They just rollin' you across at San Jon."

"Hey, what did the hooker say to the trucker's wife?"

I'll never know. They were out of range.

Seven hundred miles and counting.

I passed Santa Rosa, NM and its truck stops. The TA was old and dirty when I'd started driving, and Love's was new and dirty the day it opened for business, but there weren't as many flies competing for your food at the TA. On the north side of the Interstate, undeveloped parcels had always been used by truckers for overnight parking—red dust in summer, red mud in winter. I preferred the graveled lot directly across Route 66 from Denny's, where the coffee was liquid speed. Sipped carefully while it cooled, it gave you a jolt then a long, clean burn.

Five hundred miles and counting.

I thought back over every load, every trip, and every mile,

my life out there flashing before me. The first time I crossed Monument Pass, South Pass, Snoqualmie Pass. The first time I unloaded a trailer by myself. Ran The Bottom. Ran The Top. Saw the Blue Grass, the Blue Ridge, and the dry heart of the Dust Bowl. Chained up—atop Donner Pass. Pounded frozen brakes—in Missoula. Drove through New Mexico with Eric Le Clare and Robin Williams. First load to Canada. First solo trip across the country. Growing into competence and a new-found, middle-aged confidence. Early trips to Minnesota, Florida, Virginia, Maine, Tennessee, and Montana—all new to me then, all known to me now. People I met—the good, the bad, and the indifferent. Weather like I had never seen before: real winter, the damp heat of the southeast in high summer, and all-day, blow-your-truck-over wind on the great plains. The night I backed a trailer—no pull-ups, one clean sweep—to a tight Atlanta dock, jumped down from the cab, and bowed, laughing, to a group of drivers who offered a round of applause. The night a driver ahead of me hit two cows on I-40 and almost dropped a set of doubles in my lap. The first time I stayed out for five weeks—Sam was angry because I'd been gone so long, but he forgave me. Good dogs are like that. Rest in peace, Sammy.

Phone calls to my wife. "Don't worry." "You've got to see this." "I won't be home for another two or three weeks."

Phone calls to dispatchers and fleet managers. Dispatch busters. Irregular routes and all-nighters. My realization that the HOS regulations were unworkable. Unpaid miles, illegal dispatches, and Linehaul's lines: "Deliver on time," "Log it legal," and (my favorite), "Safety involves an attitude that is evidence by responsible, self-reliant, adult human beings."

The Treatment.

Gayle's first big trip in a big truck. "This is fun," she'd said. "I can see why you like it."

And her last. "Why do you stay with these people?"

Then I was dropping off the Sandia Mountains, down through Tijeras Canyon toward Albuquerque and the phone call that would turn Gayle's life upside down.

"Call her from Albuquerque," a voice said, "and she'll never speak to you again."

I couldn't bear it.

I passed the exit without taking my foot off the accelerator.

Four hundred miles and counting.

I rolled on through Gallup and into Arizona—my first trucking state and my last—past Holbrook, past Winslow, past Meteor Crater, past the San Francisco Peaks towering above the lights of Flagstaff. And past Little America, which serves the best truck-stop food on I-40. I turned south on I-17, watching one last time for elk before starting down Copper Canyon. I passed the truck escape ramp, where, years before, I'd seen an eighteen plow into the deep gravel.

I'd yelled, "Hey in there! Hey! You okay?"

"Yeah," the driver said. "You don't have to stop. Damn. I just . . . let it get away from me."

But that had been in full daylight. Now it was dark and I could only feel the hill, feel it pulling me down to Camp Verde, down and down to my last night under a load. I logged sleeper time but didn't sleep. I played every CD I had, played them loud, played some of them two or three times. My last all-nighter. My last sunrise on the road. An ache that wouldn't go away. Deal with it. But how?

I thought again of every experience out there and what I'd brought to trucking and what I'd picked up and discarded, and what I would carry with me all my days. I stared at my reflection in the last C-store window. Standing at my shoulder in the glass, but not—I turned to look—next to me, I saw the man who had climbed into a Volvo single-screw 10 years earlier and, next to him, the boy who desperately needed to learn how to fight.

Somewhere, the truck drivers who'd backed up on a San Francisco morning 44 years earlier were near the ends of their lives or at rest. They'd always been with me, but never more than during my years of driving. Don Emery, too, had steered me toward the road and I would never be able to thank him. I'd grabbed a gearshift or two like he'd said and I'd seen the country and now the party was over. The CD collection followed my road atlas into the duffel bag.

One hundred miles and counting.

One more slow climb and one more steep, descending grade. At the bottom of my last hill lay Phoenix and my last traffic jam in a big truck. Crush hour, good name for it. My roads didn't go on forever.

Compression.

Decompression.

Depression.

—⁂—

At the Phoenix terminal.

I drove forward into a parking space, unhooked, and pulled away from the trailer. My hands were shaking. I couldn't believe I was doing this to myself. *I couldn't believe it*. Isn't that what people always say? I'd had white-line fever and the cross-country blues for a decade and I didn't know what I'd do to replace them.

True to form, hub miles for the trip exceeded paid miles, and, true to form, I didn't log the trip the way I ran it, I logged it legal. Before sealing my trip envelope I filled in the next day's log (Phoenix to New York City, 2,494 miles, in 10 consecutive driving hours). I went to see Annie.

She said, "How do you feel about getting out? How do you *really* feel?"

"Glad to be going, sorry to be going, torn up."

I sat next to her desk while she unwrapped the award jacket, a blend of cowboy and biker styles. Black canvas. Fake leather collar. My name misspelled on the back. She opened a white gift box and, smiling, removed the award plaque. They'd spelled my name wrong on that too.

I had only asked for a plaque and a wallet card to document my safe driving and I'd said many times that I didn't want the jacket. I'd fought a running Qualcomm battle.

Beep: *What size?*

Beep: *Marc! What size?*

Beep: *You don't know what size jacket you wear?*

No.

I dropped the jacket behind a trash barrel. I kept the plaque and signed the wallet card, spelling my name correctly. All I had to do now was clean out the truck, endure the trade-prep inspection, settle my Linehaul account, and fly home. But I sat in the driver's seat for the rest of the day, unwilling to let go of the wheel, trying to answer the question I thought I'd answered: should I stay in trucking or put it behind me?

I called Gayle.

"Hi," she said. "Where are you? I miss you. When are you coming home?"

I swear, I heard Sam bark.

Tuesday morning.

I puttered in the cab then slipped into my trucker's overalls. I installed new fan belts, air filters, and windshield wipers, and replaced lamps and lens covers that didn't need to be replaced, small and simple tasks that helped take my mind off my situation. I made a point of filling the windshield washer bottle.

I drove through a truck wash. Paid two street people to spit-shine the wheels. Put the original radio back in the dash and sold the CD player to a mechanic. Placed a box of tools on a chair in a drivers' lounge, yelled, "Take what you want," and stepped back. I gave blankets and most of my clothing to a man who lived in the bushes between a truck stop and I-10. Tire chains, load locks, and the load lock holder went to one owner-operator, oil, flares, coolant, a fire extinguisher, and bags of light bulbs to another. I presented my CB and scanner to a teenager who cleaned the drivers' showers at Linehaul. "Scanner," he said. "Is that the one's got cops on it?"

Tuesday afternoon.

Sullen and suspicious, wearing pristine Linehaul t-shirts (*Been there! Hauled that!*), a rookie husband-wife team—trainer and trainee—hunched over a picnic table outside the driver center. She was unbelievably fat and barely able to move, and I tried to imagine her adjusting brakes under a trailer, fighting a frozen tandem, throwing freight, or raising her ponderous girth up to a truck cab. I couldn't guess how she'd passed her fitness test and CDL physical exam.

I heaved two bulging grocery sacks onto the table. "Here. It's all free."

The wife said, "What's this?"

"Tools. Binoculars. Maps. A spotlight. Hand cleaner. Duct tape and baling wire. You'll probably need the ice scrapers and the bungee cords someday. Wear the rubber gloves when you fuel—they'll keep diesel off your hands. Use the steel tape to measure king-pin settings."

"My trainer didn't teach that," the husband said. "Besides, we ain't moving. Been sitting here for two days. Where is all the high-mile team freight they promised?"

Tuesday night.

Stay or leave? Life was questions without answers. Unable to sleep, I walked the yard.

I watched a rookie back under a trailer. He didn't tug against the king pin to make sure the fifth wheel was locked, but it held. Beginner's luck. In a few minutes he'd join the stream of heavy traffic on I-10. His first night out there. My last.

Wednesday.

I tossed my duffel bags into a rental car, parked 22247 in front of the prep shop, lay plastic sheeting over the floor, and covered the seats one last time. As they had done with 21127—as they did with all lease turn-ins—mechanics would examine the truck in PDI-like detail. Once again, Allen Dobbs and I would discuss findings and money.

They backed 22247 out of the shop and left me alone with the truck. The seats and sleeper carpet were still covered and unsoiled, but someone had managed to leave grease on the pedals. I wiped them clean, pulled the plastic from the floor and the captain's chairs and sat for awhile where I belonged—in the driver's seat. The interior was spotless—as always—but I gave it one final touch-up with a dust cloth just to have something to do. Nothing of ours remained inside, nothing said that Gayle and I had ever been there. The interior looked new—except for a few nicks on the dash left by a careless Linehaul mechanic—and the odometer readout was well within Freightliner's mileage guidelines for trade-ins; 22247 would be the first one off a dealer's lot.

Beep: *Marc, are you in the truck? I have your numbers — Allen.*

I looked around the cab and sleeper, now bare and impersonal as a motel room. Tomorrow, shop workers would peel off our decals, reducing Mayfield Transportation to memories and the truck to just another metallic-blue Century Class tractor. If I ever saw it again, I wouldn't know I was looking at the tractor with 890896 stamped on the VIN tag. I stepped down, clicked the driver's door shut, ran a hand along a waxed fender, and walked away without the nerve to look back.

In Allen's office, a cluttered cubicle tucked into a corner at the owner-operator division.

He said, "Here's the word from the prep shop."

Replace water pump. Replace passenger-side windshield. Repair oil leak at diamond seal. Replace driver's-side fog lamp. Replace right-rear wheel seal. Repair leak at transmission-speed sensor housing. Replace oil filler-tube hose. Replace oil pan gasket. Repair worn passenger-side door hinge. Repair chipped paint. Remove decals. Fill windshield washer bottle.

The mechanics didn't notice the pitted driver's side windshield, an air leak, a sidebox door lock that had never worked, and a missing bunk safety harness, but they estimated the trade-prep charges—parts and labor, including a $1,000 credit for tires—at $2,937. I questioned some of the called-for repairs.

"Come on," Allen said. "You'd replace the water pump anyway."

"Not if it wasn't leaking."

"It *might* leak."

"It isn't leaking *today*. What's this? $11.25 to fill the windshield washer bottle? I just filled it."

He knocked $587 off the prep fees and said, "That will bring it down to $2,350, and I'm going to do you a favor—I won't bill you for the single-state registration."

As a rule, owner-operators and lease operators who left Linehaul before the end of a calendar year were charged the full annual tractor registration—$1,500, less a percentage of "recovery." (*Recovery.* Where had I heard that before?)

I mentioned John Cadger's sideshow.

"We all heard about that," Allen said. "Pathetic."

He turned to his computer, searched for accident reports linked to 22247, and brought up four. "Save these," he said, handing me copies. "They're marked 'closed.' They have a way of opening after a driver leaves. Now we need to talk about more numbers. You haven't put many miles on your truck."

"Not as many as I wanted to. There's 382,237 on the hub. That's 127,000 each year for three years, 10,611 in an average month, 2,652 in an average week—not all paid miles, of course."

"You always did know your facts and figures. Many drivers . . . ah, you wouldn't believe it."

"I'm curious. What does The Big Guy make off of us on the truck deals? Not hauling freight, just on the leases."

"Trucklease and Linehaul each make $2,500 on the truck."

"Each?"

"Each."

My work and two trucks had cost The Big Guy exactly nothing.

"Here's your total equity," Allen said. "$6,416."

"It should be an honest $10,000 and you know it. But even so, you're short—$10,000 minus $2,350 is $7,650, not $6,416."

"Well, used truck values are down. That drops your equity. It doesn't leave much."

Well, Freightliner's buyback price, $45,266, was right there on Allen's paperwork. I tapped it with my pen.

He said, "That price was worked out long before you signed your lease and before the market went into the tank."

"Right. Freightliner has to honor it. A slump in the used truck market doesn't affect The Big Guy. He's not losing anything. Where's the lower value?"

"Be glad it's as much as it is. He doesn't think he has to give any of it back."

What's yours is mine. If that wasn't theft, what could you call it?

"You know," Allen said. "There are people here who don't like you."

What was this, high school? I had been conscientious, friendly, cooperative, and—most important in trucking—safe and reliable. I kept my likes and dislikes to myself. I wasn't argumentative or demanding and I rarely turned down freight. I asked for miles. I helped out. Fleet managers said that I worked without attitude and a Linehaul regional vice-president had once remarked that he could only hope for more drivers like me.

"They say you don't work as hard as some guys."

I worked when there was work and I sat when there weren't any loads. What else was there to do? You could only keep loaded and rolling when your carrier booked freight. I thought of loads that would have delivered late if I'd been a slacker, if I'd slept, or if I'd run legal. What about the barely-break-even trips, the favors, unpaid dock delays, and unpaid miles? Hard work, some of it. I had gone farther than any Linehaul driver they could name, staying 10 years where most drivers bailed after a month or two. My safe driving contributed to the bottom line and you wouldn't find a single service failure in my file, but that wasn't good enough.

"You stood up to them. They don't like that."

I said 'no' when 'no' was the only thing to say.

"You march to a different drummer."

What of it? The owner-operator division's sales pitch was geared to different drummers. *Be your own boss. Control your own destiny as an independent contractor. Choose when you want to drive. No forced dispatch.* Lies and half-truths; the company had little use for *independent* contractors.

I handed two of my truck keys to Allen. He tagged them with my truck number and tossed them into a box that held key sets for more than a hundred tractors, bones in a boxed bone yard, keys to many highways, keys to so many highway stories you could never tell them all. I kept one key and one Freightliner fob.

Then, suddenly, I don't know why, I didn't care about the discounted refund—The Big Guy's last ambush—or any of the rest of it. Life after Linehaul was just a few minutes away. I signed my release papers and stopped by The Director's office.

I put out my hand and said, "Well, Peter French, I'm done."

No handshake. No goodbye and good luck. He didn't ask if I liked the jacket and I didn't trust myself to say anything about Sam. No sense knocking out a man's teeth at this late date.

This is how it ends, I thought. I've been cheated. I'm leaving angry, like so many others. I'd like to hit someone. I slammed the rental car door and drove away from the company that had been the center of my universe for one-fifth of my life.

I hung around Phoenix for two more days, unable to focus. I could still change my mind, tell Gayle I wasn't coming home, then ride out the storm. I stared at the ceiling of my motel room, tried to pull my feelings together, and paged through the accident reports Allen had given me.

December 2, 1998.

Laredo. Javier Garcia. A non-preventable accident and a Linehaul cargo claim, both news to me.

September 24, 1999.

Three days after I hooked a damaged trailer in Houston and sent photographs to Claims, John Cadger moved to strip $150 from my performance bond. He never said a word. Two weeks later he cancelled the charge and responsibility was assigned to "Dummy Driver."

January 28, 2000.

Recv'd msg from 22247 that he found damage on T55886. Dummy Driver again.

March 28, 2000.

John Cadger's rusty hole was written up as "prior damage," but my name remained as the responsible driver. The final report showed a preventable incident six hours before I first saw the trailer in Laredo. Under "Photos? Y / N," John Cadger had entered an "N," violating, not for the first time and probably not for the last, a company rule against making false statements in written reports.

I'll take care of it.

And The Big Guy? He and I had been cogs in each other's wheels, lessor and lessee, lessee and lessor, and he had put a hand in my pocket and taken $1,234. Drivers gave him a security deposit and he didn't think he had to give any of it back. He should have disclosed that greedy little detail up front.

When a man with money meets a man with experience, the man with the experience ends up with the money and the man with the money ends up with the experience. I laughed the first time I heard that. Now I didn't think it was funny.

I sat in the Phoenix airport, waiting for the flight to Portland and home.

Home.

Where the heart is—as good a definition as I've found. Home, where I would go to sleep and wake up in the same town every night. Home, immobile home.

The plane was half-full, a real LTL flight. We took our seats and waited for half an hour without explanation before rolling, just like real truck drivers.

I like to watch the ground fall away when a plane climbs, but I closed my eyes and followed The Bottom once more, all the way east to Jacksonville, FL. Then my thoughts carried me up I-95 and west on I-80, and I remembered all the Interstates that intersect *it* and I followed each of them north and south and then all the roads *they* meet, and I could hear my truck and feel its rumbling motion and my arm moved and my fingers twitched as if I was shifting gears and flipping the range selector and my left leg pumped the clutch pedal. I checked the mirrors.

"Nice truck, Mayfield."
Solitude.
Tight docks.
Backing up.
Sunrises and sunsets.
Out there. For years it had been out *here*.
Fading, already fading.

In the end, perhaps, a truck driver's sense of self-worth and memories of his travels are all he really takes home. He runs his race while a big guy holds the purse, succeeding in *his* own way, bound for a heavenly reward like a camel headed for the eye of a needle. I opened my eyes for a final glimpse of Phoenix and brushed The Big Guy's hand from my shoulder.

Gayle and I often said that we'd been lucky out there, that we'd gained more than we lost. I'd driven two nice trucks. There'd been some laughs, a few in-cab arguments, several close calls and a couple of smashed hoods, but no fiery crashes and no need for a wrecker or an ambulance. The journey and its rewards were ours to keep, right from the start. Loads and trips had always counted for more than miles and money.

And success? Was it 144,000 paid miles a year, your name on the doors, and a taste of freedom? Was it getting into a lease or getting out of one? What *was* success, that one-word slogan broadcast throughout the trucking industry and parroted by The Director, but never examined or defined? I knew myself better for having taken a road trip and that was my success. Our marriage was stronger and that was Gayle's.

—⚋—

The plane broke through low clouds and there below lay Portland, a kept promise of return, a new dream to wake up to, a future.

An airporter van was parked at the curb, the driver listening to talk radio and fiddling with his cell phone. "Hop in," he said. "It's another beautiful day in the Pacific Northwest. Say, why don't you sit up front? You're my only passenger and I like to have someone to talk to when I drive."

The only passenger didn't have much to say. He felt old and tired, felt that he had aged 10 years in the weeks gone by. He sagged in the jump seat and looked at 18-wheelers on the Interstate.

"Big trucks," the van driver said. "I've *always* wanted to drive one. Those guys don't have to put up with any crap. They're free as birds."

I asked to be let out three blocks from home, thanked the driver, and pressed a $20 bill into his hand.

He said, "Cool."

He said it the way people say it these days: kewl. Ten years earlier, the man would have thanked me for the tip. Now, he expected no less and I expected no more. "Thank you" had gone out of fashion while I'd been out there and had become "kewl," "there you go," or nothing at all, in a steady national depreciation of appreciation.

I walked and gripped my Freightliner fob, felt everything and felt nothing. What's the difference between truck drivers and puppies? After six months the puppies stop whining. Deal with it. Under the sun, a Red-tailed Hawk soared on late-afternoon thermals and Canada Geese flew in noisy formations. Another beautiful day in the Pacific Northwest, the first day of the rest of my life.

I turned my key in the lock. Gayle, smiling then tearful, holding me close, still not quite sure that I was no longer out there, had waited for the last time. She said, "Welcome home."

Acknowledgments

I could not have completed *In The Driver's Seat* without help from three people I've never met. Peter Stark went out on a limb for someone he didn't know. Stuart Krichevsky read two early drafts, offering critiques and sage advice. Bryan Di Salvatore's kind words, emails, and encouragement will always mean more than I can say.

I thank my wife Gayle for her natural grace, loving patience, and understanding. She is and always will be my best editor and my best companion. If only Sam had lived long enough to see me leave the road and settle down with her. He'd have loved it.

Thanks also go to Joe Konrath for leading the eBook charge and Brion Sausser of BookCreatives.com for book design and gentle humor.

13310202R00182

Made in the USA
Charleston, SC
30 June 2012